ACES OF THE RISING SUN

1937–1945

ACES
OF THE
RISING
SUN
1937–1945

Henry Sakaida

First published in Great Britain in 2002 by Osprey Publishing,
Elms Court, Chapel Way, Botley, Oxford OX2 9LP, United Kingdom.
Email: info@ospreypublishing.com

Previously published as Aircraft of the Aces 13: *Japanese Army Air Force Aces 1937–45* and Aircraft of the Aces 22: *Imperial Japanese Navy Aces 1937–45*

Cover photograph: Takeo Tanimizu and Shoichi Sugita as student pilots in May 1941. (Courtesy of T Tanimizu)

ISBN 1 84176 618 6

Editor: Sally Rawlings
Series editor: Tony Holmes
Aircraft profiles by Grant Race, Mark Styling and Tom Tullis
Figure Artwork by Mike Chappell
Scale drawings by Mark Styling
Index by Alan Thatcher
Design by Tony Truscott

Origination by Grasmere Digital Imaging, Leeds, UK
Printed in China

02 03 04 05 06   10 9 8 7 6 5 4 3 2 1

CONTENTS

THE CHINA AND NOMONHAN INCIDENTS

Japan's ambitious plan to become the master of Greater Asia laid the foundation for the build-up of its infant Army and Navy Air Forces in the 1930s. The staging area for confrontation was in the vast region of Manchuria, in northern China, which was surrounded by Inner and Outer Mongolia, the Soviet Union and Korea. Japan had defeated China during a short war in 1894, forcing the latter to cede Formosa and the Pescadores. It then went to war with Russia in 1904 and won a quick and decisive victory – the Russians in turn were forced to relinquish their lease of Manchurian territory.

Siding with the Western powers at the outbreak of World War 1, the Japanese took over German possessions in China and the Pacific, taking advantage of the weak Chinese government which was in no position to prevent Japanese expansionist policies. Through strong-armed political tactics, Japan gained interests in Manchuria, and immediately set out to gain control of the Southern Manchurian Railway.

An international agreement permitted the Japanese occupiers to raise a formidable military force known as the Kwantung Army. This rogue militia was created both to protect Japanese interests from Chinese bandits and guard the Southern Manchurian Railway. Through a series of clashes with Chinese troops, it raided and occupied key cities in Manchuria.

In 1931 Japan seized Manchuria from China and set up a puppet government. Thousands of Japanese colonists from the homeland flocked to the frontier territory in search of new opportunities. The Japanese estab-lished mines, factories and a railway system to exploit the abundant natural resources of the region.

Anti-Japanese sentiments in China came to the boil on 7 July 1937 when Japanese and Chinese troops clashed on the Marco Polo Bridge near Beijing. The local skirmish exploded into an undeclared war which gave the Japanese an excuse to grab more Chinese territory. As the Japanese military moved forward, it deployed its Air Force in ground support roles.

The standard Japanese Army Air

Ki-27-Ko 'Nates' of the 1st Chutai of the 64th Sentai are prepared for their next sortie somewhere on the Nomonhan Plain in October 1939 (*via Phil Jarrett*)

A fair chunk of the 64th Sentai's operational strength in June 1939 is seen in this view, taken from the cockpit of a 'Nate'. The machine parked up next to it is a 1st Chutai machine, whilst the next Ki-27-Ko in line belongs to the 3rd Chutai (*via Phil Jarrett*)

Having got its ever-reliable Nakajima Ha-1b radial engine ticking over nicely, Sgt Maj Hiroshi Sekiguchi poses in the cockpit of his 1st Chutai/64th Sentai Ki-27-Ko prior to taxying out for take-off at the start of yet another combat sortie in the summer of 1939. Sekiguchi achieved ace status in this conflict, and latter reached the rank of first lieutenant in New Guinea during World War 2. His total score was seven kills (*via Phil Jarrett*)

Force (JAAF) fighter at the time was the Kawasaki Ki-10 Type 95 'Perry', an advanced biplane fighter that could attain speeds of up to 248 mph at its optimum ceiling of 9845 ft, and which was armed with two 7.7 mm machine guns in the nose

The Chinese Air Force (CAF) of the Kuomintang Government was no match for the Japanese opposition, being a 'mongrel' force equipped with a mix of imported Italian, American, German and Soviet aircraft. In addition to the CAF, the various provincial warlords also had their own squadrons. These factionalised air units, along with the CAF, were principally used to further their own political interests, and when not flying against the Japanese invaders, they were fighting amongst themselves. The CAF, for example, operated against the Chinese communists in various 'Bandit Extermination Campaigns' throughout the 1930s.

The backbone of the CAF was the Curtiss Hawk II biplane fighter, whilst other aircraft in their arsenal included the Vought Corsair (biplane) and Douglas O-2. Their initial combats with Japanese naval fighters (the A5M2 Type 96 'Claude') proved disastrous, and when the remnants of the force flew against the JAAF, they fared no better.

Although the army units won battle honours in July 1937 (the 10th Dokuritsu Hiko Chutai, 33rd and 64th Sentais and the 8th Hiko Daitai being the principal units involved), it was not until 19 September 1937 that a flight from the 33rd Sentai, led by Lt Yoshio Hirosei, shot down four out of six Chinese fighters encountered during a routine patrol, and thus claim the first ever victories scored by the JAAF.

Large quantities of Soviet aircraft started pouring into China over the next few months following the signing of a non-aggression pact between China and the Soviet Union on 21 August 1937. With the agreement ratified, the former

Members of the 1st Chutai, 11th Sentai, pose for a souvenir snapshot. The aces included in this group photo could boast almost 150 victory claims between them! Some of the pilots are; Capt Kenji Shimada (sitting front – 40 kills), MSgt Bunji Yoshiyama (displaying his victim's Tokarev pistol – 25 kills), 2Lt Tomoari Hasegawa (fourth from right – 19 kills) and WO Hiromichi Shinohara (far right – 58 kills). (*via Y Izawa*)

Ranking JAAF ace Sgt Hiromichi Shinohara flew this 1st Chutai/64th Sentai Ki-27-Otsu during the first weeks of the Nomonhan Incident in the summer of 1939. It is seen here adorned with ten red victory markings (*via K Osuo*)

immediately requested military aid and duly received some 255 aircraft (155 Polikarpov I-152s and I-15s), along with over 250 'volunteer' pilots and accompanying technicians. The infusion of Soviet aircraft and pilots was quickly noted by Japanese navy pilots flying the A5M 'Claudes', and they soon reported increased resistance and aggressiveness on the part of their opposition.

However, by January 1938 the CAF had lost much of its aircraft in mêlées with the JNAF, whilst the JAAF's Ki-10's had also proved to be far superior to the CAF's American Hawks, Russian I-15s and British Gladiators. The darkening war clouds over Europe also forced the Soviet Union to cut back on aircraft shipments to China, thus accelerating the demise of the CAF as a viable force.

Despite the increasing lack of targets, Lt Kosuke Kawahara of the 64th Sentai achieved his fifth kill on 8 March 1938 to duly become the first ever JAAF 'ace' (in the Western tradition). While returning from a bomber escort mission to Sian, the 1st Chutai had encountered four I-15s, and Kawahara – who had claimed four victories from previous encounters – shot down one while his comrades finished off the rest.

With the introduction of the new monoplane Nakajima Ki-27 'Nate' in March 1938, the standard Ki-10 fighter was retired – this signalled an end to the biplane era within the JAAF. The 64th Sentai received its first Ki-27s on 3 April and immediately commenced training. Eager to test the new aircraft under combat conditions, the day of reckoning arrived just seven days later when 18 'Nates' tangled with an estimated 30 enemy aircraft and shot down 24, losing just two of their own in reply! Capt Tateo Kato, who destroyed three CAF aircraft, could not praise the new fighter enough, and shortly after the Ki-27's introduction to the frontline, what was left of Chinese airpower was decisively crushed.

NOMONHAN (KHALKIN GOL)

In May 1939 an ill-defined border between Manchuria and Outer Mongolia led to the Nomonhan (Khalkin Gol) Incident, which turned out to be yet another local skirmish that quickly flared into an undeclared war. It started on 10 May 1939 when nomadic Mongolians crossed the Khalka River to pasture their flocks, but were in turn driven back across the river by Manchurian border guards. The next day, Mongolian cavalrymen crossed the river to attack the latter, and followed up this action 24 hours later with another armed raid. The audacity of the Mongolians infuriated the leaders of the Kwantung Army, who rushed both infantry and air units to the Nomonhan Plains.

In response to this act by the Japanese, the Soviet Union was forced to enter the fray through the Soviet-Mongolian Mutual Assistance Pact of 1936 – the 1st Army was despatched to Tamsak-Bulak, which was about 60 miles south-west of Nomonhan in Mongolia itself. Along with the

infantry came two advanced fighter regiments (I-15 and I-16s) and single bomber and reconnaissance units.

The first blood shed in the aerial duel for the skies occurred on the evening of 20 May when three 'Nates' of the 24th Sentai, led by Lt Col Kojiro Matsumura, ran into two I-16s escorting an R-Z reconnaissance biplane on a sortie over the Khalka River. Following a short fight, the R-Z went down, although the Polikarpov fighters escaped. Two days later, the 'Nates' tangled with six I-16s and claimed three downed.

The 'tit for tat' skirmishes began to enlarge as more aircraft were sent to the disputed border area – these included five JAAF regiments, all equipped with new Ki-27s. The Soviet veterans who had fought the JNAF in China now found themselves duelling with the JAAF.

On 26 May the 11th Sentai received their baptism of fire in this conflict when nine 'Nates' bounced a formation of I-16s and reportedly destroyed nine of their number over Nomonhan. Two days later more than 60 Soviet fighters returned to seek their revenge, but the 11th Sentai scrambled 18 aircraft in response to this threat and claimed an incredible 42 victories for the loss of just one Ki-27. In reality the Soviets lost just ten aircraft, but the inflated claims by the Japanese had set the standard for subsequent actions.

On 22 June the biggest dogfight yet seen occurred when nearly 100

Nomonhan ace Cpl Katsuaki Kira (standing far left – 21 kills) and his fellow comrades of the 24th Sentai relax by a starter truck during the bloody summer of 1939 (*via Y Izawa*)

64th Sentai Ki-27s scramble for combat against the Soviets during mid-1939. The flat features of the Nomonhan Plain made take-off and landings easy, and pilots from both sides frequently landed to pick up downed comrades (*via Y Izawa*)

Another view of the 64th Sentai operating from Manchurian territory during the Nomonhan Incident. These 'airfields' were always temporary in nature, with all personnel (officers and ratings alike) quartered in tents. Aircraft maintenance was also performed entirely in the open, but thanks to the 'Nate's' rugged construction this posed few problems to JAAF groundcrews (*via Y Izawa*)

The 2nd Chutai of the 11th Sentai pose for a group photo in July 1939 during the height of the war with the Soviets (*via K Osuo*)

Soviet fighters crossed the Khalka River into Manchurian territory. The 24th Sentai could only muster 18 fighters in response, but during a series of running dogfights the handful of Japanese pilots claimed 47 victories for the loss of five of their own. The Soviets, on the other hand, claimed that they had lost only 11 aircraft, and destroyed 31 Japanese fighters!

While the Soviet-Mongolian ground forces fought the Japanese Kwantung Army along the Khalka River, tremendous air battles raged overhead. Acts of heroism were observed on both sides as pilots landed their fighters on the flat plains to rescue downed comrades. An example of this occurred on 26 June when the commander of the Soviet's 70th IAP fighter regiment, Maj V M Zabaluev, parachuted from his burning I-16 over Manchurian territory. His deputy, Maj Sergei Gritsevets, landed his aircraft as Japanese infantrymen advanced, and once his commander was safely sitting on his lap, took off in a hail of small arms fire.

Due to the continuing Soviet-Mongolian air offensive into Manchurian territory, the Japanese decided to escalate the air war by attacking targets across the Khalka River. During the dawn hours of 27 June, 104 aircraft of the 2nd Hikodan crossed into Mongolian territory to bomb bases at Tamsak-Bulak. As Japanese bombers blasted the airfield, Soviet fighters scrambled to do battle. What followed was an intense 30-minute dogfight involving over 150 aircraft which mesmerised troops watching the spectacle from the ground. When the bombers completed their task, the escort fighters broke off combat and accompanied the 'heavies' across the border. The Japanese lost two fighters and three bombers. Thanks to the skill of the JAAF fighter pilots, only One Type 97 bomber was forced to make an emergency landing (due to engine problems) in enemy territory, and even then another bomber landed and picked up the entire crew!

The month of July saw the heaviest fighting of the 129-day border skirmish. Soviet I-153s were mauled by the 'Nates', and their headquarters subsequently concluded that the era of biplane warfare was now well and truly over. In response to mounting losses, the Soviets now began to change their tactics, staging 'hit and run' raids with their I-16s across the border – their pilots had been warned not to dogfight with the 'Nates'. The newer *Tip* 12 and 17 models of the I-16 employed heavier armament, including ShVAK 20 mm cannon, as well as armour-plating to protect the pilot.

By August the JAAF began to experience fewer claims and more pilot casualties, and it was rapidly determined that the enemy had

The first monoplane fighter of the JAAF, the 'Nate' was armed with two 7.7 mm machine guns in the upper fuselage forward decking and could achieve a maximum speed of 292 mph at 11,480 ft. This allowed the Nakajima to more than stand its ground against the Soviet I-16, although it lacked the latter's fire-power and armour protection. However, these deficiencies were more than compensated for by the 'Nate's' unrivalled manoeuvrability, which Japanese pilots preferred in dogfighting to cannons or armour plating. This Ki-27 sports the red cowling and eagle insignia of the 1st Chutai of the 64th Sentai, and is seen here with Sgt Shigeru Takuwa at the controls (*via Maru*)

realised the inferiority of their fighters when compared with the 'Nate', and were now employing better tactics. In addition, the small cadre of JAAF fighter pilots in Manchuria had also started to succumb to battle fatigue after flying more than four missions per day for near on three months. The Japanese decided to end hostilities to save what was left of their battered ground forces, and the Soviets, stunned by the German invasion of Poland on 1 September, were only too eager to disengage. However, while peace negotiations were being conducted behind closed doors the combatants continued the fighting. The last aerial action of this incident occurred on 15 September when the 1st, 11th, 24th, 59th, and 64th Sentais were engaged in heavy combat with Soviet fighters. The following day a truce was signed, and peace returned to the border region.

Both sides made tremendous claims and minimised their losses. The Soviets believed that they had destroyed over 650 Japanese aircraft (actual documented losses put the figure at 162), whilst the Japanese claimed that they had shot down 1162 Soviet aircraft and destroyed a further 98 on the ground – the latter lost 207 aeroplanes as a result of combat. The top JAAF ace of the conflict was WO Hiromichi Shinohara, who claimed 58 victories, whilst his counterpart on the Soviet side was Maj Sergei Ivanovich Gritsevets of 70th IAP with 40+ victories.

The combat experiences gained in this 'dress rehearsal' for World War 2 gave the JAAF fighter pilots a valuable insight into their strengths and weaknesses. They now believed that speed was essential if the opponent avoided close-quarter dogfighting. In respect to their own aircraft, pilots realised that the advent of better armed, and armoured, enemy fighters, made their rifle-calibre armament virtually useless, whilst the lack of self-sealing fuel tanks in the 'Nate' made the Nakajima particularly vulnerable to cannon fire – their radio equipment was also virtually useless. While the pilots' criticisms were taken seriously by aircraft designers at the time, what they would eventually receive to replace the 'Nate' some two years later (the Nakajima Ki-43 *Hayabusa*, code-named 'Oscar') tended to indicate otherwise.

Master Sergeant Bunji Yoshiyama

One of the toughest JAAF pilots to emerge from the Nomonhan Incident was Bunji Yoshiyama, a native of Kagoshima Prefecture in Japan. He was born in 1916 and dropped out of Merchant Marine School to try his luck with the JAAF. He graduated from flight training in November 1934, and was eventually posted to the 11th Sentai at Harbin, Manchuria.

On 28 May 1939 more than 60 Soviet I-152s and I-16 fighters crossed the Khalka River into Manchurian territory, led by Maj V M Zabaluev. Smarting from their losses two days earlier, the Soviets were anxious for a rematch, and the 11th Sentai duly rose to the challenge. Yoshiyama, fly-ing with the 1st Chutai, shot down an I-152 in his first dogfight, while his squadron claimed 42 victories for a single loss – the pilot involved para-chuted to safety.

On 27 June the JAAF crossed the Khalka River into Mongolian terri-tory for the second time, despite being warned by Tokyo HQ not to take the offensive. Ignoring the High Command, the leaders of the Kwantung Army gave orders to launch a pre-emptive strike on the Soviet airfield at Tamsak-Bulak – MSgt Yoshiyama revelled in the day's action, downing four enemy fighters (three I-16s and an I-152). Prior to returning to base, he landed his aircraft east of Lake Byur and rescued MSgt Eisaku Suzuki.

On 25 July Yoshiyama destroyed three enemy fighters and again landed behind enemy lines, this time to pick up MSgt Shintaro Kajima of the 4th Chutai, who had parachuted down. As his score continued to climb so too did his reputation, and he often flew as second wingman to Capt Kenji Shimada, CO of the 1st Chutai.

In a wild dogfight on 20 August Yoshiyama damaged a Soviet fighter, which made an emergency landing. In an act of daring, or sheer foolish-ness, he landed beside his Soviet opponent and shot him dead. Yoshiyama then relieved him of his pistol and wristwatch and returned to Manchuria with them as souvenirs of their fateful encounter.

MSgt Bunji Yoshiyama disappeared on 15 September 1939 while on a bomber escort mission to attack Soviet airfields east of Lake Byur – the next day the armistice was signed. At the time of his death he had flown 90 missions and achieved at least 20 victories, possibly 25.

Major Iwori Sakai

Iwori Sakai was one of the oldest operational fighter pilots of World War 2, and his greatest contribution to the JAAF during this period was as an instructor and test pilot. He was born in Gifu Prefecture in 1909, and originally trained as a civilian pilot at Tokorozawa. In 1928, he became an NCO pilot in the reserves.

Cpl Sakai performed his military duties firstly in Korea and then Shan-tung, in China. He then returned to Japan and became an assistant instructor at the Akeno Fighter School. He entered the Army Academy in 1932 and graduated the following year, attaining a second lieutenant's commission. He then continued his teaching at Akeno and also at Toko-rozawa.

When the China War started in July 1937, the Japanese rushed troops and aircraft into the northern part of the country. Sakai's baptism of fire took place on 11 March 1938 during an attack over Sian, and exactly two weeks later he shot down his first enemy aircraft – an I-15. On 10 April, he claimed three more, followed by another on 20 May.

By the time the Nomonhan Incident started in May 1939, Capt Sakai was flying with the 2nd Chutai in the 64th Sentai, and when the CO (a Capt Anzai) of the former was killed on 1 September, he became the new commander.

Toward the later part of this conflict, Japanese pilot casualties started to increase. He recalled, 'I had to fly four to six missions a day and I was so greatly fatigued that often I could barely see to land my plane. The enemy planes came over like a black cloud, and our losses were very heavy'. Sakai

Maj Iwori Sakai was a noted instruc-tor and test pilot, as well as being a 15-kill veteran of the Nomonhan Incident. Many surviving JAAF pilots owed their lives to his training methods (*via Maru*)

flew a record seven missions in one day, and once came back with over 50 bullet holes in his fighter.

At the end of hostilities on the Nomonhan plains, Capt Sakai was transferred to Seoul, Korea, where he trained his men in the 'Sakai Method', using the latest American and British fighter tactics. In July 1941 he returned to the Akeno Fighter School, where his subsequent teachings influenced many future JAAF aces, including Maj Yohei Hinoki.

By March 1942 Sakai had attained the rank of major and he became involved in testing the new Ki-61 *Hien* ('Tony'). He considered this machine to be the equal second best fighter of the JAAF, along with the standard 'Oscar', from 1943 to the end of the war – he reserved top honors for the Ki-84 *Hayate* ('Frank'). When B-29s started to raid the homeland, he commanded an air defence unit and battled the Superfortresses. In the late stages of the war he test flew the Ki-100 *Goshikisen* and was favourably impressed, but it arrived too late to make any difference to the final outcome of the conflict.

At the end of the war Maj Sakai's personal victory tally stood at 15 (all Soviet aircraft), and he had flown a total of over 5000 hours in 50 different aircraft types.

Major Jyozo Iwahashi

A career military officer who became a distinguished fighter/leader in World War 2, Jyozo Iwahashi was born in Wakayama Prefecture, Japan, in 1912. He graduated from the 45th term of the Army Military Academy in July 1933, and was duly commissioned as a second lieutenant. He received flight training at Tokorozawa and Akeno.

At the time of the Nomonhan Incident Iwahashi was squadron leader of the 4th Chutai/11th Sentai, then based at Harbin, Manchuria. He did not participate in the initial fighting, and only became involved in the second phase which erupted in June. His first victories came on the 24th of that month when he claimed two enemy fighters shot down.

Due to Iwahashi's leadership skills, the 4th Chutai had gained over 100 victories by the time of the armistice, but because of his disdain for the Japanese media, and his refusal to permit reporters to interview him, much of his success went unrecorded. Iwahashi claimed 20 victories at Nomonhan, and was subsequently awarded the 4th Grade Order of Merit for distinguished service.

He returned to Japan to become an instructor at Akeno, before assuming the role of test pilot. As the war situation deteriorated, the JAAF's eagerness to bring the new Ki-84 into service led Iwahashi to head the inspection department which was to evaluate the new Nakajima fighter.

He was subsequently appointed commander of the newly-created 22nd Sentai on 5 March 1944, this unit being the first unit in the JAAF to receive the 'Frank'. After a brief period of familiarisation training, the sentai was ordered to central China for combat, Iwahashi flying into Hankow with 40 Ki-84s on 24 August.

Four days after arriving in-theatre, the 22nd Sentai engaged in its first combat at Yochow when it tangled with P-40Ns from several provisional squadrons of the Chinese-American Composite Wing and the USAAF's

Due to his loathing of the Japanese press, the exploits of 20-kill Nomonhan ace Jyozo Iwahashi went largely unreported during 1939. He served as squadron leader of the 4th Chutai, within the crack 11th Sentai, during the scored phase of the conflict, and later became an instructor and then a test pilot (*via Maru*)

13

118th TRS/23rd FG. Maj Iwahashi claimed one P-40 shot down.

The following month, Iwahashi and some of his men began intercepting B-29s on their way to Japan from their Chinese bases. On 21 September 1944 they were ordered to attack Xian (Sian) Airfield, and the major and his wingman strafed enemy fighters as they were taking off until the former was hit by ground fire. Iwahashi then dove his aircraft into the ground and was killed, one source claiming that he rammed a P-47. At the time of his death he had scored over 21 kills, and was subsequently promoted two ranks posthumously to lieutenant colonel.

Second Lieutenant Masatoshi Masuzawa

Masatoshi Masuzawa was one of the more colourful characters within the JAAF, comparable to the US Marine Corps' legendary ace Maj Gregory 'Pappy' Boyington. A tenacious fighter pilot who took extreme risks, and exuded an aura of invincibility, his only weakness was alcohol. Indeed, it was said that he had fought while in a drunken stupor, which was an incredible feat if true. Masuzawa was the stuff of legends.

He was born in Miyagi Prefecture in 1915, and like many of his comrades, as soon as he was old enough enlisted in the army and began his career as a common infantryman. Realising that fighter pilots were admired and treated better than foot soldiers, Masuzawa transferred to the Kumagaya Flying School and then graduated in February 1938 to fighter training at Akeno.

At the time of the Nomonhan Incident Masuzawa was a member of the 1st Sentai. He scored his first victory over Tamsak-Bulak, in Mongolian territory, on 27 June, and by the end of hostilities in September had recorded 12 kills. His dogfighting technique was simple and effective – charge into the enemy boldly, scatter them, and then pick them off. His aircraft received many hits through the employment of this tactic, but Masuzawa lived a charmed life.

After the Nomanhan Incident, the 1st Sentai was based near Harbin, in Manchuria, until November 1941. On the opening day of the Pacific War, the air group escorted a convoy of ships southward bound for the Malayan campaign. Prior to their departure for Rabaul, New Britain, in January 1943, they also saw action over French Indochina.

WO Masuzawa flew against the

Shown here soon after the Nomonhan Incident, 1st Sentai ace 2Lt Masatoshi Masuzawa (centre) lived a charmed life. He took extreme risks and returned alive every time, downing 12 Soviet aircraft in 1939 (*via Y Izawa*)

Americans over New Guinea, operating from bases at Salamaua and Lae. On 22 June 1943 he was wounded in a dogfight with P-38s of the 80th Fighter Squadron over Salamaua, claiming one Lockheed fighter shot down before being hit and severely wounded himself – Masuzawa made a forced landing at Lae and was later sent back to Japan by hospital ship.

Whilst he remained hospitalised the war effort was deteriorating for Japan. The need for experienced flight instructors finally provided the grounded pilot with the chance to fly again, and in March 1944, Masuzawa was assigned to the 39th KFR (educational training squadron) at Yokoshiba Airfield, utilising Manchurian-built Ki-79 aircraft – a redesigned trainer variant of the Ki-27 'Nate'. During this time he trained dozens of pilots for *kamikaze* suicide operations.

On 16 February 1945 American carrier aircraft attacked Japanese airfields as part of a huge fighter sweep over the Chiba Peninsula and Tokyo areas – Task Force 58's assault was the first large-scale attack by the Americans on the Japanese homeland since the 1942 Doolittle Raid.

When reports of incoming enemy aircraft reached Yokoshiba, WO Masuzawa was one of 16 instructors and trainees to scramble in defence of the airfield. In aerial combat with F6F-5 Hellcats from VF-9 and VF-80, the peerless ace claimed one aircraft shot down, despite his Ki-79 being armed with just a solitary 7.7 mm machine gun! Almost all of his comrades were shot down, but Masuzawa returned alive.

He ended the war with a total of 15 aerial victories.

Second Lieutenant Shogo Saito

Shogo Saito gained fame as the 'King of Ramming Attacks' during the Nomonhan Incident. He was born in 1918 in the Aomori Prefecture of Japan. In 1935 he entered flight training at Tokorozawa and completed the course of fighter training at Akeno in November 1936.

When conflict on the Mongolian border erupted in May 1939, Saito was a member of the 24th Sentai at Hailar, Manchuria. On 24 May he claimed his first victories when he flew straight into a formation of Soviet I-152s over Byur Lake and downed two – he had taken off late and mistook the enemy aircraft for his own squadron-mates.

The first large dogfight of the Nomonhan Incident occured on 22 June when over 100 Soviet aircraft twice crossed the Khalka River into Manchurian territory. The only Japanese sentai to oppose this raid was the 24th with 18 Ki-27s. MSgt Saito downed three enemy aircraft and forced one pilot to take to his parachute. When a further three Soviet fighters made emergency landings, he strafed and burned them.

As the combat swirled about him Saito found himself in a dangerous predicament, for he had expended all of his ammunition. He decided to flee toward base, but was soon surrounded by eight I-16s. Knowing that he had no chance of surviving such odds, he decided to ram a Polikarpov fighter. He quickly singled out his victim, and whilst attempting to collide with the Soviet fighter his right wing tore off the upper portion of the fin and rudder of the I-16, and the hapless enemy pilot lost all control of his mount – Saito had scored his fourth aerial victory for the day. In the subsequent confusion he managed to make good his escape and somehow reach home.

On 21 July Saito single-handedly destroyed four enemy fighters and

2Lt Shogo Saito was given the title 'King of Ramming Attacks' following several memorable encounters with I-16s in the summer of 1939. He became the top ace in the 24th Sentai in Nomonhan by scoring 24 kills, although contrary to his nickname, he only scored one confirmed victory through physically ramming a Soviet aircraft (*via Maru*)

claimed one probable. He also saved the life of his commanding officer when he made a ramming attempt after again expending all of his ammunition. The tactic proved successful as the enemy pilot veered away at the unexpected assault.

Two days later the Soviets staged a massive bombing attack across the Khalka River, employing over 120 fighters to escort 23 SB-2 bombers. In the largest dogfight of the conflict, the Japanese were unsuccessful in stopping the raid – MSgt Saito downed one of the bombers, but was quickly attacked by a horde of fighters and received bullet wounds to his left leg. He extracted himself from the mêlée and returned to base, where he was briefly hospitalised.

By the time the ceasefire was implemented in mid-September Saito had achieved 25 victories to become the top ace in the 24th Sentai. He went on to serve with his unit in the Philippines at the outbreak of World War 2, then transferred to New Guinea, where he claimed a B-24 amongst several other kills – the exact count is unknown. He died on 2 July 1944 whilst fighting as an infantryman against US Forces on Hollandia.

Warrant Officer Hiromichi Shinohara

Hiromichi Shinohara was the top fighter pilot of the JAAF. He gained fame during the Nomonhan Incident where, in only three months of combat, he downed 58 enemy aircraft to earn him the title of 'Richtofen of the Orient'. No Air Force fighter pilot ever broke his record of achievement.

The future 'ace of aces' was born in 1913 to a farming family in Tochigi Prefecture. He enlisted in the Army's 27th Cavalry Regiment in 1931 and did his overseas duty in Manchuria, where he was a member of an expeditionary force sent to protect Japanese settlers, and their property, from Chinese bandits. In June 1933 Shinohara entered Tokorozawa Flying School and graduated in January 1934, being assigned to the 11th Sentai and posted to Harbin in Manchuria.

When the border skirmish with Soviet-Mongolian Forces erupted on 10 May 1939, Sgt Shinohara was ready. The little 'tit for tat' confrontations on the ground soon took on serious consequences as both sides moved up fighter reinforcement along the ill-defined border. Col Yujiro Noguchi, commanding the 11th Sentai, led 20 Ki-27 'Nates' from Harbin to forward bases near the Mongolian border on 24 May, and three days later Shinohara downed four I-16s in his first combat, which unfolded over the Khalka River. Less than 24 hours later he downed an L-Z reconnaissance aircraft and five I-15 fighters.

The unbroken Japanese record of 11 enemy fighters shot down in a single day was achieved by Shinohara on 27 June 1939 over Tamsak-Bulak. This day marked the first large-scale air offensive against the enemy over their own territory, and saw a force of over 100 Japanese aircraft cross the Khalka River and bomb airfields at Tamsak-Bulak. More than 150 aircraft engaged in an immense, confusing, mêlée for over half an hour. Shinohara's tactic was simple – he would charge into a formation of enemy fighters alone, scattering them and picking them off one by one with his superb marksmanship.

The 11th Sentai nearly lost Shinohara on 25 July when he was hit in combat, the peerless ace being forced to make an emergency landing after

In an incredible combat career that lasted just three months, Hiromichi Shinohara scored 58 victories – a total which included a JAAF record 11 kills in one day. His stunning success with the 11th Sentai earned him the title of 'Richtofen of the Orient' (*via K Osuo*)

WO Shinohara was shot down by an overwhelming number of I-16s on 27 August 1939, and these charred items were recovered from the burnt-out wreck of his Ki-27. They included a Mauser Model 1914 pistol (taken from one of his victims), a watch, brass identity disk, a can opener, key and other items (via *K Osuo*)

his fighter was struck in the left fuel tank. Luckily, his squadronmate, MSgt Iwasaki, landed his aircraft and rescued his comrade as Soviet tanks advanced on them.

WO Hiromichi Shinohara's luck finally ran out on the evening of 27 August 1939 – while escorting bombers he fell victim to a pursuing fighter, but not before he had shot down three of their number. Shinohara's last diary entry listed 55 victories, to which was added the three kills achieved on this final mission. He received a posthumous promotion to second lieutenant.

Captain Kenji Shimada

Kenji Shimada had neither the appearance or the demeanour of a fighter pilot. He was overweight and mild mannered, with a gentle disposition. However, looks were most definitely deceiving in this case for Shimada went on to become one of the top-scoring JAAF aces of the Nomonhan Incident. Born in Tokyo in 1911, Shimada graduated from the Army Military Academy in July 1933 and entered the Tokorozawa Flying School. After completing various flight courses, he received further training at the Akeno Fighter School.

By March 1938 Shimada had been promoted to the rank captain and posted to the 11th Sentai as squadron leader of the 1st Chutai. He was stationed in Manchuria at the outbreak of the Nomonhan Incident, and moved his squadron to Hailar on the 24th of that month as the border skirmishes increased in intensity.

Capt Shimada's baptism of fire occurred three days later whilst leading a six-aircraft patrol over the Khalka River. His formation engaged nine Soviet I-16s, and he soon shot down three of them, whilst his comrades shared the remaining six. There was a lull in fighting after 28 May, and both sides used the time to both regroup and reassess the situation.

The border skirmish heated up again on 22 June, and from that day forward until the armistice in mid-September, Capt Shimada was engaged in regular combats. His 1st Chutai went on to score the highest number of kills in the air group, claiming over 180 enemy aircraft destroyed. Amongst his subordinates was ranking ace WO Hiromichi Shinohara – see previous entry.

On 15 September 1939 – the final day of fighting – Capt Shimada participated in a raid against Tamsak-Bulak. He was last seen engaged in aerial combat with I-16s, but following his failure to return to base the captain was declared killed in action. He received the customary one rank posthumous promotion to major.

Kenji Shimada's final score is unclear, and according to some Japanese historians he is credited with 27 aerial kills, whilst other sources say he claimed over 40 victories. Notwithstanding the confusion surrounding Shimada's own personal tally, his unit's outstanding achievement serves as a clear testimont to his extraordinary leadership qualities.

CHINA-BURMA-INDIA THEATRE

When Japan went to war with the United States on 7 December 1941, the JAAF was at the pinnacle of its existence. The veterans of the China War and Nomonhan were confident in their ability to take on their American, British and Dutch counterparts. They believed at the beginning of World War 2 that the key to victory was to engage in close-quarter dogfighting, as well as to always retain sufficient speed in combat in order to chase down a fleeing opponent – the lessons from Nomonhan were fresh in their minds. Unfortunately, the Ki-43 *Hayabusa* (Peregrine Falcon), which was given the Allied codename of 'Oscar', did not fully meet their expectations.

Although the USAAF's P-40 Warhawk was technically superior to the Ki-43 'Oscar', it was often pilot skill that determined the victory in favour of the JAAF pilot in the early war years. Here, a P-40E falls victim to an 'Oscar' attack in the early months of 1942 in the CBI (*via Maru*)

In comparison to the Navy's lithe Mitsubishi A6M Zero fighter, the 'Oscar' was even smaller and lighter. Its wide chord 'butterfly' combat flaps bestowed upon the aircraft superior manoeuvrability when deployed in the heat of a dogfight, but its 950 hp Nakajima Ha-25 engine gave it a top speed of just 308 mph at 13,125 ft, which was appreciably slower than the Zero's 331 mph.

In terms of firepower, the *Hayabusa* was a lightweight, boasting just a pair of 7.7 mm machine guns in the nose – this paltry armament caused much consternation amongst veteran JAAF pilots, who had roundly criticised the Ki-43's predecessor, the Ki-27, for its lack of offensive 'punch' several years earlier. Later models carried two nose-mounted 12.7 mm guns, but Nakajima refused to adopt wing armament like that fitted to the Zero.

In preparation for the Malay invasion, the Army's 1st, 11th, 64th and 77th Sentais were tasked with ship escort duty for the landing forces, and of these four sentais, only the 64th was flying the new Ki-43-I-Otsu – they had received them in August 1941.

On 7 December 1941, whilst the Japanese Navy struck at Pearl Harbor, the JAAF found employment supporting the landings of the 25th Army in Malaya. The RAF, handicapped by a gross lack of modern combat aircraft, was quickly neutralised by the JAAF fighters, and once the latter had secured air superiority, the fall of Malaya was secured.

Seen soon after its arrival in China in mid-1943, this factory-fresh Ki-43-II-Otsu was funded through wartime public subscription – it was christened Aikoku ('Patriotism') Aircraft No 2068 (*via Phil Jarrett*)

Wearing the distinctive red tail and fuselage stripes of the 2nd Chutai/25th Sentai, this Ki-43-II-Ko was the squadron commander's personal 'Oscar II'. It is seen parked between sorties at Hankow, in China, in 1944 (*via Phil Jarrett*)

By the end of January 1942 British and Commonwealth Forces had been forced to retreat into the protective enclave of Singapore island. From here the RAF managed to stage something of a fightback against overwhelming odds, its handful of war-weary Hawker Hurricane IIBs and Brewster Buffalos staving off defeat for a number of days until finally succumbing to the superior Japanese force.

The Hurricane had made a name for itself by helping to stem the Luftwaffe tide during the Battle of Britain in the summer of 1940. When it had entered service in late 1937 it had been the first RAF fighter capable of exceeding sustained speeds of 300 mph. Larger than the 'Oscar', and armed with an incredible (to JAAF pilots at least) eight Browning .303-in machine guns (four per wing), it easily outgunned its opposition. The Hurricane's maximum speed of 335 mph at 18,500 ft was also an unpleasant surprise to Japanese pilots.

The Brewster F2A Buffalo was the Hurricane's poor American cousin in Malaya, having been banished to the Far East due to its unsuitability for frontline use in Europe. Resembling a flying barrel, this aircraft

The complex red tail marking on this Ki-61-I denotes that its employer is the 37th Flight Training Company, based at Matsuyama Airfield, on Formosa, in March 1944. This unit relied on a cadre of ex-frontline pilots to hone the skills of newly-arrived aircrew from Home Island-based basic flying training schools. Although strictly a training unit first and foremost, operational necessities often meant that instructors from the 37th would regularly be called upon to fly Home Defence sorties. Indeed, the company was also fully committed to the doomed defence of Okinawa in 1945 (*via Phil Jarrett*)

became the first monoplane fighter to enter US Navy service in June 1939. Although it possessed a maximum speed of 321 mph at 15,000 ft and was armed with four Colt .50-in machine guns (two in the nose and one in each wing), the stubby Buffalo was not successful in American service and most were sold to overseas customers. At the time of the Japanese invasion of Malaya, the Buffalo was the most numerous Allied fighter in the Far East, serving with squadrons of the RAF, Royal Australian and New Zealand Air Forces and the Royal Netherlands Indies Army Air Division. Sadly for its pilots it proved to be no match for the 'Oscar'.

The 64th Sentai engaged Hurricanes for the first time over Singapore on 20 January 1942, claiming five and two probables – RAF fighters continued to oppose the Japanese until Singapore fell on 15 February 1942. When Lt Gen A E Percival surrendered Singapore, it became the greatest British military disaster in history, with over 130,000 British and Commonwealth soldiers being taken prisoner.

With Singapore in their hands, the Japanese prepared to attack the vital oil refineries at Palembang in the Dutch East Indies. It was imperative for the Japanese to acquire these key targets intact in order to fuel their war

A pilot receives a haircut between sorties, much to the amusement of his comrades. The famous arrow insignia of the 64th Sentai can be seen on the Ki-43 in the background (*via Maru*)

effort as Japan itself was bereft of natural oil supplies. Fighters from the 59th and 64th Sentais played a key role in providing fighter escorts for bombers attacking Allied forces defending the refineries. RAF Hurricanes sent out to repel the JAAF formations were quickly beaten back, and Japanese paratroopers subsequently captured Palembang on 15 February.

Following the capture of the oilfields, the Japanese invaded Java – there seemed to be no stopping the Japanese 'juggernaut'. With the surrender of Allied Forces in the Dutch East Indies on 12 March, the Japanese had successfully achieved their major objectives of securing the oil reserves and raw materials of the region in just three months.

To the west, the Burma Campaign commenced in conjunction with the Pearl Harbor raid and the Malayan invasion, the Japanese Army's goal being to cut off the vital Burma Road, which fed Allied war supplies to the beleaguered Chinese Army. It was in Burma that the 50th and 64th Sentais gained fame, their pilots flying both ground support missions and combat fighter patrols against RAF Hurricanes and Mohawks. They also ran into the legendary American Volunteer Group (AVG), better known as the 'Flying Tigers'.

The AVG came into being through the efforts of then Capt Claire Chennault, a former US Army Air Corps fighter pilot now working for the Chinese Air Force. He recruited 100 American pilots from the various branches of the military with promises of adventure and bonuses. Three squadrons were raised and they began operating in Burma in September 1941.

The 'Flying Tigers' claimed their first victories on 20 December southeast of their base at Kunming, China, a dozen ex-RAF/RCAF P-40Bs intercepting ten JAAF bombers and downing three for the loss of one of their own. Pushed back into Burma following the Japanese invasion, they subsequently flew with great bravery in the defence of Rangoon, but as with their RAF brethren, limited resources saw them fail in their efforts to stop the enemy advance.

This distinctively dappled Ki-44-II-Otsu was regularly flown by the CO of the 2nd Chutai within the 85th Sentai in 1942/43. It is seen here at Jogai Airfield, in Nanking, in the summer of 1943 (*via Phil Jarrett*)

Capt Hideaki Inayama (at least five kills) was a seasoned veteran of the 87th Sentai in the CBI. He fought British Fleet Air Arm Corsairs, Hellcats and Avengers on 24 January 1945 over Sumatra, downing two of the latter in his Ki-44 (*via H Sakaida*)

When Japanese troops enterered Rangoon on 8 March it was virtually deserted, its former defenders, realising the no-win situation they now faced, having given orders to abandon the city. The long retreat to India thus began. The 50th Sentai established their base at Mingaladon Airfield, in Rangoon, in mid-March, followed by the 1st and 64th Sentais in May. The Burma Road was cut later that year, forcing the Americans to fly in supplies to China over 'The Hump' (the Himalayas).

In July 1942 the AVG became a part of the USAAF's 14th Air Force, whilst its charismatic leader was given the rank of major general. They had fought early on in the war with very little support, yet had hampered the Japanese efforts in Burma. As commander of the 14th Air Force, Chennault was in a position to demand more aircraft and supplies, and despite his aggressive tactics alienating senior commanders in-theatre, he forced the Japanese to counter-attack with Operation *Ichi-Go* in 1944 – over a million battle-hardened Army troops were pulled out of Manchuria to try and destroy the 14th AF's bases in Hunan and Kwangsi Provinces.

The Americans were able to establish airfields in India in 1944 for their

The pilot performs engine power checks on his Ki-45-KAI-Otsu at an undisclosed base in Burma in 1944. This particular 'Nick' belongs to the 1st Chutai of the 21st Sentai (*via Phil Jarrett*)

One of the last surviving Manchoukuo Air Force Ki-27-Otsu-KAIs dominates this view of a base near Mukden, in northern Manchuria, in mid-1945. Neatly lined up behind the weather-beaten 'Nate' are five camouflaged Ki-84s (*via Jerry Scutts*)

B-29s, the idea being to get their aircraft and supplies into China for the purpose of eventually bombing the Japanese mainland. The 58th Bomb Wing was the first to succeed in this endeavour on 15/16 June 1944, its B-29s flying from China against industrial targets on the northern coast of Kyushu. They would also bomb targets in Bangkok, Formosa, Singapore, Saigon and Manchuria as the war progressed.

Despite the success of the 'air bridge' into China, the Americans wanted to open up the Burma Road, but the British lacked the equipment and manpower to get this job done. Finally, in late 1944 Allied troops broke out from their base in Assam, India, and plowed forward down the Burma Road, with engineers at the vanguard paving the way. By February 1945 the British had linked up with the Burma Road at Lashio.

Maj Koki Kawamoto was a highly-experienced flight instructor and aerial tactician who had served with both the famous Akeno Fighter School and the 106th Flight School in Formosa prior to seeing combat in late 1943. Due to his vast tactical experience, Kawamoto rose rapidly through the ranks of the Ki-43-equipped 50th Sentai as the unit fought defensive battles over northern Burma and French Indochina. Following the death in combat of sentai leader Maj Tatsujiro Fujii in April 1945, Kawamoto took charge of the 50th and led it through to the end of the war. He sored eight kills whilst in action, and was awarded the Bukosho (Medal of Honor, B Class) on 10 June 1945 at 5th Air Division HQ in Phnom Penh, Cambodia, by Lt Gen Takeshi Hattori (*via K Kawamoto*)

The see-saw battles between Anglo-Chinese forces and the Japanese continued to rage in the skies over China until the war ended in August 1945. Throughout this time, when Gen Chiang Kai-Shek's CAF was not fighting the Japanese it was battling the Communists. This bitter feud characterised the political infighting that raged amongst key Allied personnel on the China-Burma-India front throughout the war, the end result of which was unnecessary casualties, delays in instigating offensive operations against the real enemy and the gross waste of scarce supplies.

23

Warrant Officer Bunichi Yamaguchi

It was considered most difficult for a pilot in the lightly-armed Ki-43 *Hayabusa* to single-handedly down a B-24 Liberator, but WO Bunichi Yamaguchi managed to destroy six and live to tell the tale!

This remarkable pilot was born in 1918 in Miyazaki Prefecture, Japan, and he joined the Army in 1936. Once he had completed flight courses in 1940, Yamaguchi was posted to the 1st Chutai of the 11th Sentai on the China front. He participated in the Malay operations at the start of the war, and although his unit intercepted RAF Blenheim bombers over Palembang in the early months of 1942, Yamaguchi failed to see any combat.

In April of that year the 204th Sentai was formed at Chinsei, Manchuria, from elements of various sentais, including the 11th – Yamaguchi joined the new unit and stayed with it until the end of the war. He arrived at Mingaladon Airfield in October 1943 and flew both air defence and offensive sorties. He finally claimed his first victory – a USAAF P-40 – on 22 December 1943 over Kunming, China.

WO Yamaguchi's most notable combat occurred on the night of 29 February 1944 when a pair of 'Oscars', flown by Yamaguchi and 2Lt Hiroshi Takiguchi, intercepted a formation of USAAF B-24s. They claimed two shot down, plus another pair as probables.

Lt Gen Noboru Tazoe, CO of the 5th Air Division, presented a citation to the two pilots, which read in part, '. . . (they) engaged in battle with 10+ Consolidated B-24s which raided Rangoon during the night of 29 February 1944. They took off in an emergency and were able to fight the enemy, taking advantage of the aerial searchlights which illuminated the aircraft. Both of our fighters were manoeuvred by our pilots to take full advantage of the capabilities of the aircraft. In a matter of seconds, two enemy aircraft were positively shot down into the ground and in addition, two more aircraft were severely damaged . . . Each of the aircraft flown by Takiguchi and Yamaguchi seriously damaged the enemy tactics employed, and raised the morale of friendly forces. In addition, they created a magnificent impression on the officials and people of Burma. With their outstanding spirit and determination to ensure that each attack resulted in a certain target being shot down, tradition was magnificently exemplified by these two individuals . . .'

The news of the daring attack circulated in the CBI and Yamaguchi's fame began to spread. In August 1944 he moved to Thailand, but the 204th Sentai was soon sent to Manila when the Philippines was threatened by American Forces. The unit was badly mauled by marauding USAAF and US Navy fighters within days of its arrival, and was duly forced to withdraw to Japan where its survivors tried to rebuild the sentai. By early 1945 the 204th had assembled a sufficient number of pilots and machines to participate in the defence of Okinawa, and WO Yamaguchi was heavily involved in a number of costly actions over the islands.

The spring of that year found Japanese forces preparing for the final onslaught as the Allies closed in around the Home Islands. Units were ordered to minimise combat missions in order to save their aircraft for a *kamikaze* suicide blitz, and this directive effectively saw the grounding of Yamaguchi and the remnants of the 204th Sentai until VJ-Day.

Sgt Bunichi Yamaguchi poses in front of an 11th Sentai Ki-27 in early 1941. This remarkable pilot went on to become a renowned heavy bomber specialist in the CBI, utilising 204th Sentai 'Oscars' to down six B-24s as part of a final tally of 19 kills (*Y Izawa*)

Bunichi Yamaguchi's final score of 19 victories was all the more impressive for the fact that it included six four-engined heavy bombers, all of which he shot down in the diminutive 'Oscar'. Yamaguchi passed away in 1992.

Master Sergeant Yukio Shimokawa

'Shimokawa, The Courageous Man' was the moniker given to Yukio Shimokawa by his fellow comrades in recognition of his bravery in combat. He hailed from Fukuoka Prefecture, and realised his boyhood dream of becoming a fighter pilot when he entered the Tokyo Army Flying School in April 1938.

By March 1941 Shimokawa had completed flight courses at Kumagaya and Tachiarai, and was assigned to the 5th Sentai. In January 1942 he was transferred to the 50th Sentai in Burma, but he returned to Japan four months later when the unit flew back to the Home Islands to exchange their Ki-27 'Nates' for Ki-43-I-Heis.

Once back in the frontline, and having engaged the RAF over the Burmese jungles, Shimokawa's reputation as a fearless fighter began to grow. On 24 December 1942, whilst pursuing a Blenheim bomber, he was wounded when shot through the thigh. Shimokawa's aircraft was also mortally damaged by the well-aimed burst, and with his *Hayabusa* burning fiercely, he bailed out. Despite the nature of his wounds, Shimokawa was able to return to his unit just a week later.

He was to see much action in 1943, the highlight being an action on 26 April when he claimed two enemy aircraft shot down over Lashio, Burma. However, Shimokawa's luck finally deserted him in the autumn when he was hit and blinded in one eye by the return fire from a B-24 – despite losing a considerable quantity of blood, he just managed to return to base. Shimokawa was immediately repatriated to Japan for hospitalisation.

The chronic shortage of experienced pilots by late 1944 saw a recuperated – but still medically unfit for combat – Shimokawa gain employment as a ferry pilot flying Oscars to Taiwan and the Philippines. The war finally caught up with the Burma veteran on 19 March 1945 when American carrier aircraft raided the Japanese naval base at Kure (southern Honshu). Shimokawa jumped into a Ki-84 'Frank' and, along with nine other pilots from Ozuki Airfield, scrambled into the air to repel the American fighters.

'Over Hiroshima at 6000 metres, we dove on enemy aircraft below. There must have been over 100 of them. In the following mêlée all my comrades were shot down and I was cornered near the mountains', he recounted some years later.

After shooting up two Hellcats, Shimokawa ran into the entire squadron strength of VF-17, whose F6F-5s had launched from USS *Hornet*. The 'Frank' pilot desperately tried to escape with the Grumman fighters in hot pursuit, flying headlong into a canyon. However, as he pulled up at its end to clear the mountains, Shimokawa presented an easy target for future six-kill ace Lt(jg) Tilman E Pool, who duly fired a long burst into the Japanese fighter – it exploded in flames just as its pilot bailed out.

'Just as my parachute opened it hooked up on a tree. I was burned, but I was OK', he remembered. Shimokawa had just provided the young

Texan with his third kill barely 24 hours after he had opened his account with a pair of Zekes over Kanoya Airfield.

In recognition for his actions on 19 March, and for several years of distinguished service, Shimokawa received a personal citation from Maj Gen Akira Horiuchi, Chief of the Army Aerial Transportation Department, on 28 July 1945. His citation read, 'Upon taking part in the battle on the Southern Front, you fought bravely in aerial combats, though you lost the sight of your left eye. You never abandoned your duty as an airman. You believed your special skill to fly is a gift. Since then, you have been doing your best; that is why your skill has accelerated greatly. You belonged to the transportation department. In March 1945, when you were ordered to transport planes to Taiwan, you happened to intercept US Navy fighters over Kyushu. You dashed into them and destroyed some of them; the others flew away. Since then, you belong to the Ninth Flying Unit and are in charge of education for students as an assistant instructor. You train them keenly and seriously. You overcame your handicap. You train them day and night. You have done your duty well. It can be said that your achievement is the result of your gift, but your spirit to do your duty and efforts are remarkable. You are the ideal airman. You are hereby commended'.

MSgt Yukio Shimokawa trained pilots for *kamikaze* attacks until the war ended. He claimed over 16 enemy aircraft destroyed.

Lieutenant Colonel Tateo Kato

Tateo Kato, who became the most celebrated and distinguished fighter-leader of the JAAF in World War 2, was born in 1904 after his father, Tetsuzo, was killed in the Russo-Japanese War.

There was no doubt that the young Kato would also follow a military career, and he duly graduated in the 37th Class of the Army Military Academy in July 1925. Flying had always fascinated this young cadet, so he soon elected to transfer from the infantry to the Army Air Force. Completing·the flight course at Tokorozawa in May 1927, Kato was posted to the 6th Hiko Rentai (flight regiment) in Pyongyang, Korea. His flying skill in the Kawasaki Ko-4 biplane fighter (a licence-built Nieuport-Delage NiD 29) was shown to be so outstanding that he was awarded a gift by his superior, and allowed to perform a demonstration at graduation which left the audience enthralled.

Prior to overseas duty, Lt Kato worked as a flight instructor at the Tokorozawa and Akeno Flying Schools, and by February 1936, he had been promoted to lead a chutai within the 5th Hiko Rentai.

In July 1937 the China War began, and Capt Kato led the 1st Chutai, equipped with Ki-10 Type 95 'Perry' biplanes, from the 2nd Hiko Daitai (flight battalion) to the front. The Ki-10s quickly demonstrated their superiority over the Chinese Polikarpov I-15s, and the aggressive Japanese pilots dominated their opponents in aerial combat – Kato's best day came on 25 March 1938 when he shot down four I-15s. When the new Ki-27 'Nates' arrived the following month the Japanese became the undisputed masters of the sky. As an example of this, Capt Kato's 1st Chutai fought against eight I-15s on 10 April and the CO personally claimed three shot down. By May his unit had accounted for 39 enemy aircraft for the loss of only three Ki-27s – his chutai also received

Maj Tateo Kato led the 64th Sentai from April 1941 until his death in May 1942. One of the most highly-respected sentai leaders of the entire JAAF in World War 2, Kato had scored over 18 victories when he fell victim to an RAF Blenheim IV of No 60 Sqn over the Bay of Bengal. Despite the major's death, the lessons he had taught his unit lived on for the 64th Sentai became the most famous JAAF unit of the war (*via Maru*)

Assigned to the 2nd Hiko Daitai, the then Capt Tateo Kato poses by his Ki-10 Type 95 fighter during the China War in the spring of 1938 – he shot down four I-15s in a Ki-10 on 25 March 1938. Despite the obvious superiority of the Kawasaki biplane over the Chinese-manned Polikarpov fighters, the Ki-10 was replaced by the new monoplane Ki-27 'Nate' within a month of Kato's successful combat (*via Maru*)

two unit citations in this period. Kato returned to Japan that same month with nine victories, a score which made him the top ace of the conflict.

Prior to his appointment as commander of the 64th Sentai, Capt Kato entered the Army university and worked on the staff at headquarters. He visited Europe on assignment, and inspected the German Air Force.

When the Pacific War started, Maj Kato's group escorted naval vessels to Malaya. The 64th Sentai then became very active in the theatre, and under Kato's command they recorded over 260 aerial victories. He disallowed individual victory credits for the sake of teamwork, and led his men by example in the air – it was quite rare for an officer of his rank to fly routine combat missions.

Lt Col Tateo Kato was killed on 22 May 1942 when his fighter was hit by return fire from Flt Sgt 'Jock' McLuckie, the air-gunner in a No 60 Sqn Blenheim IV bomber that had been sent to attack Akyab Airfield on the Burmese coast. The lone bomber had originally been part of a formation of three Blenheims scheduled to set out from Dum Dum, in India, to hit the Japanese airfield, but due to technical problems only Z9808, flown by WO Huggard, had managed to reach the target. They hastily dropped their bombs at low-level and sped off out over the Bay of Bengal at wave-top height.

However, despite the element of surprise being firmly in their favour, the Blenheim crew had spotted a number of 64th Sentai Ki-43s scrambling after them as they overflew Akyab. First off in pursuit of the daring raider was 10-kill ace Sgt Maj Yoshito Yasuda, who soon caught up with the Blenheim and dived in to attack. Fortunately for the three-man Blenheim crew (Sgt Jack Howitt was the third member, serving as navigator), their turret gunner in 'Jock' McLuckie proved to be a crack shot, despite having never before fired his guns in anger. He hit Yasuda'a 'Oscar' in its first pass, and the JAAF pilot was forced to return to Akyab.

Capt Masuzo Otani then took up the attack, but he too fell victim to a well-aimed burst from the Vickers 'K' gun and had to retire back to Burma. Finally, after almost 30 minutes of constant attack, three Ki-43-I-Heis appeared on the scene, with Lt Col Tateo Kato in the lead fighter. This did not phase the brave McLuckie, however, and as Kato pulled up after making his first diving pass on the Blenheim, the gunner raked the *Hayabusa*'s exposed belly with a long burst and the Ki-43 began to burn. Realising that he would never make it back to Akyab, Kato half-looped his stricken 'Oscar' and purposely dove into the sea – he had advised his pilots on numerous occasions in the past to perform just such a manoeuvre if hit badly over the water. The remaining two JAAF pilots immediately returned to Akyab to report the terrible news.

The Blenheim returned to India unscathed by the 'Oscars'' attacks, and once British Intelligence had ascertained just who was flying the Ki-43 downed by McLuckie, No 60 Sqn received the following signal from Air Officer Commanding Burma, Air Vice-Marshal D F Stevenson, on 2 August 1942;

'Please convey my congratulations toward WO Huggard, Sgt Howitt and Sgt McLuckie on the successful action they fought against four enemy fighters which took place over Akyab on 22 May, and which resulted in Lt Col T A Keo Kato (*sic*), leader of the Japanese fighter force, being shot down.'

The death of the charismatic leader was a severe blow to the JAAF in particular, and to Japan as a whole. In recognition of his distinguished service, Tateo Kato was elevated two ranks posthumously to major general, and it was recorded at the time that he had achieved 18 aerial victories. Even today, his memory is kept alive by the popular song 'Kato Hayabusa Sentoki Tai' (Fighter Air Group Kato), sung by spirited businessmen both young and old.

Captain Yukiyoshi Wakamatsu

Yukiyoshi Wakamatsu, who became an accomplished fighter pilot in China, was one of the few veterans of the CBI to gain all of his victories without ever flying the *Hayabusa* – the JAAF's workhorse – in combat.

Born in Kagoshima Prefecture in 1911, Wakamatsu entered the 3rd Flying Regiment in 1930 as a volunteer, and graduated from the 41st term student piloting course in November 1932. After graduation, he worked at Tokorozawa and Kumagaya Flying Schools as an assistant instructor, before entering officers' flight school in May 1938 and graduating later that year as a second lieutenant.

By the autumn of 1939 the Nomonhan Incident was coming to a close, and by the time 2Lt Wakamatsu arrived at Hailar, in Manchuria, for duty with the 64th Sentai, the bloody skirmish had just two days to run before the ceasefire was declared – hence, he saw no combat.

With peace now secured on the northern border, Wakamatsu's unit moved south into China, and he served out his time there in rather uneventful fashion before returning in 1940 to Japan for further training at Akeno.

In May 1941, Wakamatsu was sent to the newly-organised 85th Sentai, which was still flying the Ki-27 'Nate' despite the fact that most other JAAF fighter units had upgraded to the modern *Hayabusa*. Promoted to captain, he was given command of the 2nd Chutai in January 1942, and he duly led his squadron down to southern China when the whole sentai was moved closer to the action. Here, Wakamatsu began to blossom into a skilled fighter pilot.

On 24 July 1943 he claimed two P-40s of the 74th FS/23rd FG over Kweilin for his first victories, followed on 20 August by two more Warhawks from the same unit over Canton. His main fighter opposition throughout this period came from the 74th, and he was involved in numerous heated engagements with them in 1944 whilst flying the Ki-44 *Shoki* over Canton, Hong Kong and Hankow.

In September of that year Capt Wakamatsu changed his mount to the Ki-84 *Hayate*, and in his very first combat in the new aircraft on 4 October over Wuchow he encountered P-51Bs of the 76th FS/23rd FG – Wakamatsu claimed two Mustangs destroyed.

On 18 December Gen Claire Chennault sent a massive air raid to strike at Hankow, 84 B-29s firebombing supply depots and other targets in the city, supported by Fourteenth Air Force B-24s and B-25s. Fighters from the 23rd FG and the Chinese-American Composite Wing provided bomber escort, plus struck at Japanese airfields in the area in order to catch enemy fighters landing to refuel between sorties.

One of the pilots to fall victim to these roving fighter strikes was Capt Wakamatsu, who took off from a satellite airfield outside of Wuchang in

Capt Yukiyoshi Wakamatsu gained most of his 18+ victories flying Ki-44s with the 85th Sentai. He became something of a specialist against the P-51B/C in China, shooting down at least nine Mustangs prior to his death on 18 December 1944 (*via Maru*)

an attempt to re-engage the B-29s, but was quickly jumped by his old enemies from the 74th FS, led by five-kill ace Maj Phil Chapman. With his Ki-84's undercarriage barely retracted and still struggling to build up speed, Wakamatsu was surrounded by at least ten P-51Cs and blasted out of the sky.

Upon his death, Army HQ recommended that he be cited and promoted two ranks posthumously to lieutenant colonel. However, due to the confusion of war, the honours were never bestowed.

Capt Wakamatsu's aerial gunnery was exceptional, and it was accepted that he had shot down more than 18 enemy aircraft – all fighters – during his career. He became a specialist hunter of the P-51B/C, and it is believed that half of his total was made up of Mustangs.

A number of postwar historians have created a myth surrounding Wakamatsu's fighting ability, labelling him the 'Red-nosed Ace' who struck terror into the hearts of his opponents – his aircraft's spinner and tail were painted red. Credence is lent to this story by the fact that the Chinese government reputedly put a price on Wakamatsu's head, such was his skill in aerial combat. An ideal fighter leader, it was only fitting that he would emerge as a legendary figure after his death.

Captain Hiroshi Onozaki

Hiroshi Onozaki was born in 1917 in Tochigi Prefecture, Japan. He entered flight training at Kumagaya in the 3rd term Youth Flight Programme in February 1936, and as an outstanding trainee, received the presentation of a silver watch. After graduation, he was sent to the Akeno Fighter School for combat training.

During the Nomonhan Incident, Onozaki was transferred to the 59th Sentai in Manchuria, but he failed to see any action. Indeed, it wasn't until December 1941 that this young pilot was thrust into combat when, as a member of the 1st Chutai, he participated in the Malayan Campaign – his unit crossed the Gulf of Siam from French Indochina and strafed airfields at Kota Baharu on the north-eastern tip of Malaya.

Capt Hiroshi Onozaki (seen here in late 1942 as a second lieutenant) became the top ace of the 59th Sentai. He exacted a heavy toll on the embattled RAF during the early months of 1942, downing eight Hurricanes and a Blenheim IV over Java (*via Maru*)

Sgt Onozaki's first dogfight occurred over the skies of Kuala Lumpur on 21 December 1941 when he was credited with shooting down a Brewster Buffalo flown by Sgt K R Leys of No 453 Sqn, RAAF – other JAAF pilots from the 59th claimed three kills from this sortie, although only two Australian Buffalos were ever engaged, and Leys was the only casualty. The 'Oscar' pilots from this unit went on to attack targets over Malaya and Singapore, as well as Dutch and British fighters sent aloft to protect the oilfields at Palembang. Over Java, Onozaki added eight Hurricanes (from Nos 232 and 258 Sqns), a Blenheim IV (of No 211 Sqn, downed on 6 February) and a Ryan STM-2 trainer to his score, and thus become the top ace of the 59th Sentai.

In May MSgt Onozaki returned to the homeland, where he entered the Army Air Academy and duly graduated six months later as a second lieutenant. He subsequently returned to his unit in Java, where he commenced flying air defence duties around Timor Island. In January 1943 his flight shot down a USAAF B-25 which was part of a formation that had come to attack the Timorese capital of Dili.

On 20 June the JAAF launched a large attack on Port Darwin, in Australia, and the 59th Sentai, operating from Timor, sortied 22 'Oscars' under the command of the CO, Maj Takeo Fukuda, in support of the raiders – 18 bombers from the 61st Sentai and a further nine from the 75th. The force was opposed by some 46 Spitfire LF VCs from No 1 Fighter Wing, RAAF, and in the bitter dogfight that ensued, Onozaki claimed to have destroyed two of the Australian fighters.

The following month his unit was ordered to New Guinea, where Japanese Army troops were struggling in the face of renewed Allied attacks, as well as the harsh tropical environment. They commenced operations from their bases at But, on the eastern coast of New Guinea, within days of arriving, and on 15 August escorted bombers sent to attack the formerly secret Allied airfield at Tsili Tsili (Fabua). The following day, when they returned to finish the job, Onozaki became embroiled in a series of running battles with P-38s from the 431st FS over Marilinan, south of Tsili Tsili. Although he claimed one Lightning downed, USAAF records have since revealed that no fighters were lost on this date. Two days later he was surrounded at low altitude by an estimated 20 P-38s from the same unit, and only managed to escape thanks to the unmatched manoeuvrability of his Ki-43 at tree-top height. The next day, he was evacuated to Rabaul due to a severe attack of dysentery.

Capt Onozaki returned to Japan to become an instructor at Tachiarai, and he ended the war with a victory tally of 14 enemy aircraft shot down.

Major Hideo Miyabe

As the last air group commander of the illustrious 64th Sentai, Hideo Miyabe was yet another great fighter leader of the JAAF. Born in Kumamoto Prefecture in January 1919, he entered the Army Air Officers' School and duly graduated in the 52nd Class in 1939.

During the early war years, Miyabe served both with the 5th Sentai and as a commander of a ward in the Army Air Officers' School. His eye for administrative detail and leadership led to his appointment as leader of the 2nd Chutai/64th Sentai in February 1943.

The harsh tropical environment of the CBI, coupled with a lack of supplies and aggressive enemy forces, served to progressively weaken his unit after March 1943. Miyabe believed that leaders should foster confidence in their subordinates by fighting from the front, and the rigorous training regimes he set for his young pilots were implemented in the belief that such tests would someday perhaps save their lives. Miyabe was also hard on himself, for he took personal responsibility for the loss of any of his pilots, and blamed himself for unsuccessful operations.

He bears the distinction of being the first pilot to reportedly attack a B-29, for on 26 April 1944 Miyabe engaged B-29 (42-6330) of the 444th BG, which was flying supplies from China to India. Flying jointly with 'Oscars' from the 204th Sentai, he led the attack and reported machine gun strikes on

Maj Hideo Miyabe (far right) was the last CO of the famous 64th Sentai. He fostered teamwork, shunned publicity and would not even acknowledge his own victories (12+), nor the award of his Bukosho (*via Maru*)

This rare shot shows Capt Hideo Miyabe on patrol in his personal Ki-43-IIIa in late 1944. The final mass-produced variant of the venerable 'Oscar' family, the IIIa made its service debut with the 64th Sentai over Thailand in late October 1944 (*via Maru*)

one of the bomber's right engines. With their fuel running low, the Japanese pilots finally gave up the chase after the B-29 lost altitude – it was later claimed by the pilots as having been destroyed. The USAAF crew, however, reported no damage on their return, although they did claim to have shot one of their assailants down – none were reported as having been lost according to JAAF records.

In April 1945 Maj Miyabe was appointed as the leader of the 64th Sentai, and on 10 June was awarded the Bukosho by Lt Gen Takeshi Hattori of the 5th Air Division. His award citation states;

'The person mentioned herewith, since March 1943 as company commander, attacked airfields near Burma, co-operated with ground defence in a joint attack with competence and bravery – the enemy lost more than ten ships, more than 100 aircraft destroyed and several hundred motor vehicles. During this period, Maj Miyabe sank a large transport ship and damaged two others; he also damaged several small boats, shot down or damaged 30 aircraft. He also dropped supplies accurately, great deeds on every mission. He became a distinguished and remarkable air group commander of this traditionally famous and highly acclaimed unit.'

Miyabe did not appreciate his own commendation, and said of his award, 'The contents of the award scroll were somewhat exaggerated I must admit!'

He ended the war fighting in French Indochina, and returned to Japan where he became president of a large paper manufacturing company. While it is believed that he downed many enemy aircraft, he never acknowledged them – historians believe he scored more than 12 victories. The beloved leader of the 64th Sentai passed away in October 1978.

Major Yasuhiko Kuroe

Maj Yasuhiko Kuroe was the top scoring fighter pilot amongst the officers' group of the Army Military Academy. He was born in February 1918, the son of an army major, and following in his father's footsteps, the young Yasuhiko also joined up and subsequently graduated from the 50th Class of the Army Military Academy in June 1937. He elected to become a fighter pilot and entered flight training at Akeno.

Upon graduation from flight training, Kuroe was assigned to the 59th Sentai in November 1938 and transferred to Hankow Air Base, in central China. Experiencing a lull in the fighting at the time of his arrival, Kuroe joined other pilots of the unit in performing numerous training exercises with their new Ki-27 'Nates'. When the Mongolian border skirmish flared into a fully-blown war in 1939, the 59th was immediately dispatched to the Nomonhan Plateau. On the final day of fighting in mid-September, Kuroe claimed his first two victories in the shape of a pair of I-15s.

In 1941, 1Lt Kuroe returned to Japan and became a flight instructor at the Army Officers' Flight Academy, being promoted to the rank of captain in May. Four months later, nine prototypes of the new Ki-44 *Shoki*

'Tojo' fighter were assigned to the experimental 47th Independent Chutai for flight testing under combat conditions, and Capt Kuroe was duly placed in charge of the programme, flying the fighters to South-east Asia – French Indochina, Malaya and Burma. There were few opportunities for combat at this early stage of the war, however, but he still managed to down three Hurricanes of No 232 Sqn over Singapore, and other adjoining areas. Despite this success, Kuroe stated that the Ki-44 did not live up to his expectations, but the Nakajima fighter was nevertheless accepted into service.

With the American and British Forces making their presence felt in the CBI, the pressure was placed on the Army's 64th Sentai to keep them in check. Following his success with the Ki-44, Capt Kuroe was transferred to the unit and given command of the 3rd Chutai. After Lt Col Tateo Kato – the CO of the air group – was killed in May 1942, Kuroe was instrumental in keeping the sentai intact essentially through the sheer strength of his personality. Always an optimist, he had nerves of steel, a personable disposition and superior organisational skills, and it was with the 64th that Kuroe made a name for himself as the model fighter leader.

On 13 September 1943, Kuroe shot down a photo-recce F-5A (unarmed P-38) of the 9th Photo Squadron, its pilot, 1Lt Frank H Tilcock, remembering;

'I never saw my attackers. My first and only indication that I wasn't alone in the sky was when my instrument panel in my airplane disappeared. Fire and smoke poured into the cockpit.'

The American parachuted to safety, being captured three days later. Kuroe later wrote in his memoirs that he met Tilcock, who shook his hands and told him that he was downed on the day of his wedding anniversary! Frank Tilcock, who now resides in Florida, confirms that he was indeed shot down on this day.

'I met a lot of Jap officials who asked a lot of questions. Perhaps Kuroe was one of them?' he now ponders.

By this stage in the air war the RAF had drafted the Mosquito into action in the CBI, and the fighter-bomber was to plague the Japanese through to VJ-Day. Indeed, it was not until 2 November 1943 that an example of the seemingly invincible de Havilland aircraft was shot down, Capt Kuroe destroying PR IX DZ697 of No 684 Sqn ,which was being flown on a photo-recce sortie to Rangoon by Flg Offs Fielding and Turton at the time. On 10 December Kuroe encountered another Mosquito from the same unit (an FB II this time) in the Rangoon area, and doggedly pursued it for over 40 minutes out over the sea.

A burst of machine gun fire finally damaged the aircraft's left engine, but the 'Oscar's' guns then jammed. However, undeterred by this turn of events, the Japanese veteran managed to bluff the British pilot (Sgt Boot, with Sgt Wilkins as his navigator) into turning back towards land. The Mosquito and 'Oscar' flew in formation back towards Kuroe's base, but when the latter motioned for Boot to land, the damaged aircraft clipped a tree and crashed in a ball of fire – 'I was very sorry for him', recalled Kuroe some years later.

In January 1944, he was recalled to Japan to become a test pilot with the Army Flight Inspection Department, his new assignment involving

Maj Yasuhiko Kuroe was the top scoring ace amongst the Army Academy graduates, ending the war with 51 kills. He was also the first JAAF pilot to down an RAF Mosquito – a No 684 Sqn PR IX – over Burma (*via Maru*)

the evaluation of both rockets and experimental high altitude twin-engined fighters, which were being designed to oppose B-29s. During one test flight on 25 March, Maj Kuroe claimed two Superfortresses destroyed whilst flying an experimental Kawasaki Ki-102 twin-engined high altitude fighter, which was armed with a single 37 mm cannon and a pair of 20 mm weapons. Although successful on this occasion, the Kawasaki design failed to reach the frontline in serious numbers due to incessant engine problems. Kuroe added two more B-29s to his kill list on the night of 23 May whilst flying an early-production Ki-84-I-Ko.

In rare recognition of his outstanding service, Kuroe was awarded a citation and a special bottle of sake (rice wine) by Lt Gen Kumaichi Teramoto of the Army Flight Inspection Department in front of 3000 men on 15 July 1945.

Maj Yasuhiko Kuroe ended the war with a score of 51 victories. During his career he had been shot down three times, wounded on three separate occasions and the aircraft he had flown in combat had been hit over 500 times by the enemy!

Kuroe's talents were not wasted when the war ended for he entered the Japan Self-Defense Air Force, where he commanded a jet fighter squadron and rose to the rank of general. On 5 December 1965 Gen Kuroe drowned while fishing off a beach.

Warrant Officer Yojiro Ofusa

Yojiro Ofusa was one of the great aces of the 50th Sentai in the CBI. Born in 1918 in Miyagi Prefecture, Japan, he had joined the Army in the mid-1930s, but unlike many of his peers, Ofusa had fought at Nomonhan as an infantryman. Although the Japanese ground troops suffered tremendous losses in the bitter conflict, their Air Force was reported by the local media to have enjoyed great successes against their Soviet counterparts. The young gunner was duly impressed by such propaganda, and decided that his future lay as a fighter pilot.

In June 1942 Ofusa entered the NCO flight training class, from which he duly graduated four months later and was assigned to an air group in French Indochina. Here, he underwent more training before being posted in January 1943 to the 50th Sentai in Burma.

He fought throughout that year until his luck finally ran out on 24 November 1943. Tackling a large formation of B-24s from the 7th BG over Meikuterra, Ofusa quickly claimed one Liberator, but was also hit by return fire from the stricken bomber. Forced to take to his parachute, Ofusa subsequently spent 41 days in hospital recuperating. Upon his recovery, he went straight back into combat and was forced down on four separate occasions, although he also tempered these minor setbacks by becoming one of the top scoring pilots in the air group.

Ofusa was awarded the Bukosho (B Class) on 10 June 1945 in Phnom Penh, Cambodia – at the time of his award, he had shot down 19 enemy aircraft, damaged another 21 and sunk a cruiser in the Akyab area of the Indian Ocean.

He ended the war on Formosa after his air group withdrew from French Indochina in July 1945. His score of 19 included five P-51s, two P-47s, four Hurricanes and a Spitfire. After the war, he changed his name to Higuchi and he now resides in his native prefecture.

WO Yojiro Ofusa proved that a lightly-armed Ki-43 in the hands of a skilled pilot could defeat technically superior opposition in the form of Mustangs, Thunderbolts and Spitfires – indeed, of his 19 kills, 12 were single-engined Allied fighters. He won the rare Bukosho for his exploits in the CBI (*via Y Higuchi*)

Master Sergeant Satoshi Anabuki

Despite being the top fighter pilot of the JAAF in World War 2, Satoshi Anabuki was not well known to the Japanese public during the war years – an ignorance equally shared by his Allied opponents. Nevertheless, within the JAAF, his exploits gained him notoriety as the 'Flower of the Youth Flyers'.

The son of a farming parents, Anabuki was born in 1921, and soon expressed a love for flying. He first joined the Army Youth Preparatory Flight Programme and entered the Tokyo Army Aviation School in April 1938. He received further training at Kumagaya and Tachiarai, and upon the completion of courses here in March 1941, was assigned to the 3rd Chutai of the 50th Sentai on Formosa in July.

On 7 December 1941 19-year-old Cpl Anabuki participated in attacks on the Philippines, his first combat taking the form of a pursuit attack against a B-17D. He scored his premier victory on 22 December when he downed a 17th Pursuit Squadron (PS) P-40E over Lingayen Gulf, the latter having just strafed Japanese naval vessels. After the invasion, the main force of the 50th Sentai shipped out to Burma, but Anabuki's chutai remained behind. Making the most of his extended stay, he downed two 17th PS P-40s over Limai on 9 February 1942, these Warhawks being amongst the last airworthy USAAF fighters left to protect the Philippines at the time.

In April Anabuki returned to Japan with his unit, the latter exchanging their obsolescent Ki-27s for new Ki-43-I-Hei *Hayabusas*. Fully equipped, they flew on to Burma in June and operated around Mingaladon Airfield on the outskirts of Rangoon.

It was in the CBI that the 'Boy Wonder' blossomed. Perhaps the best example of his skill occurred on 24 December 1942 when, after his aircraft was damaged during a bombing raid while taking off, he was forced to do battle with RAF Hurricanes with his landing gear extended. Despite this handicap, Anabuki succeeded in downing three of them – RAF losses reveal that only two Hurricane IIBs failed to return, however, one each from Nos 607 and 615 Sqns. The pilot of the former machine, Plt Off C D 'Chook' Fergusson, was thrown clear of his exploding aircraft when it blew apart just feet above a sandbank in the Iwaraji River. Although badly burnt, he was to make a full recovery from his horrific injuries.

On 26 January 1943 Anabuki downed his first B-24. Ten months later on 8 October he was to repeat this success three times over when he downed a trio of Liberators, plus two of their Lightning escorts. One of his bomber kills was achieved by ramming the right fin assembly, and despite achieving 'ace in a day' status, he was wounded in the process

The JAAF's 'Ace of Aces' in World War 2, MSgt Satoshi Anabuki is seen here posing in front of an 'Oscar' in late 1944. He is wearing the standard Air Force summer flight suit. His parachute harness is a Type 92, whilst the white identification label on the strapping itself reads 'MSgt Anabuki'. Despite being dressed in a summer suit, Anabuki is inexplicably wearing a winter flying helmet (*via Maru*)

Taken at the same time as the photo above, Anabuki strikes a typical fighter pilot's pose in between Akeno Fighter School Ki-43-IIas in late 1944. Note his bandaged left hand, which was the result of his 8 October 1944 combat with US Navy Hellcats (*via Maru*)

ing on a Burmese beach – he was rescued some three days later.

Anabuki's daring feat raised the morale of his air group, and personally brought him a number of awards. Gen Kawabe, commanding the Burma District Force, presented him with a Chinese poem which he had personally composed, whilst Gen On San, the Burmese Army commander, visited the wounded pilot in the hospital to pay his respects. Although not fully recovered, Anabuki insisted on returning to duty but was forbidden to fly.

In February 1944 he returned to Japan, where he became a valued instructor at the Akeno Fighter School. He was promoted to master sergeant in October, and while employed in the hazardous task of ferrying Ki-84 *Hayates* to the Philippines, engaged in several combats with US Navy Hellcats and managed to shoot down six of them. Anabuki then flew home defence duties until the end of the war, adding a single B-29 to his score.

MSgt Anabuki kept an elaborate diary during his career, in which he recorded 173 missions in Burma and 51 victories – 30 were officially recognised. Postwar historians have since pegged his tally at 39.

Anabuki subsequently joined the Self-Defense Air Force in the 1950s and flew helicopters. He is now retired.

Major Yohei Hinoki

One cannot talk about the exploits of the 64th Sentai without mentioning Tateo Kato (the air group commander) or Yohei Hinoki, the latter's combat experiences in the CBI and Japan rivalling those of Zero ace Saburo Sakai.

Hinoki was born in Tokushima Prefecture in 1919. He received his flight commission in June 1941 and was posted to the 64th Sentai, where he served in the Malayan campaign. Here, the young second lieutenant was coached by Nomonhan veteran, Capt Iwori Sakai, in the complex art of dogfighting.

On the opening day of the war Hinoki fought against No 34 Sqn Blenheim IVs, claiming a half-share in the destruction of one of the bombers. Assigned as wingman to Sentai commander Maj Tateo Kato, his job was to protect his commander at all costs. Opportunities to engage in free-for-all combat were therefore rather rare, but Hinoki did, nevertheless, manage to claim two No 238 Sqn Hurricane IIs shot down over Singapore on 31 January 1942.

On 10 April 1942 AVG P-40Cs clashed with the 64th Sentai over Loiwing, China, in a low altitude dogfight in the clouds. Hinoki became embroiled in a fierce tussle with 3rd AVG Sqn ace Flt Ldr Robert T Smith (eight kills). The *Hayabusa* pilot was seriously wounded in the left arm and buttocks during the clash, his parachute harness stopping a .50 cal round from lodging in his back – so badly shot up was the 'Oscar' that Smith claimed it as a probable when he returned to base, having also scored a confirmed kill during the sortie.

Despite having somehow escaped his attacker, Hinoki was disoriented and crazed with pain, and just wanted to crash his fighter into a mountain peak to end his suffering. Fortunately for him, he regained his senses and followed a river back to an air base in Thailand where, after an agonising two-hour flight, he effected a deadstick landing – his fuel supply was

Lt Hinoki prepares to board his extremely weathered 64th Sentai Ki-43-Ic in Malaya in 1942. Like many JAAF officer pilots, he would often carry his sword in his aircraft for good luck. Hinoki's flight helmet was a gift from his instructor, Nomonhan ace Maj Iwori Sakai (*via Y Hinoki*)

completely exhausted by this stage. Hinoki was hospitalised for a month.

On 25 November 1943 Hinoki may have become the first Japanese pilot to shoot down a P-51 (probably an A-36A) in the CBI. His flight was scrambled to intercept seven unidentified aircraft that had entered Burmese territory, and once in visual contact with the fighters, he rocked his wings at the lead machine in order to try and ascertain its origins. The question of identification was soon settled when Col Harry R Melton, Jr, (CO of the 311th Fighter-Bomber Group) fired at him! Hinoki replied by latching onto the tail of the colonel's aircraft and inflicting mortal damage to the Mustang as its pilot desperately attempted a 'Split-S' manoeuvre. Forced to take to his parachute, Col Melton, Jr, was soon captured upon landing.

Two days later the 311th returned in force, along with a number of B-24s, heading for targets in Insein. Hinoki claimed one P-51 and an escorting P-38, plus a Liberator confirmed and a second bomber as a probable – both came from the 308th BG. Whilst pursuing the B-24s as they fled the target area, he was attacked by a 530th FS P-51A flown by 2Lt Robert F Mulhollem (who would go on to become a five-kill ace).

During the course of the brief dogfight which ensued, Hinoki was struck by a .50 cal bullet which nearly severed his right leg, but once again the 'Oscar' ace managed to extricate himself from this predicament and make a successful landing – Mulhollem, meanwhile, claimed Hinoki as a probable, having already scored two definite 'Oscar' kills earlier in the sortie. Hinoki's leg was amputated soon after he landed, and he spent many months in the base hospital gaining sufficient strength in order to survive being shipped back to Japan.

Because of his invaluable combat experience, Hinoki became an instructor at the Akeno Fighter School. Outfitted with an artificial leg, he later went on to flying combat missions against B-29s and their escorts.

In the last major combat of his career, Maj Hinoki extracted revenge against the Mustang. On 16 July 1945 he was pitted against P-51Ds of the 506th FG over Ise (Nagoya) Bay, piloting a Ki-100 *Goshikisen*. He was forced to close to within 20 metres of his target due to a severely vibrating propeller which badly upset the accuracy of his aim. Capt John W Benbow of the 457th FS felt the full force of his mixed cannon and machine-gun armament, and his Mustang went down in a slow gliding turn, trailing smoke – Benbow was never seen again.

After the combat of 16 July, the 111th Sentai was formed with a mix of Ki-84s and Ki-100s, and Hinoki was assigned as the leader of the 2nd Daitai – it saw very little combat, however.

It is estimated that Maj Yohei Hinoki downed more than 12 enemy aircraft, and his varied combat experiences demonstrated that a skilled pilot in a lightly-armed fighter like the *Hayabusa* could destroy Hurricanes, Lightnings, Mustangs and even Liberators. A gentleman in every sense of the word, the 'Master Falcon' finally passed away in January 1991.

Warrant Officer Isamu Sasaki

Unlike many of the more famous JAAF fighter pilots of World War 2, Isamu Sasaki's extraordinary accomplishments have received very little recognition over the years.

Born in 1921 in Hiroshima Prefecture, he left technical school and

Isamu Sasaki, pictured here as a cadet at the Tokyo Army Aviation School in 1938, scored some 38 kills whilst flying Ki-43s and -84s with the 50th Sentai – a score which inlcuded the destruction of six B-29s. He was awarded the Bukosho for sustained distinguished service (*via I Hirayama*)

Sgt Moritsugu Kanai (standing) and his crew chief pose next to his 11th Sentai Ki-27 'Nate' in China in 1940. The writing on the fuselage reads 'Aikoku 437', denoting that the fighter had been 'purchased' and donated by a patriotic citizen or organisation (via Y Izawa)

joined the Tokyo Army Aviation School in April 1938. Upon graduation in March 1941, he was assigned to the 50th Sentai, based on Formosa.

On the first day of the Pacific War Sasaki took part in the invasion of the Philippines, his baptism of fire taking place on 10 December 1941 over Bigan Bay when he chased a B-17C that had made a surprise attack on the Japanese invasion fleet. He pursued the Boeing bomber towards the vicinity of Bagio, where Navy Zeroes took over the hunt.

In January 1942 Sasaki advanced into Thailand with his unit and scored his first victory over Rangoon. In the violent Burma Campaign he went on to achieve over 20 kills against fighters, as well as claiming to have destroyed more than a dozen larger aircraft. In April 1944 he returned to Japan to become an examiner of test pilots.

Sasaki's courage and elaborate skills were aptly demonstrated to the examination department on 25 May 1945 when, in a single night action against B-29s over Tokyo, he targeted the enemy by silhouetting them against the great fires below. He would then dive at his victim head-on – he shot down three Superfortresses in this fashion in a matter of minutes.

By the end of hostilities, Sasaki had destroyed six B-29s and damaged three others, bringing his total war claims to at least 38. For his actions against B-29s, allied with his distinguished record in Burma, Sasaki was awarded the Bukosho (Medal of Honour, B Class) and received a promotion to warrant officer.

After the war, Sasaki changed his name to Hirayama and joined the Japan Self-Defense Air Force. He is now retired, and resides in Hiroshima Prefecture.

Lieutenant Moritsugu Kanai

Moritsugu Kanai was one of the very few JAAF pilots in China to score consistently against the Americans throughout the later war years. Born in Yamanashi Prefecture in 1919, he joined the Youth Flying Corps of the Kumagaya Flying School in February 1937.

Kanai first saw action as a member of the 11th Sentai when posted to Manchuria during the Nomonhan Incident. As a pilot in the 1st Chutai, under the command of Capt Kenji Shimada, he often flew as wingman to the top JAAF ace, Sgt Hiromichi Shinohara. By the end of hostilities, Cpl Kanai had scored seven victories.

The 11th Sentai subsequently operated in ground support missions in central China after transferring out of Manchuria, seeing very little aerial combat whilst performing this role. Kanai was then assigned to the 87th Sentai, and promoted to master sergeant, before entering the Army Officers' Flight School in December 1942. Commissioned as a second lieutenant upon graduation, Kanai was then posted to the 25th Sentai in China.

37

On 10 March 1944 2Lt Kanai opened his scoring in World War 2 when he shot down a P-38 of the 449th FS whilst flying an 'Oscar' over Anching. On 6 May, whilst tackling P-38s from the same unit over the Hankow area, his fighter was hit in the oil tank and barely managed to make it home. Once safely on the ground, he rushed over to another Ki-43 and resumed the fight – he subsequently claimed two P-38s destroyed! By the end of 1944, his tally stood at 19, which included a B-29.

Kanai's last assignment was in Korea, and by war's end he had increased his score to 32 victories – other published sources have pegged his tally at 26. After the war, Kanai joined the Japan Self-Defense Force. Sadly, he was killed in an accident in August 1972.

Captain Ryotaro Jobo

Ryotaro Jobo has been listed at one time or another in Japanese publications as having scored either 70 or 76 kills, and while his victory tally may be the topic of some conjecture, his accomplishments as a fighter pilot most certainly are not.

Jobo was born in 1916 in Shiga Prefecture. At the age of 18 he entered the Tokorozawa Army Flying School, and in January 1935 he graduated and was assigned to the 6th Flying Regiment at Pyongyang, in Korea. In January 1936 he graduated from the Akeno Fighter School, and in August 1937 Jobo joined the 9th Chutai and went to fight in the China War. One year later he became a member of the 64th Sentai.

When the latter unit was thrust into the aerial battles against Soviet-Mongolian forces at Nomonhan, Jobo soon proved his ability as a fighter pilot by scoring his first victory (an I-16) on 3 August 1939. Eleven days later he added another Polikarpov to his tally.

On 21 August the JAAF crossed the Khalka River to strike at Soviet bases at Tamsak-Bulak in an all-out attack. Over 50 Japanese heavy and light bombers and close support aircraft, protected by 88 Ki-27 'Nates', engaged more than 250 Soviet aircraft over a period of 13 hours. In the midst of the wild and confusing dogfights, Jobo managed to shoot down two I-16s, but was hit numerous times and suffered shrapnel wounds to his face.

By the time a ceasefire had been brokered between the Nomonhan protagonists in September 1939, Jobo had claimed 18 Soviet fighters shot down. From Nomohan, the 64th Sentai moved to southern China, and he returned to Japan in February 1940 and entered the Army Officers' Flight Academy – he graduated from here in July 1941. Jobo was assigned to the 33rd Sentai and posted back to southern China, where he fought until September 1943. While in-theatre he claimed two P-40s.

Lt Jobo went on to become a specialist against B-29s in the CBI, joining the 1st Field Reserve Squadron, which was equipped with Ki-43 *Hayabusa* and Ki-44 *Shoki* fighters – the latter were fitted with experimental rocket launchers under the wings so as to stand a better chance of bringing down the heavily-armed B-29s.

In June 1945 Jobo was promoted to captain and posted into the Pacific to take part in the Okinawan campaign – despite the general carnage of the late war struggle to defend the Home Islands, he survived to see peace once more.

Jobo's comrade, the great 'B-29 killer' Capt Isamu Kashiide, believes

Capt Ryotaro Jobo had nerves of steel and was a master swordsman. His final tally of 30+ victories included over a dozen B-29s either shot down or damaged in the CBI (*via R Jobo*)

that he downed 76 enemy aircraft, a figure that Gen Kanshi Ishikawa (former major and CO of the 246th Sentai) agrees with. According to Jobo's memoirs, however, he more modestly states that he downed over 30 aircraft, including 18 Soviet fighters at Nomonhan, two P-40s in China and two B-29s in the CBI, plus another ten Superfortresses probably destroyed or damaged. Ryotaro Jobo resides in Nagoya, Japan.

Warrant Officer Kosuke Tsubone

Kosuke Tsubone was one of the most talented aces in the 64th Sentai, but due to his CO's disdain for publicising the exploits of his pilots, the former's war career has remained relatively unknown.

He was born in Fukuoka Prefecture, Japan, and in February 1938 he entered the Youth Preparatory Flight Programme. Upon completion of this course, he moved on to the Kumagaya Flight School and graduated from here in July 1939. His first assignment was with the 13th Sentai, and at the start of the Pacific War, he was to be found in Taiwan undergoing training.

Tsubone was transferred to the 64th Sentai in April 1942, his first combat occurring on 5 May when he participated in a bomber escort mission to Paoshan, China. Engaged by P-40Cs from the 2nd AVG Sqn, his aircraft was hit in the fuel tank and forced to make an emergency landing. Despite this rather inauspicious start, Tsubone went on to complete many successful missions until war's end.

On 10 June 1945 MSgt Tsubone was awarded the Bukosho (B Class) for distinguished service in Phnom Penh by Lt Gen Takeshi Hattori, the 5th Air Division CO. At the same time, three other aces (WO Yojiro Ofusa and Maj Koki Kawamoto of the 50th Sentai, and Maj Hideo Miyabe of the 64th) were also decorated with the Bukosho.

WO Kosuke Tsubone achieved over ten victories in the CBI. He died in June 1990.

Kosuke Tsubone (far left) poses with fellow 64th Sentai pilots prior to flying the next over the Chinese plains in mid-1942. He finished the war with over ten kills, all scored flying Ki-43s (*via H Sakaida*)

1
Ki-27-Otsu of the 1st Chutai/11th Sentai, flown by WO Hiromichi Shinohara, Nomonhan, June 1939

2
Ki-27-Otsu of the 2nd Chutai/24th Sentai, Nomonhan, 1939

3
Ki-43-I of the 3rd Chutai/64th Sentai, flown by Capt Katsumi Anma, Ipoh Airfield, Malaya, January 1942

4
Ki-43-I of the 3rd Chutai/64th Sentai, flown by 1Lt Shogo Takeuchi, Malaya, early 1942

5
Ki-43-I of the 1st Chutai/50th Sentai, flown by Sgt Isamu Sasaki, Burma, 1942

6
Ki-43-I of the 3rd Chutai/50th Sentai, flown by Cpl Satoshi Anabuki and 1Lt Shigeru Nakazaki, Burma, January 1943

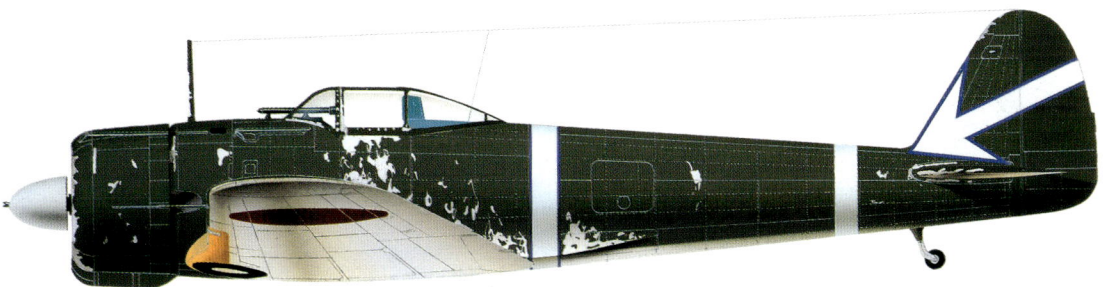

7
Ki-43-I of the 64th Sentai, flown by Group CO Maj Tateo Kato, Burma, Spring 1942

8
Ki-43-I of the 2nd Chutai/25th Sentai, flown by Sgt Kushiro Otake, Nanking, China, Summer 1943

9
Ki-43-II of the 3rd Chutai/54th Sentai, flown by MSgt Akira Sugimoto, northern Japan, late 1943

10
Ki-43-II of the 64th Sentai, flown by Capt Hideo Miyabe, Burma, Spring 1944

11
Ki-43-II of the 2nd Chutai/64th Sentai, flown by Capt Hideo Miyabe, Palembang Airfield, Sumatra, Summer 1943

12
Ki-43-II of the 3rd Chutai/64th Sentai, Lt Yohei Hinoki, Mingaladon Airfield, Burma, November 1943

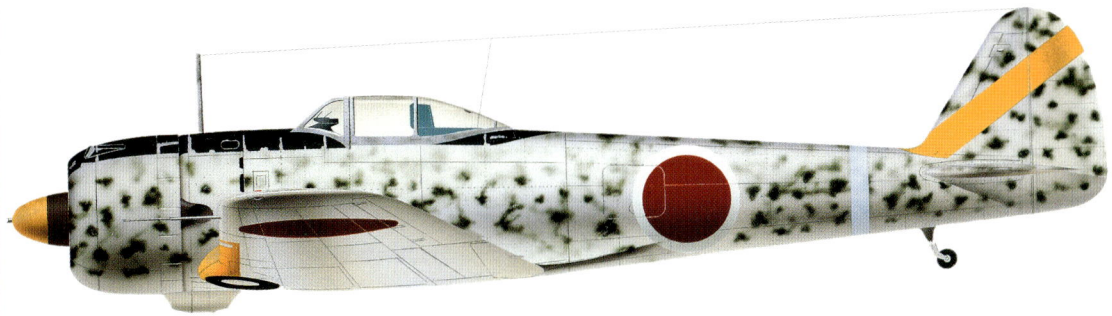

13
Ki-43-II of the 3rd Chutai/59th Sentai, flown by MSgt Tomio Hirohata, New Guinea, Summer 1943

14
Ki-43-II of the 1st Chutai/33rd Sentai, flown by Capt Kiyoshi Namai, Gelunbang Airfield, Sumatra, Summer 1944

15
Ki-43-III-Ko of the 2nd Chutai/64th Sentai, flown by WO Kosuke Tsubone, Krakor Airfield, Indochina, May 1945

16
Ki-43-II-KAI of the 1st Chutai/64th Sentai, flown by Chutai CO Maj Toyoki Eto, Saigon, Indochina, July 1944

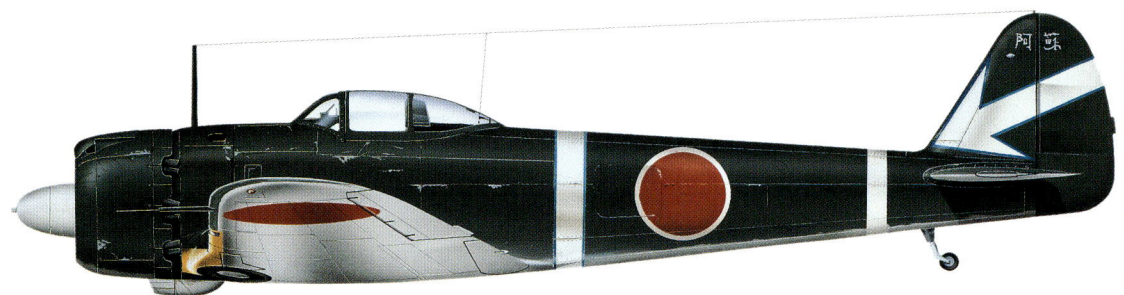

17
Ki-43-III-Ko flown by the 64th Sentai CO, Maj Hideo Miyabe, Krakor Airfield, Indochina, May 1945

18
Ki-43-II of the 2nd Chutai/59th Sentai, flown by Capt Shigeo Nango, But Airfield, New Guinea, September 1943

19
Ki-43-II of the 25th Sentai, flown by Maj Toshio Sakagawa, Hankow Airfield, China, Spring 1944

20
Ki-44-II-Hei of the 3rd Chutai/70th Sentai, flown by Capt Yoshio Yoshida, Kashiwa Airfield, Japan, June 1945

21
Ki-44-II-Hei of the 3rd Chutai/70th Sentai, flown by 2Lt Makoto Ogawa, Kashiwa Airfield, Japan, June 1945

22
Ki-84-Ko of the 246th Sentai, flown by WO Kenji Fujimoto, Taisho Airfield, Osaka, Japan, July 1945

23
Ki-45-KAI-Ko of the 3rd Chutai/5th Sentai, flown by Chutai CO Capt Fujitaro Ito, Kiyosu Airfield, Japan, March 1945

24
Ki-45-KAI-Hei of the 4th Sentai/Kaiten Tai, flown by Lt Miosaburo Yamamoto, Japan, early 1945

25
Ki-45-KAI-Ko of the 2nd Chutai/4th Sentai, flown by Lt Isamu Kashiide, Kozuki Airfield, Japan, 1944-45

26
Ki-45-KAI of the 2nd Chutai/4th Sentai, flown by WO Sadamitsu Kimura, Kozuki Airfield, Japan, January 1945

27
Ki-45-KAI of the 2nd Chutai/4th Sentai, flown by Lt Hannoshin Nishio, Kozuki Airfield, Japan, June 1945

28
Ki-45-KAI of the 3rd Chutai/53rd Sentai, flown by Sgt Nobuji Negishi, Matsudo Airfield, Japan, November 1944

29
Ki-61-I-Hei of the 244th Sentai, flown by Sgt Masao Itagaki, Chofu Airfield, Tokyo, January 1945

30
Ki-61-I-Hei of the 2nd Chutai/244th Sentai, flown by MSgt Tadao Sumi, Chofu Airfield, Tokyo, November 1944

31
Ki-61-I-KAIc No 3295 of the 244th Sentai, flown by Group CO Capt Teruhiko Kobayashi, Japan, January 1945

32
Ki-61-I-KAIc No 3024 of the 244th Sentai, flown by Group CO Capt Teruhiko Kobayashi, Japan, December 1944

33
Ki-61-I-KAIc No 3024 of the 244th Sentai, flown by Group CO Capt Teruhiko Kobayashi, Japan, April 1945

34
Ki-61-I-KAIc of HQ flight/244th Sentai, flown by TSgt Kiyoshi Ando, Japan, January 1945

35
Ki-61-I-Otsu of the 2nd Chutai/68th Sentai, flown by Capt Shogo Takeuchi, Wewak, New Guinea, October 1943

36
Unmarked Ki-84-Ko of the Army Flight Test Centre, flown by MSgt Isamu Sasaki, Fussa Airfield, Tokyo, 1945

37
Ki-84-Ko of the 1st Chutai/103rd Sentai, flown by Capt Tomojiro Ogawa, Itami Airfield, Japan, January 1945

38
Ki-84-Ko of the the HQ Chutai/ 50th Sentai, flown by Maj Koki Kawamoto, Phnom Penh, Indochina, April 1945

39
Ki-84-Ko of the 3rd Chutai/103rd Sentai, flown by 1Lt Shigeyasu Miyamoto, Itami Airfield, Japan, January 1945

40
Ki-84-Ko of the 1st Chutai/103rd Sentai, flown by Capt Tomojiro Ogawa, Itami Airfield, Japan, January 1945

1
Sgt Satoshi Anabuki, seen at the Akeno Fighter School in February 1944

2
MSgt Masatoshi Masuzawa of the 1st Sentai in his flying gear as worn during the Nomonhan Incident in 1939

3
Cpl Susumu Kajinami of the New Guinea-based 68th Sentai models his lightweight flying suit in late 1943

4
Capt Fujitaro Ito of the 5th Sentai
prepares to enter his Ki-45 at Kiyosu
Airfield, Japan, in March 1945

5
2Lt Yohei Hinoki of the 64th Sentai in
service dress in China in the spring of
1942

6
WO Makato Ogawa of the 70th
Sentai, based near Tokyo on home
defense duties in 1945

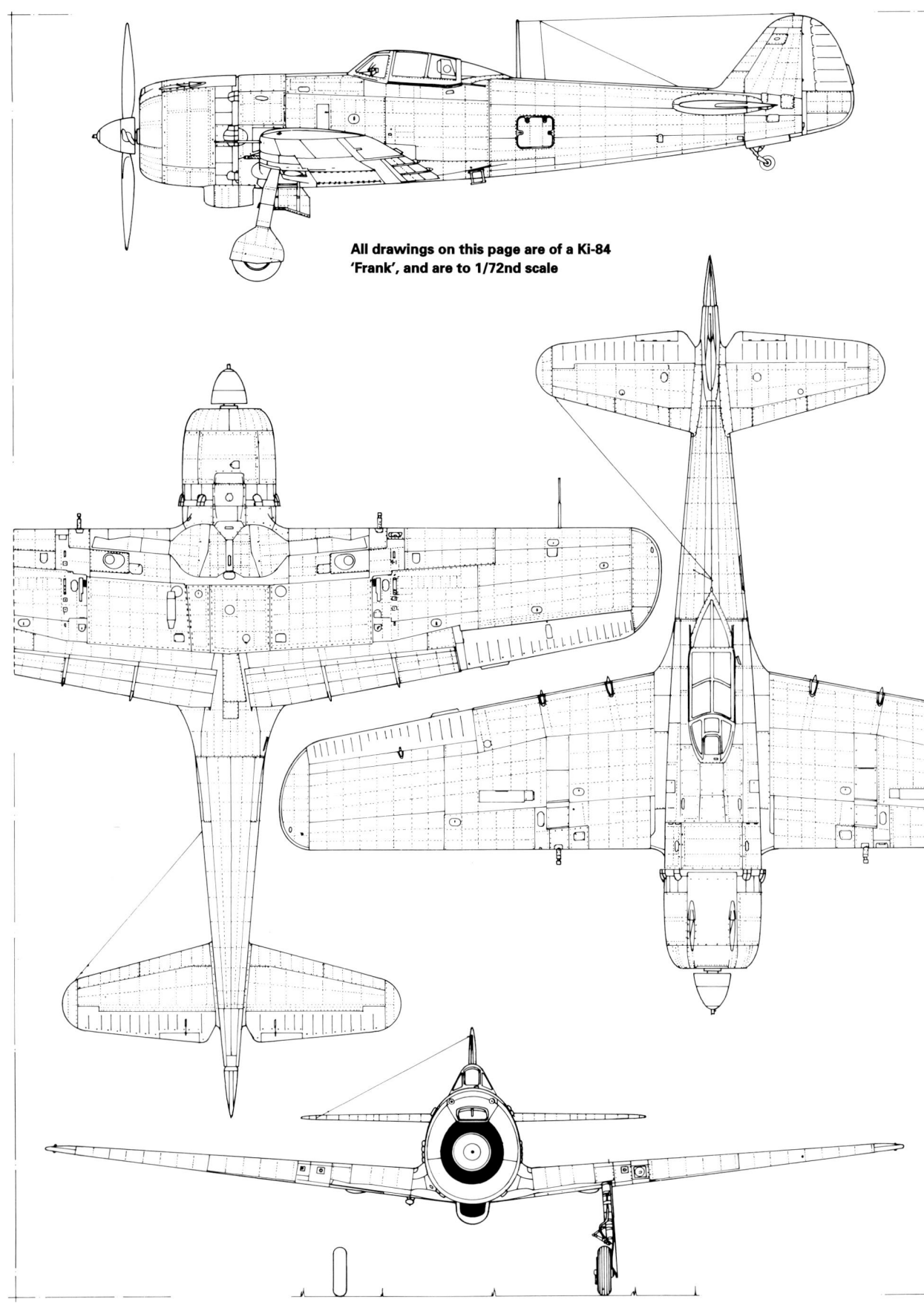

**All drawings on this page are of a Ki-84
'Frank', and are to 1/72nd scale**

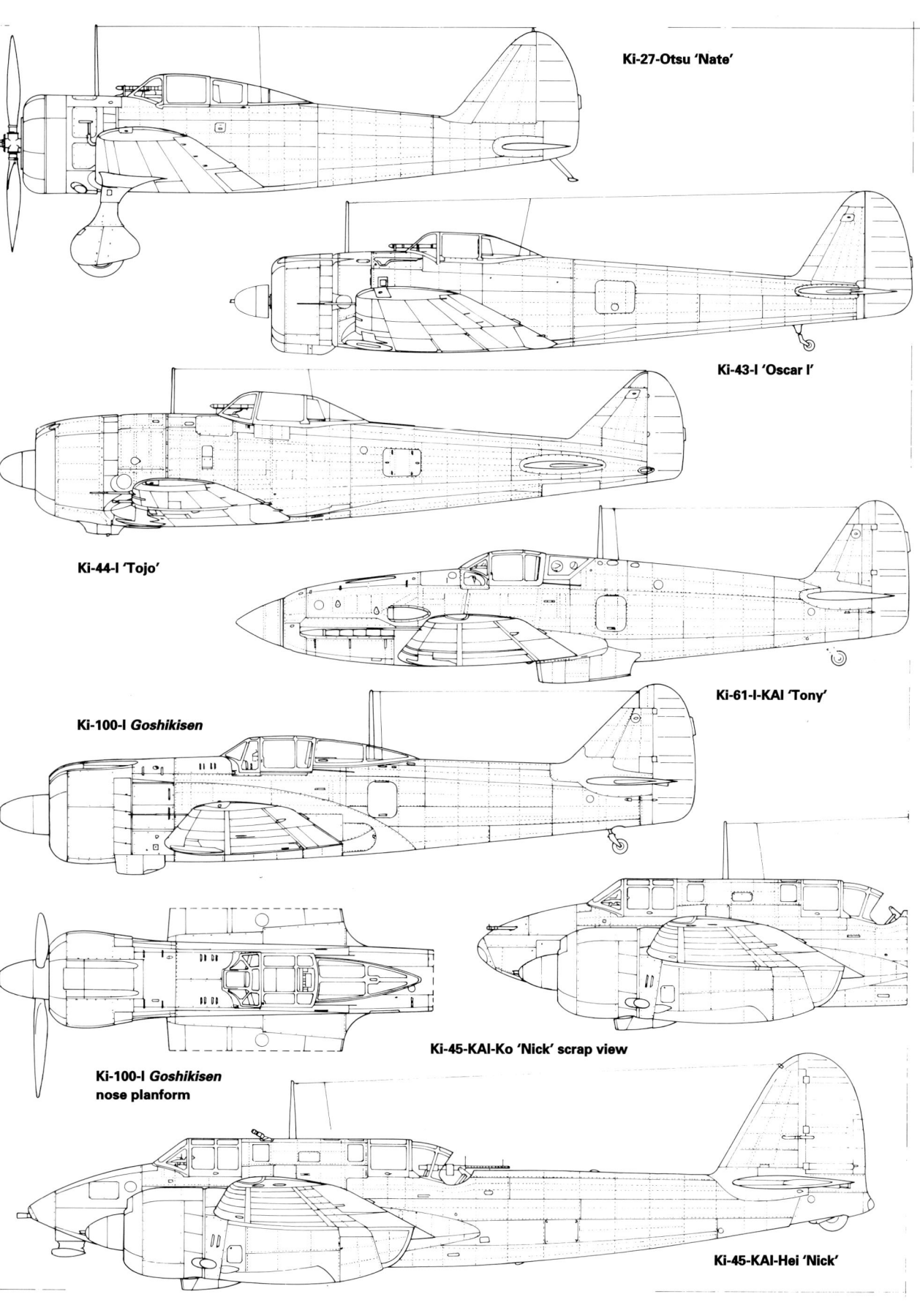

Ki-27-Otsu 'Nate'

Ki-43-I 'Oscar I'

Ki-44-I 'Tojo'

Ki-61-I-KAI 'Tony'

Ki-100-I *Goshikisen*

Ki-45-KAI-Ko 'Nick' scrap view

Ki-100-I *Goshikisen*
nose planform

Ki-45-KAI-Hei 'Nick'

COLOUR PLATES

1

Ki-27-Otsu of the 1st Chutai/11th Sentai, flown by WO Hiromichi Shinohara, Nomonhan, June 1939

The white lightning bolt markings on the tail of this 'Nate' indicates that the aircraft belonged to the 1st Chutai. Pilots flew the 'Nates' on an availability basis, and some painted red stars on the fuselage behind the cockpit to indicate victories over their Soviet opponents. This particular aircraft was lost on 25 July 1939 when Hiromishi Shinohara was forced to make an emergency landing after combat. He abandoned his aircraft and was picked up by a comrade as enemy tanks advanced on them. Shinohara set a JAAF record by downing 11 enemy aircraft in one day on 27 June (perhaps in this very Ki-27), and had amassed 58 victories by the time of his death in action on 27 August 1939.

2

Ki-27-Otsu of the 2nd Chutai/24th Sentai, Nomonhan, 1939

The kanji characters read 'Aikoku 318 (Dai Go Kaishima)' or 'Patriot 318 (No 5 Kaishima)' on this fighter. Kaishima was an organisation which had donated funds for the purchase of this aircraft, which was a common practice during the early war years. This particular 'Nate' was flown at various times in combat by Sgt Chiyoji Saito (21 victories), 2Lt Hyoe Yonaga (16 victories) and Sgt Goro Nishihara (12 victories).

3

Ki-43-I of the 3rd Chutai/64th Sentai, flown by Capt Katsumi Anma, Ipoh Airfield, Malaya, January 1942

In the spring of 1938 Anma claimed his first victory (a Chinese I-16) and went on to score five kills at Nomonhan. In August 1940 he became CO of the 3rd Chutai, and after claiming 32 victories was shot down and killed by P-40s of the AVG over Loiwing, China, on 8 April 1942.

4

Ki-43-I of the 3rd Chutai/64th Sentai, flown by 1Lt Shogo Takeuchi, Malaya, early 1942

Although Shogo Takeuchi is believed to have downed more than 30 enemy aircraft with the 64th, his sentai CO, Lt Col Tateo Kato, would not permit pilots to paint victory markings on their aircraft, choosing instead to emphasise the teamwork aspect of his command. When Takeuchi transferred to the 68th Sentai in New Guinea, he promptly painted red eagle victory markings from his 64th Sentai combats onto his new Ki-61 Hien!

5

Ki-43-I of the 1st Chutai/50th Sentai, flown by Sgt Isamu Sasaki, Burma, 1942

Isamu Sasaki's 'Oscar' exhibits extreme weathering from the tropical environment endured by the sentai in Burma. The white kanji character on the fighter's tail reads 'Tobi', which is Japanese for black kite (a bird of prey within the hawk family) – 1st Chutai aircraft within the 50th were usually named after birds. Sasaki gained over 20 victories against Allied fighters in the CBI, and finished the war with at least 38 kills.

6

Ki-43-I of the 3rd Chutai/50th Sentai, flown by Cpl Satoshi Anabuki and 1Lt Shigeru Nakazaki, Burma, January 1943

Satoshi Anabuki painted three victory roundels on the tail of this 'Oscar I' to denote the P-40 he shot down on 25 October 1942 (his first kill in this machine) and a pair of Hurricanes destroyed on 19 January 1943. Shigeru Nakazaki added a further nine roundels before he was killed on 16 January 1943 in another Ki-43-I. This aircraft has been nicknamed *Fubuki* (snowstorm), which is painted in white kanji on its tail.

7

Ki-43-I of the 64th Sentai, flown by Group CO Maj Tateo Kato, Burma, Spring 1942

Unlike most other sentai commanders, Tateo Kato forbade his pilots from painting victory markings on their aircraft. This Ki-43-I (serial number 318) was adorned with a broad white diagonal band on the upper portion of each wing, thus allowing 54th Sentai pilots to readily identify his aircraft in flight.

8

Ki-43-I of the 2nd Chutai/25th Sentai, flown by Sgt Kushiro Otake, Nanking, China, Summer 1943

This sentai formed at Kanko as part of the Chinese occupation force in October 1942, and were issued with 'Oscar Is' as their equipment. They retained Ki-43 until receiving Ki-84s in the final months of the war.

9

Ki-43-II of the 3rd Chutai/54th Sentai, flown by MSgt Akira Sugimoto, northern Japan, late 1943

This aircraft was flown on numerous occasions by Akira Sugimoto on rather monotonous home defence patrols along the northern coast of Japan during 1943/44. He finally saw action when the unit was posted south to the Philippines in late 1944, and on 7 January 1945 he took on a quartet of P-38s from the crack 431st FS over the Negros Islands. He was belatedly aided in this combat by the 71st Sentai's TSgt Mizunori Fukuda in a Ki-84. During the swirling low-level dogfight, Sugimoto managed to force a P-38 into a fatal stall, its pilot, 431st CO Maj Tom McGuire (38 kills), crashing to his death. The 'Oscar II' had been badly shot up during the engagement, however, and its pilot, realising that he would never make it back to base, force-landed the stricken fighter in a jungle clearing. Despite landing safely in a textbook wheels up landing, Sugimoto was shot to death by Philippino guerillas as he tried to extricate himself from his crashed fighter (see *Aircraft of the Aces 14 Lightning Aces of the Pacific and CBI* for more details).

10

Ki-43-II of the 64th Sentai, flown by Capt Hideo Miyabe, Burma, Spring 1944

Hideo Miyabe became the 64th Sentai's executive officer in April 1944, and then assumed command of the unit some 12 months later. Despite scoring more than a dozen victories, he refrained from coveting publicity, and never visibly denoted his aerial successes on his 'Oscar II'. Note also that this aircraft lacks the traditional flight leader's diagonal fuselage stripe.

11

Ki-43-II of the 2nd Chutai/64th Sentai, flown by Capt Hideo Miyabe, Palembang Airfield, Sumatra, Summer 1943

This 'Oscar II' served as Miyabe's mount during his time as chutai leader in the East Indies in mid-1943. The diagonal stripe absent in the previous profile is plainly obvious here, its purpose being to aid in quick aircraft recognition during formation and combat flying.

12

Ki-43-II of the 3rd Chutai/64th Sentai, Lt Yohei Hinoki, Mingaladon Airfield, Burma, November 1943
Capt Yasuhiko Kuroe flew this aircraft as chutai leader until March 1943 when 2Lt Takeshi Endo became the new CO. Following the latter's death in combat on 15 May 1943 over Kunming, China, in another aircraft, 1Lt Yohei Hinoki inherited this battle-proven 'Oscar II' when he assumed command of the chutai. The 'Master Falcon' was flying this machine on 25 November 1943 when he shot down a P-51A flown by Col Harry Melton, CO of the 311th Fighter-Bomber Group.

13

Ki-43-II of the 3rd Chutai/59th Sentai, flown by MSgt Tomio Hirohata, New Guinea, Summer 1943
Tomio Hirohata was tutored in the ways of combat by veteran ace Yasuhiko Kuroe whilst based in China, and he later put these lessons to good use by surviving the deadly combats fought over New Guinea. He escaped the final slaughter of this campaign, and returned to Japan to fight in the equally one-sided Okinawan battles. By the time of his death on 22 April 1945, Hirohata had amassed 14 victories.

14

Ki-43-II of the 1st Chutai/33rd Sentai, flown by Capt Kiyoshi Namai, Gelunbang Airfield, Sumatra, Summer 1944
Kiyoshi Namai served as 1st Chutai leader from June 1943 through to May 1944, and in that time he scored the majority of his 16 kills. Denoting his position as chutai leader, Namai's 'Oscar II' is marked with a very wide fuselage band.

15

Ki-43-III-Ko of the 2nd Chutai/64th Sentai, flown by WO Kosuke Tsubone, Krakor Airfield, Indochina, May 1945
Kosuke Tsubone scored over ten kills and duly won the Bukosho for distinguished service in the CBI, receiving the award in Phnom Penh on 10 June 1945 from Lt Gen Takeshi Hattori, CO of the 5th Air Division. He ended the war at Krakor Airfield, and returned to Japan in May 1946.

16

Ki-43-II-KAI of the 1st Chutai/64th Sentai, flown by Chutai CO Maj Toyoki Eto, Saigon, Indochina, July 1944
Toyoki Eto was CO of the 64th Sentai from June 1944 until April 1945, when he returned to Japan and commanded the Ki-100-equipped 1st Daitai (squadron) of the 111th Sentai from July 1945 until war's end. He achieved at least 12 victories, two of which were scored whilst flying 'Nates during the Nomonhan Incident.

17

Ki-43-III-Ko flown by the 64th Sentai CO, Maj Hideo Miyabe, Krakor Airfield, Indochina, May 1945
The kanji character on the tail of this 'Oscar III' reads 'Aso', after Mt Aso of Hideo Miyabe's native prefecture in Japan. By this period in the war the 64th Sentai was seeing very little aerial combat, which was probably a good thing considering the obsolescence of their mount. It is believed that the last pilot casualty suffered by the sentai was Sgt Hideo Kato, who was shot down by P-51Ds of the 26th FS/5th FG over Vinh Airfield, Indochina, on 11 July 1945.

18

Ki-43-II of the 2nd Chutai/59th Sentai, flown by Capt Shigeo Nango, But Airfield, New Guinea, September 1943
A dedicated leader of men, Shigeo Nango virtually took over the running of the entire 59th Sentai when all the unit's senior officers either fell ill or were killed in action. He gained all of his 15 victories over New Guinea (many in this 'Oscar II'), and was finally fell to his death after attacking B-24s over Wewak in 23 January 1944.

19

Ki-43-II of the 25th Sentai, flown by Maj Toshio Sakagawa, Hankow Airfield, China, Spring 1944
The double zero tail marking on this Ki-43-II was quite unique, and denoted that the fighter was the personal mount of sentai commander, Toshio Sakagawa. A ruthless pilot when in combat, this veteran pilot knew exactly how to wring every last ounce of performance out of his obsolescent mount when embroiled in a turning dogfight with a USAAF fighter. Indeed, he managed to down three P-51B/Cs in May 1944 alone over Hankow – quite probably in this very 'Oscar II'. Sakagawa had claimed 49 victories by the time he was killed in an operational accidentin the Philippines whilst flying as a passenger in a JAAF transport aircraft in December 1944.

20

Ki-44-II-Hei of the 3rd Chutai/70th Sentai, flown by Capt Yoshio Yoshida, Kashiwa Airfield, Japan, June 1945
This was the personal aircraft of Yoshio Yoshida, who commanded the chutai from February 1945 until war's end. The first two victory markings were dated 13 and 15 April 1945, and he survived the conflict having destroyed six B-29s, plus damaged a seventh – no mean achievement in the obsolescent *Shoki*. He also won the Bukosho.

21

Ki-44-II-Hei of the 3rd Chutai/70th Sentai, flown by 2Lt Makoto Ogawa, Kashiwa Airfield, Japan, June 1945
This weary combat veteran was the personal mount of Makoto Ogawa, who preferred to record his B-29 victories using stylised eagles. As the leading B-29 'killer' of the 70th Sentai, he downed seven Superfortresses plus two Mustangs. He too won the Bukosho.

22

Ki-84-Ko of the 246th Sentai, flown by WO Kenji Fujimoto, Taisho Airfield, Osaka, Japan, July 1945
This aircraft was flown on occasion by Kenji Fujimoto, who destroyed three B-29s (two by ramming on 13 and 16 March 1945) and duly won the Bukosho. He was killed in aerial combat with P-47Ns near Lake Biwa (north of Kyoto) on 14 August 1945 – just 24 hours before war's end.

23

Ki-45-KAI-Ko of the 3rd Chutai/5th Sentai, flown by Chutai CO Capt Fujitaro Ito, Kiyosu Airfield, Japan, March 1945
Totaro Ito used this aircraft to destroy the bulk of his 13 bomber kills, a tally which included no less than nine B-29s – understandably, he was awarded a Bukosho for his feats in combat. The white kanji characters on the tail reads 'Kuzuryu', which was a nine-headed dragon in Japanese mythology.

24

Ki-45-KAI-Hei of the 4th Sentai/Kaiten Tai, flown by Lt Miosaburo Yamamoto, Japan, early 1945
Miosaburo Yamamoto has had his surname written in Japanese phonetics on the tail of this Ki-45, which was a

somewhat common practice amongst suicide pilots. Yamamoto was killed in this machine during a ramming attack on a B-29 over Fukuoka Prefecture on 18 April 1945.

25
Ki-45-KAI-Ko of the 2nd Chutai/4th Sentai, flown by Lt Isamu Kashiide, Kozuki Airfield, Japan, 1944-45
Isamu Kashiide used this machine to perfect his lethal method of head-on attacks against B-29s over Japan in 1944-45. He enjoyed considerable success with this technique, claiming to have downed some 26 Superfortresses. Kashiide's 'Nick' boasted a 37 mm cannon as its primary weapon, his observer's hand-held single 7.92 mm machine-gun proving next to useless in fending off P-51D and P-47N escort fighters.

26
Ki-45-KAI of the 2nd Chutai/4th Sentai, flown by WO Sadamitsu Kimura, Kozuki Airfield, Japan, January 1945
This aircraft has a pair of obliquely-mounted (at an angle of 70°) Ho-5 20 mm cannon fitted in place of the 59 Imp gal upper fuselage tank. This arrangement was put to deadly use by Sadamitsu Kimura, who claimed to have destroyed 22 B-29s before he was shot down and killed by Superfortress gunners on the night of 13/14 July 1945.

27
Ki-45-KAI of the 2nd Chutai/4th Sentai, flown by Lt Hannoshin Nishio, Kozuki Airfield, Japan, June 1945
The kanji writing on the rear fuselage of this Ki-45 denotes that it was a donated aircraft, purchased for the JAAF by an organisation in Yamaguchi Prefecture near to where the 4th Sentai was based. Its regular pilot, Hannoshin Nishio, downed at least five B-29s in the final months of the war.

28
Ki-45-KAI of the 3rd Chutai/53rd Sentai, flown by Sgt Nobuji Negishi, Matsudo Airfield, Japan, November 1944
The operators of this 'Nick' marked all their aircraft with a stylised number 53 on the large vertical surface. Also fitted with 20 mm cannon, the Kawasaki 'heavy' fighter was utilised by leading sentai ace Nobuji Negishi, who destroyed six B-29s and damged seven others.

29
Ki-61-I-Hei of the 244th Sentai, flown by Sgt Masao Itagaki, Chofu Airfield, Tokyo, January 1945
Masao Itagaki belonged to a B-29 air-to-air ramming squadron called the Shinten Seiku Tai. The white phonetic katakana character on the tail is the 'ee' in Itagaki. On 3 December 1944, Cpl Itagaki rammed and damaged a B-29 of the 498th BG ('T Square 49' *Long Distance*) over Tokyo, and managed to parachute to safety – he won the Bukosho for the attack. On 27 January 1945, he rammed another B-29 and again escaped by parachute to win his second Bukosho. From March to May, Itagaki flew *kamikaze* escort missions to Okinawa. He survived the war as one of only two known double Bukosho recipients.

30
Ki-61-I-Hei of the 2nd Chutai/244th Sentai, flown by MSgt Tadao Sumi, Chofu Airfield, Tokyo, November 1944
Tadao Sumi became a master the *Hien* in combat, and took his skills to the 56th Sentai in December 1944, where he had downed five B-29s and a single P-51D by war's end.

31
Ki-61-I-KAIc No 3295 of the 244th Sentai, flown by Group CO Capt Teruhiko Kobayashi, Japan, January 1945
This was the 'Tony' used by Teruhiko Kobayashi to ram a B-29 at 30,000 ft over Mt Fuji on 27 January 1945. He safely parachuted from the stricken *Hien*, having suffered the smallest of cuts across the bridge of his nose.

32
Ki-61-I-KAIc No 3024 of the 244th Sentai, flown by Group CO Capt Teruhiko Kobayashi, Japan, December 1944
This colourful *Hien* carries four silhouettes denoting Kobayashi's rising tally of B-29 claims. Whenever he obtained another aircraft, Kobayashi had his crew chief immediately apply his victory tally to the new fighter. By war's end his final Ki-61 would boast 14 victory markings, a total which also included those aircraft he had simply damaged. Many postwar historians have misinterpreted this total, thus giving Kobayashi credit for downing 14 aircraft, when in reality his final score was five exactly – three B-29s and two Hellcats, plus a further nine Superfortresses damaged.

33
Ki-61-I-KAIc No 3024 of the 244th Sentai, flown by Group CO Capt Teruhiko Kobayashi, Japan, April 1945
This profile again depicts No 3024 but at a latter date, with ten B-29 silhouettes and a pair of Hellcats detailed beneath the cockpit. Kobayashi's sixth kill is further embellished with a red Ki-61 sprayed over the white planform of a B-29 – this elaborate marking denoted the Mt Fuji ramming attack. To instill morale in his pilots, the sentai leader had the word 'Hissho' ('confidence of victory') emblazoned on the rudder of his fighter in white paint.

Back Cover
Ki-61-I-KAIc of the 244th Sentai, flown by Group CO Capt Teruhiko Kobayashi, Japan, March 1945
Yet another Ki-61 associated with Kobayashi, this aircraft may have been the *Hien* he bailed out of on 12 April 1945 after it was badly shot up by B-29 gunners during an attacking pass. Due to the intense media interest in the exploits of the 244th Sentai, Kobayashi ensured that every aircraft he flew reflected the success of 'his' unit.

34
Ki-61-I-KAIc of HQ flight/244th Sentai, flown by TSgt Kiyoshi Ando, Japan, January 1945
Whilst serving as wingman for Capt Kobayashi, Kiyoshi Ando also rammed the B-29 over Mt Fuji on 29 January 1945 in this very *Hien*, but unlike his commander, the latter was killed in the crash.

35
Ki-61-I-Otsu of the 2nd Chutai/68th Sentai, flown by Capt Shogo Takeuchi, Wewak, New Guinea, October 1943
Most JAAF aces preferred the Ki-61 to the Ki-43 due to the former's increased armament, better armour protection and higher diving speeds. One of those who made effective use of the Kawasaki fighter was Shogo Takeuchi, who was quite probably the highest scoring JAAF ace in New Guinea. He had scored in excess of 30 kills in both the latter conflict and the CBI prior to his death on 15 Decmeber 1943. Takeuchi was lost when his badly shot up Ki-61 crashed short of the Hansa Airfield runway.

36
Unmarked Ki-84-Ko of the Army Flight Test Centre, flown by MSgt Isamu Sasaki, Fussa Airfield, Tokyo, 1945
Sasaki claimed three Superfortresses on the night of 25 May 1945 while flying this aircraft. A veteran of various campaigns during the Pacific War, his total score had reached at least 38 by war's end. Within this total were no less than six B-29s (he damaged a further three), the destruction of which earned him the Bukosho.

37
Ki-84-Ko of the 1st Chutai/103rd Sentai, flown by Capt Tomojiro Ogawa, Itami Airfield, Japan, January 1945
The white kanji character on the tail reads 'Mutsu' after Tomojiro Ofusa's native prefecture back in Japan. These names were added both for morale purposes and as a good luck symbol, the aircraft being christened jointly by the pilot and his crew chief. Most of the aircraft in the 1st Chutai were named after birds, Ofusa won the Bukosho on 10 June 1945 for distinguished service. Amongst his 19 victories were five Mustangs and two Thunderbolts.

38
Ki-84-Ko of the the HQ Chutai/ 50th Sentai, flown by Maj Koki Kawamoto, Phnom Penh, Indochina, April 1945
Koki Kawamoto flew this aircraft upon assuming command of the 50th Sentai in April 1945, the white kanji character on the tail reading 'Oni' (devil). The chutai colours on the fuselage lightning bolts were blue (HQ), red (1st), yellow (2nd) and white (3rd).

39
Ki-84-Ko of the 3rd Chutai/103rd Sentai, flown by 1Lt Shigeyasu Miyamoto, Itami Airfield, Japan, January 1945
Shigeyasu Miyamoto's first combat came in January 1945 when he intercepted B-29s over Japan. On 15 April he led eight fighters on a bombing raid against the north airfield on Okinawa, and on his return had to fight off the attention of a F6F-5 Hellcat. Miyamoto was wounded in the engagement and was forced to make an emergency landing in his 'Frank' on Tokuno Island. He won the Bukosho on 4 May for heroism during the Okinawan battles and survived the war.

40
Ki-84-Ko of the 1st Chutai/103rd Sentai, flown by Capt Tomojiro Ogawa, Itami Airfield, Japan, January 1945
Yojiro Ogawa participated in the Okinawan battles, leading his unit as they escorted *kamikaze* suicide aircraft to their targets, then confirming the results of these attacks – his chutai also strafed ships once the *kamikaze*s had completed their attacks. On 29 April he was awarded the Bukosho from Lt Gen Michihiro Sugawara, CO of the 6th Air Division, for heroism. Capt Ogawa survived the war.

Figure Plates

1
Sgt Satoshi Anabuki, top ace of the JAAF during World War 2, is depicted during his time as an instructor at the Akeno Fighter School in the spring of 1944. His flying suit is typical JAAF summer issue, which was sadly far from fireproof. Anabuki's leather boots are standard 'Air Force' brown, as opposed to the identical black versions worn by Navy pilots. His parachute harness is a Type 97, which came equipped with a quick release mechanism centrally placed over his stomach. The white cloth attached to the harness reads 'Sgt Anabuki', and acted as a warning to students not to borrow the instructor's flying equipment! As can be seen here, Anabuki was still wearing a glove over his slowly-healing left hand, which had been badly wounded during his legendary 'ace in a day' mission, flown on 8 October 1943 off the Burmese coast.

2
Seen in typical 1939 Nomonhan Incident flying apparel, MSgt Masatoshi Masuzawa was one of the leading aces of the 1st Sentai. The weather on the Mongolian border was often bitter, and in order to stave off the cold when flying at altitude, pilots were issued with winter flying suits made of gabardine wool and lined with fur – the exposed collar on this suit shows the lining off well. A matching fur-lined flying helmet was also a must, as were leather suede gloves. This early suit also has flaps over the trouser pockets. These often proved a hinderance in flight, and so were deleted on World War 2 issue suits. Note the static line running from Masuzawa's Type 97 right harness buckle to his parachute, and the pilot's rank insignia on his arm.

3
From one extreme to the other – the tropical environments of New Guinea and the CBI rarely made rabbit fur-lined flying suits a necessity. Indeed, a lightweight uniform that consisted of little more than a loose-fitting olive drab shirt and a pair of trousers soon proved to be the order of the day. Here, Cpl Susumu Kajinami of the New Guinea-based 68th Sentai models his faded flying suit in late 1943. There was no standard placement for rank insignias within the JAAF, pilots tending to pin them onto their sleeve, collar or chest.

4
Capt Fujitaro Ito of the 5th Sentai prepares to enter his Ki-45 at Kiyosu Airfield, Japan, in March 1945. The high altitude battles fought between USAAF B-29s, and their escorts, and the JAAF, forced the latter aircrew to wear electrically-heated flying suits like this. The wiring contained within these one-piece suits made them incredibly bulky, whilst the fur lining that dated back to the pre-war period made them even more unwieldy. An officer carrying his ceremonial sword into combat with him had no practical purpose other than to act as a symbol of authority, plus perhaps bring its bearer good luck 'in the hunt'. Ito is wearing his rank insignia on his left sleeve.

5
2Lt Yohei Hinoki of the 64th Sentai is seen in service dress in China in the spring of 1942. A distinguished ace who was embroiled in many an action, Hinoki gained fame later in the war as Japan's 'Douglas Bader', for he too lost a leg (to a P-51A attack). Depicted devoid of flying gear, Hinoki has exchanged his battered flying boots for the service issue 'high boot' variety. He is also wearing a 'soft' cap and has his cere-monial sword in his left hand. The former item is adorned with the Army's yellow star – the equivalent head gear in the Navy replaced the star with an anchor. The pilot's highly coveted 'wings' are sewn over his right breast pocket.

6
WO Makato Ogawa was the top scoring pilot in the Ki-44-equipped 70th Sentai, downing seven B-29s and two P-5IDs. He is wearing a standard issue flying suit without the fur-lined collar, and has the 'meatball' flag sewn onto his left sleeve, denoting that he is a home defence pilot. In February 1945 the JAAF's GHQ ordered that all pilots involved in home defence had to wear this recognition symbol following the tragic death of a critically-burned Japanese pilot who, being mistaken for an American airman, was beaten to death by irate farmers. Some pilots wore flags on both sleeves, whilst others even painted them on the top of their flying helmets. As noted earlier, the later flying suits boasted slash pockets without flaps (as seen here), in which were stored the pilot's gloves, maps or first aid bandages. Ogawa's black neck scarf is a personal item of clothing.

NEW GUINEA

'No one ever returns alive from New Guinea' was the often-heard saying uttered by the Japanese during the war. If there ever was a 'Russian Front' for their army in World War 2, then the 'green desert' of New Guinea was it. Entire units, ill-equipped and cut off from their main forces, simply disappeared into the thick tropical environment never to be seen again.

Ambitious pre-war plans to threaten Australia made the capture of New Guinea a necessity for the Japanese. On 8 March 1942 their forces landed at Salamaua on the eastern coast of New Guinea, their objective being Port Moresby, some 200 miles to the south on the west coast. This strategic port was considered to be the gateway to Australia, and Allied Forces prepared to defend it tenaciously.

At the time of the invasion, the air war over New Guinea was a JNAF affair, as the Japanese Army had no established airfields to operate from. Navy aircraft rotated between bases at Lae and Salamaua, along the eastern coast of New Guinea and Rabaul, on New Britain. In April a naval air group (the Tainan Kokutai) arrived at Lae from Rabaul, and they immediately set to work flying bomber escort missions to Port Moresby, as well as undertaking routine combat patrols.

In response to these attacks, the Australians doggedly defended Port Moresby with the limited resources they had at hand. Indeed, so desperate was the need to provide some form of air defence for the beleaguered troops that the RAAF's No 75 Sqn was pressed into service after a crash training programme on Kittyhawk Mk IAs that lasted just nine days! Led into action by Sqn Ldr 'Old John' Jackson, who had become an ace in 1941 whilst serving with No 3 RAAF Sqn in North Africa, the unit managed to keep the JNAF at bay for 44 days. In that time its pilots shot 18 aircraft down, and destroyed a further 17 on the ground, but in turn suffered heavy losses. The survivors of No 75 Sqn were withdrawn on 7 May, replaced by USAAF units rushed into the area from Australia.

Although the Australian troops and aircraft had hindered the Japanese invasion on land, the fate of Port Moresby was finally sealed during the Battle of Coral Sea, which took place to the north-east of New Guinea in early May. The Japanese invasion convoy was stopped cold by a US Navy task force led capably by Adm Chester Nimitz. However, those troops already on New Guinea would not give up, and proceeded to hack their way overland towards their objective some 200 miles to the south of Salamaua.

One of the first pieces of real estate that had to be captured was Buna, which was at the head of the Kokoda Trail to Port Moresby. Both the Australian and the Japanese armies made a rush for the town, and in a series of skirmishes, the latter pushed the Allies back down the trail, but at a terrible cost in human life. Despite having lost Buna, Australian and American forces waged a continual guerrilla which seriously hampered the Japanese advance southward. To add to this, thousands of Japanese infantrymen perished from tropical diseases and widespread malnutrition.

Despite these setbacks, the Japanese had advanced to the outskirts of Port Moresby by 17 September. This was as far as they got, however, as Allied Forces, bolstered by fresh troops shipped in from Australia, began their counteroffensive and eventually pushed their opponents back into the jungle from whence they had come. The Japanese finally lost Buna on 2 January 1943.

Milne Bay, at the tip of New Guinea, gained importance when the Japanese march to Port Moresby over the Kokoda Trail became almost insurmountable. The Australians were not about to let the enemy establish a base there, for that could then be used as a launch pad for aircraft to strike at Port Moresby. Despite the fact that there were more than 8700 Allied troops at Milne Bay, the Japanese Army thought that they could easily overwhelm the garrison. During August and September 1942 both sides fought furiously to gain the upper hand, Allied aircraft strafing and bombing landing convoys and supply areas with devastating results. These sorties inflicted serious losses on the attacking troops, and allied with Japanese forces being tied up in the Solomons attempting to defend Guadalcanal, it soon became obvious to senior army officers that there was no hope of reinforcements arriving to make good the numbers. The order to retreat was given on 5 September.

The first JAAF unit to arrive in the New Guinea theatre of operations was the 11th Sentai (a proud veteran of the Nomonhan Incident), which flew into Rabaul with its Ki-43-I-Heis on 18 December 1942 from Surabaya, Java. Two days after Christmas they flew their first joint mission with Navy Zeroes, escorting 'Val' dive-bombers to Buna. En route they were intercepted by P-38s from the 9th FS, and in the wild dogfight that ensued, 2Lt Richard I Bong (who would later become the top Amer-

This factory-fresh Ki-61-I was photographed enroute to New Guinea, and the 68th or 78th Sentais, in early 1943. Once in-theatre, the sleek 'Tony' would be hastily daubed with dark green paint so as to give it a modicum of invisibility from the prying eyes of USAAF fighter and bomber crews when parked on the ground (*via Phil Jarrett*)

ican ace of World War 2 with 40 kills – see *Aircraft of the Aces 14 Lightning Aces of the Pacific and CBI* for more details) achieved his first victories when he claimed a Zero and a 'Val'. Capt 'Tommy' Lynch became the first ace of the 39th Fighter Squadron when he downed two 'Oscars', and he would go on to score 20 victories before being killed in action in March 1944. Overall, the Americans claimed 13 enemy aircraft destroyed with no loss, but in reality the Japanese Navy lost just one Zero and had another force-landed, whilst the 11th Sentai also suffered a single casualty – WO Tadashi Yoshitake.

The brunt of the early JAAF effort in New Guinea was borne by the 11th and 1st Sentais, their main task being to provide air cover for the ground troops. The 1st Sentai – another ex-Nomonhan unit – flew into Rabaul with its 'Oscars' in January 1943, and proceeded immediately to Guadalcanal. On 12 April, the sentai departed for Wewak. In August 1943 the JAAF activated the 4th Air Army at this base, its main operating airfields being at Hansa, Wewak, But and Aitape. Other bases included Hollandia (to be used for withdrawal purposes), Lae, Madang and Salamaua. Between 10 August and 20 September, JAAF aircraft from Rabaul flooded into New Guinea.

This theatre became the combat testing ground for the new Kawasaki Ki-61 *Hien* (Swallow), which was given the Allied codename 'Tony' under the mistaken belief that it was of Italian origin! The only 'Tony' units to operate in New Guinea were the 68th and 78th Sentais, the former being the first air group to receive the new Ki-61-I fighter in late 1942. Both units transferred to Wewak during the summer of the following year.

The 'Tony', with its liquid-cooled Kawasaki Ha-40 inline engine (a licence-built derivative of the Daimler-Benz DB 601A), armour protection and self-sealing fuel tanks was a radical departure from the standard *Hayabusa*. Resembling the German Messerschmitt Bf 109 thanks to their shared powerplant, the Ki-61-I was armed with two nose-mounted 12.7 mm machine guns and a pair of 20 mm cannon (again licence-built German MG 151 guns) in the wings, thus giving it a far greater 'punch' than its Ki-43-II predecessor. With a maximum speed of 368 mph at 15,945 ft, it was also considerably quicker than the 'Oscar II', which could manage just 329 mph at 13,125 ft. Indeed, the latter only retained the upper hand over the Ki-61 in terms of its unmatched manoeuvrability and impressive range.

The air war over New Guinea had worsened for the Japanese as 1943 progressed, and it was hoped that the new Ki-61 would tip the balance back in the JAAF's favour. However, like all new types, the 'Tony'

Below and right
This amazing pair of genuine combat photos show a Ki-43 attacking a low-flying B-25 somewhere off the coast of northern New Guinea in 1943. On this occasion the Mitchell crew managed to escape (*via Maru*)

initially suffered from teething troubles, particularly in relation to the poor quality of the fuel available in New Guinea and chronic overheating problems associated with the aircraft's ineffective radiators. As an example of this, 1Lt Mitsuyoshi Tarui (a veteran pilot of the 68th who scored 38 victories before he was killed) was forced down three times in just a matter of weeks due to engine problems. Pilots soon became distrustful of the *Hien*.

American fighter pilots were also unfamiliar with the Ki-61, the 39th FS first encountering the sleek new aircraft on 18 July when they engaged elements of the 78th Sentai between Lae and Salamaua. 1Lt Gene Duncan stated that he had damaged an aircraft which 'resembled a Me 109', whilst his fellow squadronmates claimed the destruction of two Ki-61s, along with four probables and two damaged – the Japanese suffered no losses. However, the 78th Sentai claimed its first victory courtesy of 1Lt Fujishima. Two days later the 68th Sentai scored its first kill in New Guinea when the unit attacked Allied positions at Benabena. Capt Shogo Takeuchi's (30+ kills) five-aircraft formation attacked and shot down a B-24.

The second American claims for this new enemy fighter occurred 24 hours after the 68th Sentai's B-24 kill when P-38s from the 39th and 80th FSs encountered 'Tonys' (of the 68th and 78th Sentais) and 'Oscars' between Ramu Valley and Madang. The Japanese fighters had been scrambled to intercept B-25s attacking the Japanese base at Bogadjim, and in the subsequent mêlée, American pilots claimed 22 victories without suffering a single loss. Again, USAAF overclaiming was rife, for only four Japanese fighters were downed, including two 'Tony' pilots from the 78th Sentai. Their Japanese opponents put in claims for two Lightnings destroyed.

With the fall of Buna, the main battleground became the Lae-Salamaua-Markham Valley region. By this stage in the campaign Japanese supply convoys from Rabaul were struggling to make it to New Guinea

due to marauding Allied submarines and surface vessels dominating the sea lanes. As a result of this naval blockade, most units were suffering from a lack of spare parts. The loss of skilled mechanics killed in endless bombing attacks also drastically reduced the effectiveness of various air groups. Col Rinsuka Kaneko, a staff officer of the 4th Air Army in New Guinea, recalled;

'Up until April 1943 about 50 per cent of aircraft on hand were in normal operation. Subsequent to that time only about 25 per cent of the total aircraft on hand were in full operation. This figure became even lower as the war progressed.'

The Allied amphibious landing south of Salamaua on 29-30 June

1943 was just another in a sequence of defeats inflicted upon the Japanese during the space of 12 months. Salamaua fell on 11 September, and the Allied Force advanced and took Lae five days later. By 2 October they had captured Finschhafen.

On 11 October 1943 the 14th Air Brigade suffered a great loss at the hands of 22-kill ace Col Neel Kearby of the 348th FG. Japanese radar detected the approach of P-47D Thunderbolts and scrambled 'Tonys' (68th Sentai) and 'Oscar IIs' (13th Sentai) for an interception near Wewak. Kearby recalled soon after the sortie;

'At 1115 one Zeke (actually a 'Tony') was sighted at 9 o'clock below at 20,000 ft. I came in on him from 7 o'clock above and opened fire at 1500 ft. He took no evasive action, caught fire, and dived into the sea.'

His victim was Col Tamiya Teranishi, and Kearby went on to claim a further five victories in this single sortie, thus earning him the Medal of Honor.

With the Japanese bastion at Rabaul isolated, its forces on New Guinea were rapidly declining. Gen Douglas MacArthur systematically bypassed pockets of enemy troop concentrations and let them perish through lack of supplies. B-24s and B-25s had been employed, meanwhile, to break the back of the JAAF. The air blockade of New Guinea was so complete by

The end of the line for a 68th Sentai pilot. On 10 December 1943 Maj Gerald R Johnson of the 9th FS shot down a 'Tony' near Gusap whilst flying a P-47D-4, thus recording his 11th victory. The pilot bailed out and Johnson called back to base on the radio to ask them to send a patrol out to capture his erstwhile foe. Australian troops on the ground duly found the Japanese pilot, who was observed to be moving around under his parachute – he was was possibly wounded. Not prepared to take any chances, the soldiers gave him a burst from their Tommy guns, and he was killed outright. Johnson was not pleased upon hearing this news as he wanted to meet his worthy opponent (*via J R Bruning*)

the end of 1943 that mass-starvation and disease destroyed entire units. The Japanese Navy also abandoned New Guinea to their doomed army brethren in order to concentrate their forces in preparation for the anticipated defence of the Marianas.

On 22 April 1944 the American 1st Corps landed at Hollandia, and the 68th Sentai was forced to evacuate their air base. The 14th Air Brigade commander, Col Kenzo Ondo, was quickly killed in the ground fighting, and pilots and groundcrews discarded their aircraft and fled into the jungles.

The 68th Sentai (along with the 77th, 78th and 248th) was disbanded on 25 July 1944, and the many surviving ground- and aircrews joined the ranks of the infantry. Despite doing their level best to avoid offensive manoeuvres against overwhelming Allied forces, thousands died in the jungles simply trying to survive through to VJ-Day.

Warrant Officer Katsuaki Kira

Katsuaki Kira has the distinction of being one of just a handful of fighter pilots who survived six years of continuos combat in the various campaigns contested by the JAAF. Born in Kumamoto Prefecture, Japan, in 1919, he graduated from flight school in July 1938 and was sent to the Akeno Fighter School for combat training. Once he had successfully completed the course, Kira was sent to Hailar, Manchuria, to join the 24th Sentai.

Soon after his arrival the Nomonhan Incident flared up, but Cpl Kira did not participate in the initial combats. In June, a second major skirmish ensued, and his sentai was despatched to the frontline. Kira downed his first enemy fighter – an I-16 – over the Khalka River on 22 June, and by the time of the ceasefire in mid-September he had amassed nine victories, and a wealth of valuable combat experience.

When the Pacific War began in December 1941, Kira participated in the attack on the Philippines, but returned to Manchuria after the swift conclusion to the campaign. His next taste of action came when his sentai was involved in the air defence of the Palembang oilfields in the former Dutch East Indies.

In May 1943 the 24th Sentai, recently re-equipped with new Ki-43-II-Ko 'Oscar IIs', was sent to But Airfield in New Guinea – Kira found himself embroiled in bitter dogfights with USAAF P-38s almost immediately. On the 24th of the month, whilst preparing to land at Madang Airfield, he was notified that an enemy bombing raid was in progress at the base. Kira immediately throttled up on his aircraft and commenced a steep climb for altitude. Once he had gained sufficient height, he searched out a formation of fleeing B-24s and repeatedly attacked them, damaging two in a running gunfight.

On 3 August Kira succeeded in shooting down a B-17 over Madang Airfield, followed just days later by a duel to the death over Lae with a P-38. He managed to down his opponent, but in turn was forced to belly land on the airstrip due to the severe damage inflicted to his 'Oscar II'.

In October 1943 Kira departed New Guinea with his squadron for Manila, in the Philippines. A year later he was transferred to the 200th Sentai, which was in the process of forming at Akeno. This new elite unit, comprised of veterans from various frontline sentai and instructors from

WO Katsuaki Kira, seen here during the Nomonhan Incident in 1939, survived the 'killing fields' of New Guinea. After escaping to the Philippines, Kira and his unit (the 24th Sentai) came directly up against the top American ace of the war, Maj Richard I Bong (*via Maru*)

the Akeno Fighter School, was armed exclusively with the Ki-84 and rushed to the Philippines, where it initially flew escort missions for the remnants of the Japanese naval fleet.

Kira's sentai encountered P-38 ace Maj Dick Bong, now of the 5th Fighter Command, as well as the high-scoring squadrons of the 49th FG around Leyte. During combat with Lightnings in the Philippines, the veteran pilot received a rare citation from Gen Tominaga, CO of the 4th Air Army, for single-handedly engaging ten USAAF fighters and shooting down two. Kira was also promoted to the rank of warrant officer.

In January 1945 WO Kira withdrew to Taiwan with the survivors of his unit, the 200th Sentai having been nearly destroyed in the fighting for the Philippines – at the end of its first month in action, for example, only nine serviceable fighters were left.

Katsuaki Kira's final combat was in the bitter air battle over Okinawa as a member of the 103rd Sentai. He survived the war with a score in excess 21 kills (nine at Nomonhan, seven in New Guinea and at least five in the Philippines and during home defence duty).

After the war he served in the Japan Self-Defense Air Force.

Warrant Officer Kazuo Shimizu

Kazuo Shimizu became famous for his expertise in the use of aerial burst bombs (Ta-dan) against American aircraft in New Guinea. He was born in Tokyo in 1918 and started his army career as a private in the field artillery. He graduated from flight school at Tachiarai in May 1941, and in February of the following year was assigned to the 59th Sentai.

Due to the lull in fighting following the initial invasion of the Dutch East Indies, Shimizu saw little combat during the many fleet escort missions and air patrols he participated in around Java. Indeed, it wasn't until early 1943 that he recorded his first kill in the defence of Timor.

WO Kazuo Shimizu (squatting center holding a sign) with members of the 3rd Chutai of the 59th Sentai, Ashiya Airfield, Japan, in December 1944. The placard reads 'Inouye Squadron' (*via Y Izawa*)

When the JAAF sortied against Darwin on 20 June 1943, the 59th Sentai's 22 Ki-43-II-Kos were given the responsibility of escorting 27 bombers to the target. Unlike the surprise raids of the previous year, when JNAF machines had caused much devastation to northern Australia with relative impunity, the RAAF had since bolstered its air defences in the region – 46 Spitfire LF VCs of No 1 Fighter Wing were waiting for the approaching raiders.

In the subsequent action, the Japanese claimed 15 victories for the loss of a fighter and a bomber, whilst the Australians claimed nine bombers and five fighters destroyed in return for the destruction of two Spitfires. Shimizu participated in this dogfight, but his claims are unknown.

In July, the 59th Sentai moved to their new base at But, on the northeastern coast of New Guinea, but Shimizu fell ill with dysentery soon after his arrival and was grounded for some time.

Having regained his strength after several months out of the cockpit, Shimizu returned to action in early November. On the 9th of the month he single-handedly took on a formation of six USAAF P-40Ns of the 35th FS near Alexishafen and subsequently claimed one shot down.

Around this time word filtered through to But of the successful deployment of aerial burst bombs against large formations of enemy bombers by JNAF units in Rabaul. The JAAF duly decided to try the new weapon against the increasing hordes of B-25s and B-24s being encountered over New Guinea, and on 14 February 1944 Shimizu dropped a Ta-dan on a formation of Mitchells over But and observed three bombers crash as a result of the weapon's detonation. The next day he repeated the attack on a formation of P-47 Thunderbolts, and two fell from the sky. However, on this occasion Shimizu's 'Oscar II' was badly shot up in the subsequent counter-attack by the surviving P-47s, and he barely made it back to But. Based on his achievements over a 48-hour period, WO Shimizu was awarded a rare commendation.

The 59th Sentai, decimated by the ceaseless heavy fighting against overwhelming numbers of Allied aircraft, left New Guinea four days after the second Ta-dan attack and headed for Ashiya Air Base in Kyushu, Japan. Shimizu continued fly with the sentai in the home defence role until war's end, by which stage he had achieved at least 18 victories, of which half were bombers.

Captain Shigeo Nango

Capt Shigeo Nango was one of the very few JAAF aces who gained all of their victories in New Guinea, this great fighter leader receiving much publicity during World War 2. Born in Tokyo in 1917, he was the younger brother of the great naval fighter leader, Lt Cdr Mochifumi Nango (he scored eight victories but was killed in action over China on 18 July 1938), and graduated from the Army Military Academy in April 1939. He undertook a course of fighter training at Akeno before being posted to the 33rd Sentai.

When the Nomonhan Incident erupted in May 1939 Nango went to Manchuria, but the young officer did not participate in the fighting, rather spending his days honing his skills as a fighter pilot in myriad training flights.

In January 1942, Capt Nango became a squadron leader of the 2nd

Capt Shigeo Nango gained all of his 15+ victories against the Americans over New Guinea. Despite this success in the air with the 59th Sentai, he fought a losing battle against both the USAAF and the tropical environment. Nango was finally killed whilst attempting to repel an overwhelming force of B-24s on 23 January 1944 (*via Y Izawa*)

Chutai/59th Sentai, and he led the unit in the Dutch East Indies on convoy escort patrols and ground support sorties. Eighteen months later he participated in the large June raids against Darwin. The following month he was posted into the frontline in New Guinea along with the rest of the 59th Sentai, and it was in this theatre that he blossomed into a first-rate fighter pilot and leader, flying daily sorties from But Airfield.

The Allied Forces needed an advanced fighter base to assault Lae and Salamaua, so they began to carve out an airfield at Tsili Tsili, 50 miles west of Lae. The secret airstrip was soon discovered by the Japanese, and on 15 August seven Ki-21 'Sally' bombers, escorted by 36 fighters from the 59th and 24th Sentais, raided the site. The JAAF arrived just as transport aircraft were landing, and Capt Nango subsequently shot down a C-47 (confirmed through USAAF records).

The Americans were quickly stung into action by the attacking force, P-39Ns from the 40th and 41st FSs intercepting the Japanese Force as it retreated westward back to But. In the ensuing 'slugfest', the Japanese lost three fighters and six bombers, whilst the Americans had four fighters shot down, although only one USAAF pilot was killed. Nango's Ki-43-II-Ko had been covered with oil from the exploding C-47 and he thought he had been hit. Rather than crash land in enemy territory, he decided to dive into a suitable target, but when Nango realised that his aircraft had not actually been damaged, he extracted himself from combat and returned to base.

Less than 24 hours later, the 59th was once again back over Tsili Tsili, but this time the Americans were waiting for them. P-38s of the 431st FS and P-47s from the 340th intercepted the incoming force of 33 'Oscar IIs' and three Ki-21s, and although the Americans claimed over a dozen fighters and two single-engined bombers shot down, Japanese losses were restricted to just three Ki-43-II-Kos. Similarly, despite Capt Nango reportedly causing two American fighters to collide, and other 'Oscar II' pilots claiming a further 19 USAAF aircraft destroyed, there were no American losses.

As August progressed the 59th Sentai lost a number of veteran pilots, including two chutai leaders. The unit's Ki-43-II-Heis simply could not compete with the newer versions of P-38 and P-47 appearing in New Guinea, and Japanese morale soon faltered. The lack of supplies and rampant tropical diseases also began to sap the strength of the 59th, and under extreme hardship, Nango began taking over duties for all of the squadrons within the sentai.

On 23 January 1944 Capt Nango was shot down and killed while intercepting B-24s, and their escorting fighters, over Wewak. Ironically, Army HQ had planned to transfer him back to Japan at the end of the month for eventual leadership of the Akeno Fighter School. On 29 April 1944 Shigeo Nango received a posthumous citation and was elevated two ranks to lieutenant colonel. It is believed that he had shot down over 15 American aircraft in New Guinea.

Sergeant Susumu Kajinami

This young pilot has the distinction of being one of the few veteran aces to survive the air battles over New Guinea. Susumu Kajinami was born in October 1923 in Okayama Prefecture and entered the Army in April

1940. In November 1942 he was sent to Kumagaya Flying School, and eventually received his combat training with the 246th Sentai on Ki-27 'Nates'.

In August 1943 Kajinami was assigned to the 68th Sentai and was posted to the 2nd Chutai in Wewak, where he flew the Ki-61 *Hien*. His first claim was a P-40N over Hansa Bay, and during his time in New Guinea fought many types of American aircraft – he considered the P-47 Thunderbolt his deadliest foe. He claimed one such Republic fighter shot down in combat, but was nearly killed himself when another put 29 holes in his 'Tony' whilst chasing him over the jungle.

In February 1944 Sgt Kajinami left New Guinea and was employed until VJ-Day ferrying aircraft between Korea and Tachikawa Air Base in Japan.

By his own reckoning, he shot down the following aircraft – six P-40s, six P-38s, one P-47, two F4Us, three F6Fs, one F4F, two B-24, two B-25s and one unidentified transport aircraft. Kajinami was officially credited with eight kills, plus 16 unofficially.

He changed his name after the war to Koyama, and today is still flying as a commercial pilot from Matsuyama Airfield in Kyushu.

The then Cpl Susumu Kajinami poses next to a Ki-27 of the 246th Sentai at Kakogawa Airfield, in Japan, in 1943 (*via S Koyama*)

Cpl Kajinami with 2nd Chutai/68th Sentai Ki-61 No 888 at Kagamihara Airfield in the Gifu Prefecture, Japan, just prior to flying out to Wewak in August 1943. Although Kajinami claimed 24 victories while flying the Ki-61, his official score is a more modest eight (*via S Koyama*)

Captain Shogo Takeuchi

Capt Takeuchi, who was probably the leading JAAF ace over New Guinea, was born in 1918 in Kyoto. He graduated in the 52nd term class of the Army Aviation Academy in September 1939 as a second lieutenant, and was posted to the 64th Sentai.

His unit ranged all over the CBI during the early war years, Takeuchi sharpening his dogfighting skill under the tutelage of the sentai's CO, Maj Tateo Kato, and his 3rd Chutai leader, Capt Katsumi Anma (32 victories). The young protégé of the air group's two distinguished aces developed into a remarkable marksman. Indicative of his budding skill was the dogfight of 31 January 1942 over Singapore that saw his chutai intercept a dozen Hurricane IIs from Nos 232(P) and 238 Sqns, hell-bent on shooting down a formation of Ki-21 bombers being escorted by the 'Oscar' pilots. In the brief dogfight that ensued, Takeuchi quickly dispatched three of the Hawker fighters, much to the amazement of Maj Kato.

In April 1942, Lt Takeuchi was transferred to the newly-formed 68th Sentai. The unit converted to the Ki-61 *Hien* later that year, and plans were made to send them to New Guinea. In preparation for the deployment, the sentai spent much of the autumn and winter familiarising themselves with their new mount, and in December Takeuchi took over the 2nd Chutai as a captain.

The 68th Sentai finally arrived at Wewak, via Rabaul, in June 1943, and almost from the start of combat operations, pilots complained about radiator and fuel problems with their new aircraft. The pilots' collective lack of confidence in their fighters was disturbing to Takeuchi, who immediately set about raising morale. On 20 July there was a brief moment of jubilation when the five-aircraft formation from the 2nd Chutai downed a B-24 on a mission to Benabena, this kill providing the unit with its first victory. It also shattered the myth of the Liberator's invincibility

The daily grind of combat over New Guinea, coupled with the Allied counter-offensive in the autumn of 1943, took a toll on members of the 68th Sentai. Many of its senior officers were killed in action or grounded due to tropical illnesses, whilst aircaft went unserviceable due to a lack of critical spares. Despite these hardships, Capt Takeuchi continued to lead by example, and in October he was wounded in combat and hospitalised for 15 days.

Although grounded by the sentai's medical officer, he left the hospital and declared himself fit for combat, despite being swathed in bandages. Such was the morale-boosting effect of his return to the frontline that groundcrew and officers alike cheered him as he climbed back into his Ki-61, adorned with 58 red eagle victory markings, at the commencement of his first sortie back at Wewak Airfield.

By December 1943 the 68th Sentai had only three pilots left, and Capt Takeuchi's days were numbered. On 15 December US Forces landed at Arawe Peninsula on the southern coast of New Britain Island and the Japanese counter-attacked. Takeuchi escorted light bombers to the enemy landing area, but they were attacked by a large force of P-47s. He reportedly claimed one enemy aircraft destroyed – none were lost – before rushing to the aid of Maj Kiyoshi Kimura (the sentai CO), who was in grave danger of being shot down. Takeuchi managed to save him by fending off the persistent P-47, but he sustained hits to his own aircraft in the process.

Disengaging, the wounded ace retreated alone across the strait towards New Guinea. As he was landing at Hansa Airfield, the engine in his Ki-61 seized and Takeuchi crashed into trees – he was pulled from the wreckage fatally wounded, and died three hours later.

According to Maj Kimura, Takeuchi had flown about 90 missions while in New Guinea and shot down 16 enemy aircraft, with a further ten as probables. Taking his earlier service in the CBI into account, historians state that he shot down, or damaged, over 30 enemy aircraft whilst with the 64th Sentai. Although Takeuchi received a posthumous promotion to the rank of major, a proposed individual citation for distinguished service was not realised.

Another view of Cpl Kajinami, this time whilst he was training to flying Ki-27 fighters at the Akeno Fighter School in April 1943 (*via S Koyama*)

Maj Shogo Takeuchi was an inspiration to his men, and aside from being an adept fighter leader, he was probably also the leading JAAF ace in-theatre with 30+ kills (*via Y Izawa*)

HOME DEFENCE

When Lt Col Jimmy Doolittle led a dozen B-25s in the first attack against Tokyo on 18 April 1942, the psychological effect the raid had on the Japanese public far outlasted any material damage inflicted by the Mitchells' meagre bomb load. Not only had the Americans violated the sacred homeland, but the poor state of the nation's air defence system was clearly exposed. It proved to be a source of acute embarrassment for Adm Isoroku Yamamoto, whose naval aviators had failed miserably in their efforts to protect the Imperial capital.

In response to the 'Doolittle Raiders', the Japanese war cabinet's reaction was overwhelming. The JAAF was ordered to recall the 47th Independent Chutai from Burma and place it under the command of the 17th Air Brigade (who also commanded the 5th and 244th Sentais), which had in turn been given the task of defending the Tokyo region. JAAF training schools also participated in home defence patrols, but it would be more than two years before any of these units would get to fire their guns in anger.

By early 1944 the strategic situation in the CBI had deteriorated so badly for the Japanese that Tokyo GHQ deduced correctly that the next bombing raid on Japan would be flown by four-engined bombers from their bases in China before the end of the summer. The target would be industrial sites in northern Kyushu.

Their ominous predictions were proved correct on the night of 15/16 June when 58th Bomb Wing B-29As attacked the Imperial Iron and Steel Works at Yawata on Kyushu. Of the 62 bombers that had set out from bases in the Chengtu area of China, 47 reached

Although principally assigned the task of turning novice aviators into competent combat pilots, instructors from the Akeno Fighter School were also required to support front-line units in the defence of Japan when the need arose. The principal fighter employed by the school in the final years of the war was the 'Oscar II', these examples being Ki-43-II-Kos (*via Phil Jarrett*)

Natural-metal Ki-44-IIs of the 2nd Chutai/47th Sentai run up prior to taking off on yet another practice interception from Narimasu Airfield in late 1943. Descended from the famous 'Kingfisher' Company that had first blooded the *Shoki* in combat over Malaya in early 1942, the 47th Sentai had been ordered back to Japan in the autumn of the following year to help bolster the defences of the Home Islands (*via Phil Jarrett*)

69

A large number of Ki-61-lb-Kais were also on strength with the Akeno school from early 1944 until war's end, and these advanced Kawasaki fighters proved far more effective against USAAF bomber raids than the more common, but decidedly obsolescent, Ki-43-IIs (*via Phil Jarrett*)

The third model 2 Ki-44 evaluation prototype is run up at a JAAF airfield on the outskirts of Yokota in mid-1942. Production of the fighter got underway soon after this photograph was taken, and it proved to be quite successful at home defence duties in 1944/45 (*via Phil Jarrett*)

This mottled *Shoki* models the scheme worn by a number of Ki-44s encountered over the Philippines in late 1944. Indeed, this aeroplane may have ended up fighting in the skies over Clark Field, although at the time the photo was taken in the spring of 1944 it was very much an Akeno-based machine (*via Phil Jarrett*)

Yawata and bombed the primary target. Twin-engined Ki-45 *Toryu* ('Nicks') from the 4th Sentai sortied to do battle, but of the seven B-29s lost on this mission, none fell to fighters. Nevertheless, the JAAF crews claimed five shot down and five damaged.

Capt Isamu Kashiide, a veteran of Nomonhan, recalls the shock of encountering the Superfortress for the first time on this historic night;

'I was flying over the industrial area of northern Kyushu. The unit commander gave the order "Enemy planes invading an important area, every flight attack!" At the same time, ground searchlights lit up the sky. Finally, I sighted an enemy four-engined bomber. I was scared. It was known that the B-29 was a huge plane, but when I saw my opponent it was much larger than I had ever expected! There was no question that when compared with the B-17, the B-29 was the Superfortress! The

figure that appeared in the searchlight made me think of a great whale in the ocean . . . I was astounded by its size!'

After returning to base following this first combat, Kashiide was extremely critical of the small-calibre weapons found on JAAF aircraft:

'Against larger aircraft, the 7.7 mm and 13 mm machine guns proved ineffective. Even the 20 mm cannon did not produce good results. Against B-29s, we armed our planes with the 37 mm anti-tank gun. "One shot – One hit" was our philosophy.'

As B-29 raids increased on Japan, the invasion of Saipan began when Marines from the 5th Amphibious Corps landed on Garapan, south of the main island, on 15 June. Two days of heavy fighting resulted in the capture of Isley Field, which would eventually be used by B-29s to bomb the Home Islands.

The staple training tool for the Akeno school in the early years of World War 2 was the Ki-27 'Nate', which had been widely replaced in the frontline by the Ki-43 soon after hostilities had commenced. Wearing the distinctive circular badge of Akeno on their rudders, these two Ki-27-Otsus belong to the 2nd (two red stripes) and the 3rd (three white stripes) Chutais repectively (*via Phil Jarrett*)

Right and below
The Ki-100-I-Otsu was undoubtedly one of the best piston-engined fighters of World War 2, but like a crop of excellent Japanese aircraft, it arrived too late to have any great impact on the eventual outcome of the bomber battles over the Home Islands. These shots show *Goshi-kisen* of the 5th Sentai, based at Kiyoso, north of Nagoya, during the last weeks of the war. 'White 39' was the personal mount of Maj Yasuhida Baba, Hikotai-cho of the 5th, who had previously served as CO of the 1st Chutai between March 1943 and March 1944. Whilst leading the 5th, he had seen his sentai claim 40 B-29s destroyed and a further 100+ damaged – all for the loss of ten pilots killed in action and a further six in operational accidents (*both photos via Phil Jarrett*)

Hopelessly outclassed by virtually all Allied fighters by this stage of the war, ex-CBI Ki-43-I-Heis were gain-fully employed as target tugs for the newer *Shokis* within the 47th Sentai in the autumn of 1943. This photo was taken at Narimasu Airfield, north-west of Tokyo
(*via Phil Jarrett*)

Another view of the 3rd Chutai/47th Sentai machine seen above, although this time framed by the tail section of a Ki-44-II-Otsu from the same chutai. The latter fighter is having maintenance work carried out on its retraction mechanism
(*via Phil Jarrett*)

The first daylight bombing of the Japanese mainland by B-29s occurred on 20 August 1944 when the 58th Bomb Wing (BW) returned to Yawata to finish the job. In this engagement, the first intentional air-to-air ramming against a B-29 by a JAAF aircraft occurred. Sgt Shigeo Nobe, of the 4th Sentai, flew his 'Nick' on a collision course with *Gertrude C* of the 794th Bomb Squadron (BS), striking the bomber in the left wing. Both aircraft exploded in flames, and the flying debris struck Capt Ornell Stauffer's *Calamity Sue* a fatal blow. Nobe's destruction of two B-29s resulted in a rare double rank posthumous promotion.

On 1 November 1944 F-13 42-93852 *Tokyo Rose* (B-29 recce variant) of the 3rd Photo Recon Squadron, commanded by Capt Ralph Steakley, flew over Tokyo. It was the first enemy aircraft that had been seen over the Imperial Capital since the 'Doolittle Raiders' of April 1942, and in response this bold action, Capt Sunao Shimizu of the 47th Independent Chutai led his comrades in pursuit of the intruder in their Ki-44-II-Otsus. However, try as they might, the pilots could not reach sufficient altitude to engage the high-flying F-13, and Capts Shimizu and Mat-suzaki could do little more than to point the noses of their respective 'breathless' Nakajima interceptors in the general direction of the Super-fortress and fire blindly. The recce aircraft, never in danger of being hit, leisurely cruised away having successfully completed its mission – aerial

This view of a 53rd Sentai Ki-45-KAI-Hei reveals the twin obliquely-mounted 20 mm cannon fitted into the fuselage between the radio mast and the pilot's cockpit
(*via Phil Jarrett*)

This impressive air-to-air view shows a Ki-45-KAI-Hei of the 3rd Chutai/53rd Sentai out on a patrol from its Matsudo base, on the outskirts of Tokyo, in late 1944. This particular machine wears a red (outlined in yellow) chutai leader's diagonal command stripe across its centre fuselage (*via Phil Jarrett*)

photos taken during the sortie revealed crowded factories and airfields loaded with aircraft.

The JAAF began its defence of the Philippines on 7 November 1944, and their naval counterparts shocked the American fleet on 25 October when their *kamikaze* aircraft sank the escort carrier USS *St Lo* and damaged six others. The JAAF quickly formed their own suicide squadrons, with many pilots volunteering, or being selected, to crash their bomb-laden aircraft into enemy warships.

Despite the desperate measures employed by pilots in the Pacific, the Allied noose continued to tighten around the Japanese Home Islands. Tokyo GHQ, anticipating a new phase in the aerial bombardment of the mainland, desperately formed five air-to-air ramming sentais within the 10th Air Division on 5 December 1944. These new units were equipped with specially-lightened Nakajima and Kawasaki fighters that had had all unnecessary weight removed in order to maximise their climbing performance.

Wearing external fuel tanks so as to increase its range for the impending staged flight from southern Japan to the Philippines, an early-build Ki-84 of the 52nd Sentai taxies out at the start of its hazardous overwater crossing in mid-1944 (*via Phil Jarrett*)

The deteriorating war situation began to erode the morale of the pilots, and in an attempt to stem flagging spirits, Emperor Hirohito issued an

Imperial edict on 7 December 1944 that established the award of the Bukosho for military merit. In the past, the traditional way of honouring the military dead had been to give the deceased an immediate one rank promotion, whilst the award of the Kinshi Kunsho (Order of the Golden Kite) was bestowed upon the lower ranks.

The Bukosho, which was the

This gaudily-decorated Ki-45-KAI-Hei was assigned to the 'Shinten-Seiku' ('Special Attack') Shotai of the 53rd Sentai at Matsudo. This elite flight's only method of attack was to ram the enemy, which usually took the form of a B-29 – the fuselage motif denoted the shotai's rather drastic *modus operandi* (*via Phil Jarrett*)

Seen at Ashiya Airfield, in the Fukuoka Province, soon after VJ-Day, Ki-61-I-Otsu No 776 has a unique bomb over a 'Kikusui' (floating chrysanthemum) emblem on its tail. Mysteriously, this motif appears to be newer than the paint applied to the rest of the fighter – the 'Tony' was probably operated by a *kamikaze* flight (*via Jerry Scutts*)

equivalent of the US Medal of Honor or the British Victoria Cross, broke with tradition through the fact that it could be presented to a living recipient. It could also be awarded on the spot by the unit commander at his discretion. Almost all of the 89 known recipients of the award were aviators, the majority of whom had scored heavily against B-29s over the Home Islands.

The first recipients were Cpl Masao Itagaki and Sgt Matsumi Nakano of the 244th Sentai's air-to-air ramming unit who, on 3 December 1944, had claimed a B-29 apiece in ramming attacks – Nakano managed to land his stricken 'Tony' while Itagaki made a parachute descent.

The initial *kamikaze* suicide attacks held promise, but the Allied Forces quickly countered with combat air patrols. By this stage in the war the quality of JAAF pilots had deteriorated to the point where they could not hope to pierce the overwhelming Allied fighter screen thrown up around the carriers. Hundreds of young pilots were sacrificed many miles short of their targets in a futile attempt to stem the Allied advance toward the Japanese homeland.

Also seen at Ashiya at the same time as 'Tony' No 776, this Ki-61-I provides more of a clue as to the previous owners of the former fighter. This forgotten machine also bears the bomb emblem on its rudder, as well as the remnants of the original 3rd Chutai/59th Sentai diagonal stripe on the fin. The faded red lightning bolt (outlined in yellow) on the fuselage further identifies this *Hien* as the chutai commander's aircraft (*via Jerry Scutts*)

Ki-84s of the 102nd Sentai jockey for postion as they prepare to take-off on yet another sortie in late 1944. This unit was one of the most unsuccessful late war sentais in the JAAF, failing to score even a single victory during numerous home defence patrols over Japan between December 1944 and March 1945. It did, however, contribute six pilots to the *kamikaze* operations off Okinawa (*via K Osuo*)

Ki-84 *Hayate*s of the 2nd Chutai/73rd Sentai in late 1944. Hastily organised and rushed into service in May 1944, this unit had been virtually destroyed by March 1945 following a series of one-sided actions in the Philippines. This aircraft has been left unpainted except for the black anti-glare panel along the nose and the sentai marking on the tail (*via K Osuo*)

The JAAF's Okinawan Campaign began on 14 January 1945 and continued well into July, although within weeks of the offensive commencing, it soon became obvious to both air force commanders and frontline pilots alike that its outcome would be little different to the disaster recently experienced in the Philippines. Employing tactics that had worked a treat in the latter battle, Allied forces began targeting airfields in Kyushu that were being used as launching points for *kamikaze* flights.

Akeno Fighter School Ki-44 *Shoki*s seen openly parked on the ramp in March 1944, prior to bombing raids forcing the widespread dispersal of all JAAF aircraft (*via K Osuo*)

All the while the bombing campaign aimed at the Japanese mainland was increasing in its intensity. Indeed, if one raid could symbolise the 'beginning of the end' for Japan it would be the devastating 'fire bomb' attack flown on the night of 9/10 March 1945, for it saw the USAAF bomber force embrace 'total war' on a broad scale for the first time.

The reason behind the change in the tactics employed by the Americans was simple – air force generals were becoming increasingly alarmed at the growing number of losses being inflicted on the B-29 force by the combination of Japanese fighters and intense flak, particularly in light of

B-29 'killers' of the 4th Sentai pose together for a photo at Ozuki Airfield in Yamaguchi Prefecture, Japan, in early 1944. Back row, left to right; Sgt Shigeo Nobe (destroyed two B-29s in the first ramming attack by JAAF), Sgt Hannoshin Nishio (five victories), and Sgt Shinji Mori. Front row, left to right; Sgt Minoru Uchida (three victories) and Lt Isamu Kashiide (26 victories) (*via H Sakaida*)

The Bukosho (B Class depicted) was Japan's equivalent of the British Victoria Cross or the American 'Medal of Honor'. Most were awarded to pilots who were successful against the B-29s (*via H Sakaida*)

1Lt Toru Shinomiya (left) and Sgt Masao Itagaki both claimed to have destroyed a B-29 apiece through ramming on 3 December 1944 over Tokyo. They belonged to a specialist unit within the 244th Sentai which specialised in such extreme methods of attack, and although Itagaki was forced to abandon his stricken Ki-61 moments after hitting his target, Shinomiy somehow managed to return to base with a large chunk of his port wing missing – as can be clearly seen here. Both were awarded a Bukosho each for their daring feats of bravery (*via M Katoh*)

the fact that bomber crews were failing to consistently hit pin-point industrial targets from high altitude.

Operational tactics had to be altered, and these changes were instigated when Gen Curtis LeMay arrived in-theatre to take over control of XXI Bomber Command from Gen Haywood Hansell in late January 1945. Having studied the poor results being achieved by the command, he decided that precision attacks were too difficult for his crews to prosecute, and reasoned that the destruction of generalised urban targets would achieve better results. He also decided that these raids should be flown at night in order to increase the protection available to his bombers. By using the cover of darkness to help hide their position, raiders could also reduce their attacking altitude (down to 7800 ft on the Tokyo mission) in order to improve weapons drop accuracy, thus alleviating the problems posed by severe jetstreams encountered at high altitude – these had

plagued daylight operations since they had commenced in mid-1944.

Finally, in order to maximise the damage inflicted on the timber buildings that proliferated in the urban areas of Japan, it was obvious that the type of weapon used had to be changed from high explosive munitions to an incendiary device like the recently developed 500-lb 'pyrotechnic gel' bomb. These had been dropped in small numbers on earlier raids, but on this occasion many more rained down on Tokyo than had ever been pre-

viously deployed, resulting in 16 square miles of the city being gutted at a cost of over 100,000 lives. Fourteen B-29s were lost to all causes.

Now that the USAAF had switched to night raids, the bombing onslaught could not be stemmed by Japanese air defences. A number of 'quick fix' types were rushed into service as nightfighters, including the twin-engined recce Mitsubishi Ki-46 'Dinah' fitted with obliquely-mounted 20 mm cannon installed to fire into the undersides of the bombers – it achieved little success, however. A small batch of Ki-44s

The 55th Sentai's 2Lt Takeo Adachi, and his crew chief Sgt Kanzaki, paint a victory mark on his Ki-61 'Tony' following his success on 3 January 1945. Adachi was killed in aerial combat over Nagoya some 16 days later (*via Y Izawa*)

This Ki-100 *Goshikisen* of the Akeno Fighter School was flown by 1Lt Mamoru Tatsuda on the famous 16 July 1945 dogfight over Nagoya Bay when the instructor's flight was led into combat against P-51Ds of the 457th and 458th FSs by Maj Yohei Hinoki (*via Y Hinoki*)

Below left
Pilots and observers of the 4th Sentai at Kozuki Airfield in Yamaguchi Prefecture, Japan, in January 1944. Capt Masaji Kobayashi (CO) returns his mens' salute before their training sortie (*via Maru*)

Below
Pilots of the 4th Sentai are interviewed by a newspaper reporter on the afternoon of 16 June 1944. The previous night B-29s from the 58th BW had raided northern Kyushu – the first Superfortress raid on the Japanese mainland. Although the 4th Sentrai claimed five shot down and another five damaged, none were actually lost. Left to right; Capt Kobayashi, Maj Isao Abe (CO of the sentai), chief of staff of the 19th Air Brigade, 1Lt Isamu Kashiide, Capt Toshio Sassa and WO Sadamitsu Kimura. The newspaper reporter has his back to the camera (*via Y Watanabe*)

To bolster morale in the 70th Sentai, pilots painted victory markings on their Ki-44 'Tojos'. Here, MSgt Kitao Osakabe stands alongside Sgt Sadao Miyazawa's aircraft, the latter having downed a Hellcat on 17 February 1945 in this machine (*via K Osakabe*)

Maj Toshio Sakagawa was a tough fighter leader of the 25th Sentai in China between November 1942 and July 1944. In that time he reportedly downed 49 enemy aircraft, before being transferred back to Japan to serve as executive officer of the newly-formed 200th Sentai, equipped with the Ki-84. Sent to the Philippines soon after their establishment, the unit was badly mauled by USAAF and US Navy fighters. Ironically, Sakagawa himself was not lost in combat, but was instead killed when the transport aircraft he was a passenger on crashed on 19 December 1944 (*via Maru*)

Eight-kill ace Capt Tsutae Obara of the 244th Sentai paints a victory marking on his Ki-61. He was killed on 25 July 1945 over Yokaichi Airfield when his chutai fought a swirling dogfight with Hellcats from VF-31. Whilst attempting to evade a chasing F6F-5 in his Ki-100, Obara collided with yet another US Navy fighter flown by Ens Ed White. Both pilots were killed instantly (*via H Sakaida*)

were outfitted with monstrous 30 and 40 mm cannon mounted in the wings, but the dramatic increase in weight associated with these 'field pieces' made the 'Tojos' almost impossible to manoeuvre once aloft. Aerial burst bombs were also dropped on bomber formations, although with dubious results.

The ceaseless haemorrhaging of aircrew in both suicide and conventional attacks had also begun to take its toll on frontline JAAF units by the early spring of 1945. In the past it had been the policy of the army to utilise wounded veteran pilots in the role of instructors once they had recovered, but now that the frontline had arrived at Japan's 'doorstep', these seasoned aviators were unleashed on the enemy once again.

Men like Capt Yohei Hinoki, who had lost his right leg to a Mustang in Burma in late 1943, took up the challenge of engaging hordes of B-29s as they sortied over his base. Sgt Yukio Shimokawa had had an eye shot out over Burma by a B-24 in the autumn of 1943, but this disability was ignored as he sought out the enemy whilst ferrying fighters to the outlying islands in 1945. Similarly employed delivering replacement 'Franks' (this time to the Philippines in late 1944), combat-weary Sgt Satoshi Anabuki proved he too had not lost his touch by downing six Hellcats.

The final wartime duty performed by these hard-core veterans of countless dogfights in China, Burma and New Guinea was to invariably lead young trainees with minimal flying experience to their deaths in the skies over Japan as they vainly attempted to defend their homeland.

To add to the JAAF's problems US Navy aircraft appeared over Japan for the first time on 16-17 February 1945 during a two-day assault which wrecked airfields in the Tokyo area. Those Japanese pilots unfortunate enough to be flying 'Oscar IIs' and 'Tojos' were hard-pressed to survive attacks by F6F Hellcats and F4U Corsairs.

The fall of Iwo Jima only caused more headaches for home defence pilots as American single-engined fighter aircraft could now escort the B-29s to their target and back. The first such mission occurred on 7 April 1945 when 7th Fighter Command P-51Ds escorted 73rd BW B-29s to Tokyo, the Mustang 'jockeys' claiming 26 victories in the morning skirmish alone. On subsequent missions P-47D/N Thunderbolts joined in, and just as the Luftwaffe's Bf 110 and Me 410 'heavy' fighters had proven no match for USAAF single-seater types in the skies over western Europe, so twin-engined JAAF interceptors like the 'Nick' became easy prey for US pilots.

Two Japanese types that proved to be anything but cannon fodder for USAAF fighters were the Ki-84 *Hayate* (Gale) and the Ki-100 *Goshikisen*. With skilled pilots at the controls, both aircraft could more than hold their own against the

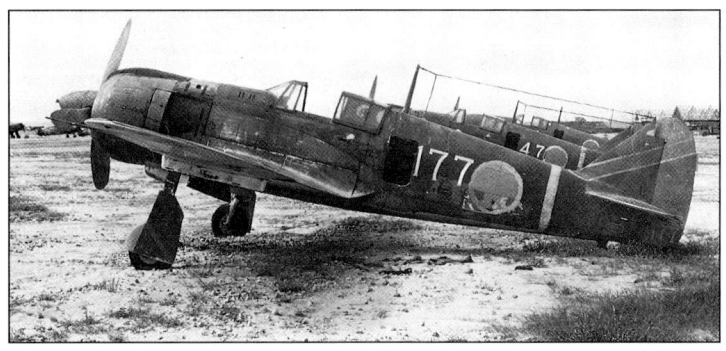

Ki-100-I-Ko *Goshikisen* of the 1st Chutai of the 59th Sentai sit in readiness for a rapid scramble from Ashiya Airfield in Fukuoka Prefecture, Japan, in June 1945. Known as the 'Tony II,' the Ki-100 was basically a K-61 airframe outfitted with a Mitsubishi Ha-112-II 14 cylinder, air-cooled, radial engine. The Ki-100-I-Ko was the most common *Goshikisen* of them all, with some 272 airframes having been built by war's end (*via Maru*)

A Ki-45 *Toryu* of the 4th Sentai takes off to do battle with B-29s over Kyushu in late 1944. Originally designed as a long-range escort fighter, the 'Nick' failed miserably in its intended role due to to its lack of performance when compared with more agile Allied fighters. However, it made its mark as a B-29 interceptor, particularly under the cover of darkness (*via H Sakaida*)

feared Hellcat, Corsair or Mustang. However, the 'Frank' never arrived in sufficient numbers to offer anything but a token resistance, and likewise Kawasaki's Ki-100 (essentially a Ki-61 'Tony' airframe fitted with a 1500-hp Mitsubishi Ha-112-II radial engine) only began to enter service after March 1945. Although these aircraft were capable of inflicting severe damage on B-29 formations, the efforts of the few who got to fly them in combat were quickly thwarted after April 1945 by overwhelming numbers of escort fighters.

The last major combat between the JAAF and the Americans occurred on 25 July 1945 when 18 Ki-100s of the 244th Sentai encountered ten F6F-5 Hellcats of VF-31 over Yokaichi Airfield on an early-morning raid. In a fierce dogfight, Capt Tsutae Obara (eight kills) collided with Ens Edwin White and both were killed. Soon after WO Shin Ikuta and Ens Herbert Law were downed, the former dying in the subsequent crash, but Law surviving to return to the America from a PoW camp after the war.

Capt Chuichi Ichikawa (see page 80), pictured here as an aviation cadet in 1937, was one of just a handful of pilots to survive combat over New Guinea and return to Japan to fight in the home defence. He won the Bukosho for downing nine B-29s whilst flying with the 244th Sentai (*via Y Izawa*)

The 244th claimed 12 Hellcats destroyed for the loss of two pilots, whilst VF-31 counter-claimed with eight kills and three probables for the loss of two. As the most successful home defence unit of the war, the 244th Sentai ended the conflict with claims of 102 B-29s shot down and 192 damaged.

Capt Nagao Shirai (see page 81) became the top ace of the 244th Sentai whilst serving as leader of the 3rd Chutai. He joined the unit soon after its formation in 1942, and served exclusively with this sentai. Postwar, Shirai shunned publicity and refused to talk about his combat career, thus relegating him into historical obscurity (*via H Sakaida*)

Major Teruhiko Kobayashi

Teruhiko Kobayashi became a dashing hero in the latter part of the Japanese home defence. Born in 1920, he had entered the Army Military Academy in the late 1930s and graduated in the 53rd Class. Initially appointed as a second lieutenant in artillery, Kobayashi soon changed courses to light bombers and was assigned to the 45th Sentai upon graduation.

On the opening day of the Pacific War he participated in the bombing of Hong Kong, and by April 1943 had become a seasoned veteran of many operational sorties with the 66th Sentai in Manchuria. When the air group enlarged, he decided to convert to fighters and was posted to the Akeno Fighter School. A promotion to captain came in November 1943, and upon the completion of his course in June 1944, Kobayashi was retained in Japan to serve as education officer with the school.

In the latter part of November 1944 he became an assistant to the commander of the 244th Sentai, this unit becoming the darling of the general public as it strove to defend Japan from enemy bombers. Armed with the sleek Ki-61-I-KAI *Hien*, the unit provided protection for the Tokyo area from their base at Chofu Airfield in the western suburbs of the city.

At the age of 24, Capt Kobayashi became the youngest air group commander in the JAAF, leading the sentai by example. His unit gained considerable fame against the B-29s, and by war's end the 244th Sentai could boast a number of Superfortress 'killers'.

Kobayashi himself shot down a B-29 in a single pass on 3 December 1944, while his group claimed six additional aircraft on the same sortie through ramming attacks (all the pilots survived). On 22 December he

Capt Teruhiko Kobayashi poses for an official photograph to celebrate his receiving the Bukosho (pinned to his left chest) in May 1945 (*via H Sakaida*)

damaged a B-29 over Akumihan Island and then on 9 January he damaged another Superfortress, although on this occasion his *Hien* was hit by return fire and he was forced to make an emergency landing. Eighteen days later Kobayashi destroyed a B-29 through ramming, escaping death by taking to his parachute – his only injury was a cut over his nose.

This beautifully painted Ki-61-I-KAI *Hien* of the 244th Sentai shows the spirit of the unit through its distinctive markings. It also sports the silhouettes of 12 B-29s and two Hellcats under the cockpit, thus denoting that it was flown by sentai commander, Capt Teruhiko Kobayashi. The air group operated from Chofu Airfield on the outskirts of Tokyo, and received much publicity during 1944-45 for its heroic struggle against B-29s over the Imperial capital (*via Maru*)

Kobayashi and his crew chief pose in front of his 'Tony' (*via Maru*)

The exploits of the 244th Sentai were published daily in newspapers at the time, and Kobayashi's fame continued to grow. On 12 April he damaged yet another B-29, but was wounded in the leg by return fire and forced to take to his parachute once again. The following month his unit received a letter of commendation from the Army High Command, and at the same time his deeds were recognised by the award of the Bukosho.

On 25 July Maj Kobayashi disobeyed orders by taking off to intercept marauding Hellcats over Yokaichi Airfield, having been instructed to stay on the ground to await incoming bombers. He and his men were by this late stage in the war flying the superlative Ki-100 *Goshikisen* (Type 5 Fighter), and as previously noted in this chapter, in the dogfight that took place at hangar-top height, the 244th Sentai pilots reportedly shot down ten of the VF-31 Hellcats that had sortied over Japan from the carrier USS *Belleau Wood* – the real score was just two for two on both sides.

Newspapers trumpeted the rout, but a court martial was planned for the young commander, which carried a very serious penalty. However, news of his great deed reached the Emperor, and words of Imperial approval were spoken in respect to Kobayashi's actions – the court martial was quickly dropped.

Maj Kobayashi scored five victories in total (three B-29s and two F6F Hellcats), although postwar Japanese historians have erroneously credited him with 10 B-29s and two fighters. This latter score, which would have made him the top JAAF B-29 'killer', is based on self-serving statements by Kobayashi's widow and photos showing numerous victory markings on his aircraft. Extensive investigation by Japanese historian Takashi Sakurai has subsequently shown that the lower score is correct.

After the war, Kobayashi joined the Self-Defense Air Force, but on 4 June 1957 was killed in a training accident when the T-33 he was flying crashed on approach to landing at Hamamatsu Air Base in bad weather. He had earlier ordered his subordinate to eject from the aircraft when it had developed a technical problem in flight. Teruhiko Kobayashi remained a hero to the end.

Captain Yoshio Yoshida

Yoshio Yoshida was one of the top B-29 'killers' of the JAAF. Born in 1921 in Hiroshima City, he entered the 55th Class of the Army Officers' Flight Academy in 1939, and upon graduation in March 1942 was sent to the Akeno Fighter School for additional training prior to being posted to the 70th Sentai.

When the USAAF's 20th Air Force sent 96 B-29s to attack targets in Anshan, Manchuria, for the first time on 29 July 1944, the 70th Sentai was transferred into the region the following month so as to provide some form of defence for the Japanese colonial territory – the air group was equipped with the Ki-44-II-Hei.

On 8 September a force of 108 B-29s raided Anshan for a second time, and in the subsequent engagement between the Superfortresses and the 'Tojos', 1Lt Yoshida managed to claim one as a probable.

The thundering hordes of B-29s started to raid the Tokyo region in November 1944, and in an attempt to counter the menace, the 70th Sentai was transferred back to Kashiwa Airfield, near the capital, where they swapped their near-useless 'Tojos' for the far superior Ki-84 'Frank'.

Two views featuring Kobayashi in different Ki-61-I-KAIs at varying stages in his career. The top shot shows a scoreboard denoting six B-29 kills, with the last one further embellished with a red Ki-61 silhouette to denote that it was achieved through ramming – this combat took place on 27 January 1945 over Mt Fuji. The second photo reveals a different style of victory marking application. Kobayashi did not differentiate between destroyed and damaged in his kill markings, and the reasoning behind a solid white silhouette as opposed to just an outline is unclear (*both via Maru*)

Capt Yoshio Yoshida stands proudly by his Ki-44. The two victory markings are dated 13 and 15 April 1945, and are detailed with both his name and rank. He claimed six B-29s and one probable (*via Maru*)

Yoshida was given command of the 3rd Chutai in February 1945, and immediately began to hone his attacks against the four-engined bombers. On 13 April he shot down a B-29, followed by another two days later, and then between 10 March and 25 May Yoshida claimed six Superfortresses in night actions. As a result of his extraordinary successes, the award of the Bukosho was bestowed upon him.

As the second-highest B-29 'killer' of the 70th Sentai, Yoshida score totalled six bombers destroyed and one probable. He is now deceased.

Warrant Officer Tadao Sumi

Tadao Sumi was born in 1916 in Gifu Prefecture. He joined the army in the mid-1930s, and had seen service as an infantryman during the sieges of Shanghai and Nanking prior to transferring to flight training in February 1941. Sumi graduated in November of that year, and was eventually assigned to the air defence of the Tokyo region with the 244th Sentai when it formed in the aftermath of the Doolittle raid in April 1942.

It wasn't until Sumi started flying against B-29s towards the end of 1944 that he became a hero in the eyes of the Japanese public. Having joined the Ki-61-equipped 56th Sentai just prior to the first raids, he subsequently fought the B-29s on a near-daily basis until war's end.

Sumi's greatest moment came during a series of night action fought on 13 March 1945 over Osaka, the master sergeant making repeated lone attacks on the B-29 force. He succeeded in shooting down four bombers, and damaging three others, before he was forced to take to his parachute when his Ki-61 ran out of fuel. However, as he undid his straps and prepared to vacate his fighter, Sumi became disoriented through an attack of vertigo. This momentarily delayed his jump to the point that when he did part company with the Ki-61, he struck his shoulder on the tailplane as the aircraft flew on. Sumi was forced to spend three months in hospital recuperating.

In recognition of his heroic deed, Gen Kawabe, commander of the 15th Military District, awarded the warrant officer a letter of commendation. On 21 June 1945, Sumi received the Bukosho (Medal of Honour, A Class – he was one of the very few recipients to receive the highest grade of this decoration).

Sumi went back into combat later that month, and despite being wounded again, continued to fly. By war's end he had downed five B-29s and damaged four more, plus destroyed a P-51. He passed away on 25 July 1985.

WO Tadao Sumi was one of just a handful of pilots to earn the Bukosho, A Class, which was awarded following his destruction of four B-29s in a single night mission over Osaka on 13 March 1945 (*via Y Izawa*)

Captain Fujitaro Ito

Although a relative unknown when compared to the more famous B-29 'killers' profiled in this chapter, Capt Fujitaro Ito may just be the top four-engined bomber destroyer of the entire JAAF. Born in 1916 in Fukui Prefecture, he enlisted in the Army in the mid-1930s and initially served in the 36th Infantry Regiment. In April 1939 he entered the NCO flight training course, and duly graduated from Kumagaya Flying School in December. Ito was then posted to the 5th Sentai, a unit with which he stayed until war's end.

Having seen several years of frontline service with this sentai, Ito then entered the Aviation Commissioned Officers' Academy as a candidate for second lieutenant in June 1942. He graduated in November of that same year, and three months later received his commission.

In July 1943 Ito departed with his unit for duty south of Java, and was engaged in various combats. By 19 January 1944 the 5th Sentai was based at Rian Air Base, on Ambon Island, in the East Indies. The unit had been equipped with the Ki-45 prior to deploying to Rian, thus becoming the first sentai in the JAAF to receive the new heavy fighter in the process.

Ito's first combat with the 'Dragon Slayer' occurred soon after his arrival in the East Indies, his chutai responding to a surprise raid staged by a formation of B-24s on the airfield. Seven Liberators fell to the heavily-armed Ki-45s, three of them to 2Lt Ito and his observer, Sgt Masanori Nozaki. They had taken on a four-bomber formation and quickly despatched a trio of B-24s using the fighter's 37 mm cannon. His own air-craft was hit in the right engine, however, and they were forced to make an emergency landing at Seramu Island. Due to the bravery shown in the face of overwhelming odds, both Ito and Nozaki received personal com-mendations from Gen Tsukuda, the regional air commander.

In mid-May 1944, Ito and Nozaki again encountered enemy bombers, but this time their 'Nick' was hit before they could inflict any damage on the formation. They were forced to make an emergency landing in the sea, but were quickly rescued. Ito later flew air defence patrols around Nanking before returning to Japan.

In December 1944 Marianas-based B-29s started to attack Nagoya, and the recently-promoted 1Lt Ito was in the vanguard thrown up by the JAAF in an attempt to thwart their efforts. Over the next eight months he would tackle USAAF bombers in Ki-45s, Ki-61s and finally Ki-100s. In January 1945 he took control of the 3rd Chutai, and proceeded to lead it until the end of the war – he had shot down more than nine B-29s by VJ-Day. In light of his efforts in the final desperate months of war, Ito was awarded the Bukosho on 7 July 1945.

Capt Ito shot down more than 13 enemy aircraft, all of which were bombers. He passed away on 15 May 1983.

Captain Isamu Kashiide

Known as the 'King of B-29 Killers', Isamu Kashiide's name became well known in the JAAF during the latter part of the home defence campaign. Born in 1915 in Niigata Prefecture, the young Kashiide's boyhood dream of becoming a fighter pilot became a reality when he entered aviation

Capt Fujitaro Ito became a four-engined specialist over Japan, knocking down at least three B-24s and nine B-29s whilst flying Ki-45s, Ki-61s and finally Ki-100s with the 5th Sentai. After the war, he became a proud member of Lions International (Japan) (*via F Ito*)

Capt Isamu Kashiide became famous as the 'King of B-29 Killers', and he is seen here wearing an electrically-heated flight suit. Such gear was mandatory when engaging B-29s at very high altitudes in the freezing skies over Japan (*via Y Izawa*)

Capt Kashiide's Ki-45-KAI-Hei at Kozuki Airfield in 1945. He believed in hunting 'big game' with a 'big gun', his aircraft boasting a Ho-203 semi-automatic recoil-operated 37 mm anti-tank cannon. This weapon was fed from a magazine that held just 25 rounds, so every shot had to count. Nevertheless, this combination was considered by many within the JAAF to be the most effective at countering the B-29 threat (*via Y Izawa*)

school in February 1934. He graduated in November of the following year, and then joined the 1st Air Regiment.

In July 1938 Kashiide was assigned to the 59th Sentai in northern China, but by the time he arrived in-theatre there was no opportunity for him to experience action against the Chinese Air Force. However, in September of the following year his Ki-27-equipped unit went to Nomonhan, and this time he saw enough combat to make up for the disappointment of the year before. On the very last day of fighting he became involved in a mêlée with eight I-16s and managed to shoot down two of his assailants, although he was nearly shot down himself.

At the end of the Nomonhan Incident, Kashiide returned to Hankow, in central China, with seven victories to his credit. He was assigned to the Formosa-based 4th Sentai in the spring of 1940, and the outbreak of the Pacific War found him performing air defence duties in obsolescent Ki-27s. Within weeks his unit was taking part in the invasion of the Philippines, although the sentai returned to Kozuki Airfield, in Japan, before Kashiide could add to his Nomonhan tally.

The 4th Sentai was equipped with the Ki-45 *Toryu* in mid-1943, but the twin-engined fighter escort soon proved to be ill-suited to its designated role. However, when outfitted with a 37 mm cannon in the nose and rear-upward firing 20 mm weapons in the fuselage, the Kawasaki type indeed metamorphosed into a 'Dragon Slayer'.

As mentioned earlier in this chapter, on the night of 14/15 June 1944 China-based B-29s commenced their first attacks on the Japanese homeland. Their mission was to destroy the Imperial Steel and Iron Works at Yawata, and opposing them was 1Lt Kashiide and his squadron, amongst other JAAF units. Once the resulting interception was over, he reported having shot down two bombers, and was uncertain about the fate of a third. Kashiide followed up this success on 20 August when he claimed three B-29s shot down and a further trio damaged during a daylight raid.

He soon developed his own style of combat through countless encounters with the Superfortresses, and drilled his subordinates hard in his unique teachings. Years after the war had ended, Kashiide recalled the following instructions;

'Manoeuvre from within 1000 meters. The B-29s have 13 machine guns – in a head-on attack, you will be faced with 10 of them. I will always fly in front and I will always be the first to attack. I am showered with tracers every time. Tracers coming toward you in a criss-cross pattern are very frightening. I feel that my vision is shot away in the screen of bullets. It is not a good feeling to have. In such cases, close your eyes and count to three. When you open your eyes, the enemy will be within 200 metres of you. Adjust your sight to within 150 to 200 metres of the target. At 100 metres, lower your plane. At 80 metres, fire, then dive your plane quickly – go straight down.'

On 27 January 1945 Kashiide shot down a B-29 of the 878th BS/499th BG over Tokyo, a 37 mm round hitting 'T Square 27' *Rover Boy Express* squarely in the nose.

One of the crewmembers that managed to bail out of the stricken B-29 was a young 22-year-old navigator by the name of Raymond 'Hap' Halloran.

For distinguished service against hordes of B-29s, 1Lt Kashiide received the Bukosho on 8 May 1945 from Lt Gen Isamu Yokoyama. His citation read;

'This distinguished person, on 27 March 1945, at the time of the assault of northern Kyushu by American Air Force B-29s over the air of the protected area, carried on

Capt Kashiide's victim over Tokyo on 27 January 1945 was 'T Square 27' *Rover Boy Express* of the 878th BS/499th BG, shown here streaming smoke having received a direct hit from a 37 mm shell. Six crewmen died in the subsequent crash, but five survived, including Raymond 'Hap' Halloran, who shook hands with Kashiide in 1985 (*via R Halloran*)

his daredevil attack, shooting down three B-29s and damaging others, and achieved this glorious result. His actions were based on severe fighting spirit and techniques which enabled him to defeat many enemy planes. His feat glorifies the spirit of the Imperial Army combat squadrons. His military record is outstanding. Therefore, he is hereby awarded the Bukosho B Class.'

By war's end Kashiide had claimed to have destroyed 26 B-29s over Japan, plus of course the seven Soviet fighters he had shot down at Nomonhan. His score is widely disputed by historians and former pilots alike, and today it is widely believed that he scored no more than seven B-29s, plus two fighters in 1939. Even if this were true, it was still an incredible accomplishment since most JAAF pilots agreed that it was almost an impossible task for a single pilot to bring down a B-29.

Kashiide was also an eyewitness to the beginning of the atomic age, for he viewed the nuclear destruction of Hiroshima and Nagasaki from the air.

On 17 September 1985 Capt Kashiide met Raymond F 'Hap' Halloran, the navigator aboard *Rover Boy Express* which he had shot down over 40 years before. They shook hands in the spirit of friendship brought by decades of peace, and marvelled at how they had both survived the war.

Second Lieutenant Makoto Ogawa

Makoto Ogawa was born in 1917 in Shizuoka Prefecture. He joined the 7th Air Regiment at Hamamatsu in 1935 and eventually transferred over to fighters. In August 1938 Ogawa graduated from the Kumagaya Aviation School in the 72nd term class, but instead of being posted to a frontline unit, he was employed as an assistant flight instructor at his old school. Finally, towards the end of 1941 he was transferred to Manchuria to serve with the 70th Sentai.

For the first three years of the Pacific War the 70th Sentai fulfilled the air defence role for the northern extremities of Manchuria, but in the autumn of 1944, it was brought back to defend Tokyo – it re-equipped with Ki-84s to perform this task. After more than seven solid years as a pilot, Ogawa had attained a high level of proficiency, and during night operations against B-29s, he quickly developed a method of frontal assaults. During daylight missions, however, Ogawa would only commence his attack once the bombers had started to drop their load, as the

One of the best combat pilots in the JAAF in the final months of the war, 2Lt Makoto Ogawa shot down seven B-29s and two P-51Ds in his decidedly inferior Ki-44-II-Otsu 'Tojo', and duly became the top pilot in the 70th Sentai. The weathered grey eagles on the fuselage of his aircraft represent B-29 victories (*via Y Izawa*)

B-29 pilots would be forced to maintain level flight during the release. This made them easy targets for Ogawa, and he downed two Superfortresses using this method of attack. By war's end he had destroyed seven B-29s and two P-51Ds, a score which made Ogawa the top pilot of the 70th Sentai. On 9 July 1945 he was awarded the Bukosho from Gen Seiichi Tanaka, and promoted to second lieutenant.

Ogawa is now a businessman, and he resides in Tokyo.

Sergeant Nobuji Negishi

Nobuji Negishi became the top B-29 'killer' of the 53rd Sentai during the home defence period. He was born in 1924 in Saitama Prefecture, and entered the Tokyo Army Aviation School in October 1939. Upon graduation in 1942, Negishi was assigned to the 244th Sentai, which had just been formed to guard the capital. After a short while he transferred to the 18th Sentai, before moving to the 53rd – both units were Japan-based.

The latter sentai had been formed specifically on Ki-45s so as to counter the B-29 forays over Japan. Sgt Negishi's first night mission on 10 March 1945 yielded instant success, for when ground searchlights lit up a formation of Superfortresses, he succeeded in knocking down two with precision shooting.

On 9 July 1945 Negishi was decorated with the award of the Bukosho for his successful missions against the B-29s. He ended the war with six Superfortress kills, and had damaged a further seven bombers.

He resides in his native prefecture.

Captain Chuichi Ichikawa

Chuichi Ichikawa became one of the great single-engined Superfortress killers in the final months of the war, overflying his native Tokyo. Born in the capital in 1918, he entered Kumagaya Army Flight School as a Youth Flight Programme cadet in February 1936, and after graduation the following year, joined the 9th Sentai.

The Nomonhan Incident was coming to a close by the time Ichikawa arrived in Manchuria to join his unit, and he duly failed to see any action. This was probably a fortunate thing for his sentai was still equipped with old Ki-10 Type 95 biplane fighters in September 1939, having still to transition to the newer monoplane Type 97 'Nates'.

In 1941, Ichikawa was assigned to the Air Inspection Division, where he test flew new aircraft and worked on their combat capabilities. In December 1942 he entered the Army Flight Academy, and upon graduation the following June, was assigned to the Ki-43 'Oscar II'-equipped 78th Sentai in Rabaul. Soon after his arrival, Ichikawa's unit shipped out to New Guinea – a theatre which soon earned the grim nickname of the 'Graveyard of Army Fighter Pilots'.

After several months of near-constant action, Ichikawa was seriously burned when his fighter was set alight during aerial combat. He somehow managed to survive the fierce blaze, however, and was sent back to the homeland for further hospitalisation. Upon recovery, Ichikawa joined the 244th Sentai, defending the Imperial capital.

It was in the home defence role that Ichikawa quickly made a name for himself, fighting bravely with remarkable skill. On the night of 15 April 1945 he downed two B-29s and damaged another, destroying one of the

Sgt Nobuji Negishi use the Ki-45 to down all six B-29s that he claimed to have destroyed – he also damaged a further seven Boeing bombers. This score made him the leading 'bomber killer' within the 53rd Sentai (*via Y Izawa*)

bombers through ramming it with his Ki-100 – he parachuted down from the collision badly wounded. Ichikawa received the Bukosho as a result of this action, being one of just five pilots known to have received the A Class award. He was also promoted to captain in June. By the end of the war Capt Ichikawa had claimed nine B-29s shot down and six more damaged, plus destroyed a single Hellcat.

He was killed in an air crash in September 1954 while working as a private pilot.

Captain Nagao Shirai

It is only recently that the wartime career of Capt Shirai has come to light, principally due to the research of Japanese aviation historian Takashi Sakurai of Tokyo. The latter has now established the fact that Shirai was not only the ranking ace of the 244th Sentai, but also possibly the leading B-29 'killer' of the JAAF.

Nagao Shirai was born in Hyogo Prefecture and graduated from the Army Military Academy in the early 1940s. He was assigned to the 244th Sentai in November 1942, but saw no real action until the bombing raids commenced on Tokyo in mid-1944. In October of that year he became the squadron leader of the 3rd Chutai, which he headed until the end of the war.

This capable fighter leader should have received more recognition than he has been accorded, for by war's end he had achieved 11 B-29 and two F6Fs kills, plus had damaged a further six enemy aircraft – all these victories were achieved using Ki-61 and Ki-100 aircraft.

After the end of the war Shirai avoided contact with his old comrades, and he never talked about his years in combat. He passed away in 1974.

Second Lieutenant Sadamitsu Kimura

Sadamitsu Kimura became one of the top JAAF B-29 'killers'. Born in Chiba Prefecture on 19 August 1915, by May 1938 he had entered flight training and was assigned to the 4th Sentai in 1942.

Kimura's entire war career centred around home defence duties and fighting B-29s. When the Boeing bombers first raided Japan on the night of 14/15 June 1944, Kimura took off in his Ki-45 from Kozuki Airfield to intercept them, and by the time he returned had claimed two B-29s shot down and three damaged. This was his unit's first major success up to that date, and he was duly awarded a ceremonial sword. Kimura also received a personal citation from Gen Shimomura of the Western Military District.

On 27 March 1945 he flew three missions during the night and claimed an incredible five B-29s shot down, with a further two damaged. On 1 May he was awarded the Bukosho for distinguished service.

On the night of 13/14 July 1945 313rd BW B-29s mined the Shimonoseki Straits, and Kimura reported by radio that he had damaged a Superfortress and was going in to finish the stricken bomber off – this was his last transmission.

Capt Isamu Kashiide, another great B-29 'killer' and a squadronmate of Kimura's, wrote in his postwar memoirs that the latter had shot down some 22 B-29s. Japanese historians have attributed him with eight victories, however.

THE CHINA WAR

It was inevitable that Japan and China would eventually go to war. Japanese economic ambitions in China and throughout Greater South-East Asia could not be supported without a modern military, and the backbone to any large-scale land occupation lay in the invading force's ability to support such actions through the use of air power. Japan had gained concessions in China by siding with the Western powers in World War 1, and with China itself being politically weak and having little say in governing her own internal affairs, the time was ripe to strike.

The first step to occupation was taken when Japan's Kwantung Army marched into Manchuria and turned it into a puppet state, thus souring relations between the two countries. China appealed to the League of Nations, who started a boycott of Japanese goods. On 18 January 1932 rioting broke out in Shanghai against the invading army, and to quell this disturbance, Japan landed an expeditionary force near the port city.

The first meaningful aerial engagement between the two force occurred on 5 February when two bombers and three fighter escorts from the carrier *Hosho* encountered a Blackburn F.2D Lincock III biplane fighter (one of only two supplied to China) over Shingu. The pilot, Tsu Dah-Shien, played 'tag' with the formation through the clouds until he was hit and wounded after his guns jammed – he managed to return to base.

Also embroiled in this escalating conflict were a handful of mercenary pilots employed by the Chinese to oppose the occupiers, and they were involved in the first real 'bloodletting' on 22 February over the Souchow Railway Station. American mercenary Robert Short, flying a Boeing P-12 biplane, intercepted carrier bombers from the *Kaga* and destroyed the lead aircraft. However, he in turn was duly shot down by a trio of escort

A5M4 Type 96 'Claudes' of the 12th AG are seen flying a patrol over China in 1939. Initially, JNAF pilots were reluctant to transition from the well-liked 'Claude' to the new Zero fighter, as in mock dogfights with the the latter type the Type 96 won every time. However, the spectacular first combat success enjoyed by the Zero in September 1940 eventually changed pilots' minds once and for all (*via Robert C Mikesh*)

pilots, thus becoming the first victory of the JNAF in China. Skirmishing around Shanghai lasted until May when Japanese forces were withdrawn.

By July 1937 relations between the two nations had deteriorated to a point where armed conflict seemed inevitable, and on 7 July a local skirmish between opposing forces on the Marco Polo Bridge, south-west of Beijing, provided the spark to ignite the China War. This event united all Chinese – despite their differing ideologies – against the Japanese.

The state of military aviation in China was very poor, with regional warlords having purchased foreign aircraft on the basis of corruption rather than performance. As a result there was no standard fighter, nor a cohesive organisation. Chinese pilots were not properly trained either, the Chinese Air Force (CAF) also suffering through corruption and political meddling which saw officer pilots owing their allegiance to their local warlords rather than the nation as a whole.

The first large-scale CAF counterattack following invasion occurred on 14 August when then Capt Claire Chennault (acting as operational CO of the fragmented air force under authority of Chiang Kai Shek) launched 60 fighters against the Japanese fleet. CAF aircraft failed to hit any ships

China War veteran Matsuo Hagiri poses with his favourite A5M4 whilst part of the *Soryu* Fighter Squadron
(*via Aerospace Publishing*)

Squadronmates of Matsuo Hagiri pose in front of Hideo Oishi's A5M4 aboard the *Soryu* during a 1939 deployment. Like Hagiri, Oishi was one of the pilots made famous by the audacious Taipingsze airfield attack on 4 October 1940
(*via Aerospace Publishing*)

With their Nakajima Kotobuki 41 engines clattering away, a clutch of 'Claudes' prepare for launch from *Soryu*'s deck during a fleet training exercise in early 1940
(*via Aerospace Publishing*)

in their dismal bombing attacks, Chinese pilots also mistakenly attacking the British cruiser HMS *Cumberland,* but fortunately their bombs fell wide of the vessel. They also dropped bombs into the Shanghai city centre, accidentally killing more than 1700 civilians and wounding a further 1800. In the first JNAF victory of the renewed conflict, a Nakajima floatplane shot down a Curtiss Hawk III. Subsequent bombing raids against Chinese targets in the far interior of the country proved costly for the JNAF, and it didn't take long for Naval GHQ to realise that unescorted bombers were vulnerable to attack from CAF fighters. Conversely, those bomber groups escorted by fighters were seldom attacked.

In September 1937 the Second Combined Air Flotilla returned to Shanghai with a new weapon – the Mitsubishi A5M Type 96 'Claude' monoplane fighter. For the JNAF the age of the biplane was over. With a speed in excess of 250 mph, the 'Claude' out performed any enemy biplane and held its own against the Soviet I-16. Within two months of the the Type 96's introduction, fighter opposition had drastically reduced.

Despite the advent of the 'Claude', Chinese fighters remained active during 1938, aided by aggressive Soviet 'volunteers' in their I-16s. And although it was widely reported in the Japanese press that 1227 CAF were destroyed in 15 months of fighting, the actual number was much less.

The Japanese never expected to conquer all of China, for it was simply too vast. However, they concentrated on holding major cities in the interior and ports along the coast, and by 1940 the war was at a stalemate. Two years earlier, the Japanese government had attempted to negotiate an end to the conflict but had been thwarted by a militant faction of the army and certain influential Chinese who wanted to keep the war going.

In September 1940 the JNAF introduced the new Zero fighter into the combat arena, and contrary to popular belief, pilots were initially not impressed with the new mount, preferring to keep their Type 96s. In mock combats between the Zero and the 'Claude', the old monoplane won every dogfight thanks to it being lighter and more manoeuvrable. It would have to take some extraordinary event to change the pilots' minds.

The first combat between the Zero and CAF fighters occurred on 13 September 1940 over Chunking when 27 I-15s and I-16s were engaged. In the subsequent action the Japanese claimed all 27 fighters destroyed without loss, WO Koshiro Yamashita becoming the first JNAF 'ace in a day' with five kills. The news spread like wildfire, and showed that what the Zero lacked in manoeuvrability when compare with the Claude, it made up for in firepower and speed. Lt Cdr Iyozoh Fujita summed it up best when he said, 'The Type 96 was very easy to control, and in a mock dogfight with a Zero it was superior. But the Zero was better than the Type 96 in total performance, so I liked the Zero'.

The combat experience gained by the JNAF during the China War would later prove to be invaluable to naval aviators during the opening months of the Pacific War, pilots believing that their beloved Zero could out perform any fighter in the world. Navy pilots also boasted that their training was superior to their army counterparts, and proved it time and again by defeating those who rose to the challenge in mock dogfights.

Fired up with naval pride, experienced in combat and with extreme confidence in their new Zero fighter, the JNAF pilot was a dangerous opponent heading into 1941.

Lieutenant Mochifumi Nango

The elder brother of Japanese Army Air Force (JAAF) pilot Shigeo Nango, Mochifumi emulated his sibling by becoming a model fighter-leader in the JNAF. Born in Hiroshima Prefecture in July 1906 as the son of a rear admiral, it was only natural that Mochifumi would enter the Naval Academy at Etajima – he duly graduated in the 55th Class in 1927, and went on to complete his flight training in November 1932.

Later in the decade Lt Nango went to England and served as an assistant naval attaché at the Japanese Embassy in London. Here, he refined his scholarly manner, improved his English speaking ability and showed a great attention to detail, all of which marked him out as a natural leader.

With the China War only three months old, Lt Nango went into battle as division officer in the 13th Air Group (AG) in October 1937, and it wasn't long before the 31-year-old aviator made a name for himself. On 2 December he led six 'Claudes' against an estimated 30 CAF fighters, downing two himself (out of thirteen claimed) and bringing honours to his unit. CO of the China Area Fleet, Adm Kiyoshi Hasegawa, issued the following citation, dated 5 December 1937, as a result of the engagement;

'The time when the Chinese Air Force was trying to regain its power through aggressive attacks with the latest imported fighters, you (Nango) on 2 December 1937, supported the raid on Nanking and battled 30 enemy fighters which began attacking you and your six fighters. Your unit downed 13 enemy fighters and made them loose spirit. Your continuous contribution to these missions are great. Your military service record is outstanding. You are hereby commended.'

Lt Nango was transferred to the carrier *Soryu* to become division officer later that month, and he served in this capacity until July 1938 when he was moved to the newly-organised 15th AG to become group leader. Based on land at Anking, his group flew both ground support missions for army troops against Hankow and air defence patrols to protect shipping along the Yangtze River. A rudimentary forward airfield with few creature comforts, the unsanitary conditions at Anking brought illness to the pilots of the new unit, Nango included. However, he refused to be side-lined and continued to fly missions. It was to have its consequences.

On 18 July 1938, whilst flying over Lake Poyang, Lt Nango dived on an I-15 piloted by Soviet volunteer Valentin Dudonov. The Russian was unaware that he was under attack until bullets started striking his seat armour plate. Before he could react, the JNAF pilot crashed into his fighter, and although Dudonov baled out and survived, Nango was killed when his shattered 'Claude' plunged into the lake. The cause of Nango's collision was attributed to vision problems brought on by ill health – he had been unable to judge the separation distance.

Eight victories have been attributed to *Gunshin Nango Shosa* (War God Lt Cdr Nango).

Warrant Officer Kiyoto Koga

The honour of becoming the first JNAF ace belongs to Kiyoto Koga, who was born in Fukuoka Prefecture in June 1910. Exactly 17 years later he joined the navy at Sasebo, and in May 1931 became a fighter pilot.

Lt Mochifumi Nango was one of the JNAF's most accomplished fighter-leaders during the China War. A scholar and a gentleman, who spoke excellent English, his devotion to duty eventually cost him his life in July 1938 (*K Osuo*)

Kiyoto Koga became the first ace of the JNAF on 24 November 1937 when he shot down an I-16 over Nanking. As a result of this achievement he received a rare personal citation from the CO of the China Area Fleet, Adm Kiyoshi Hasegawa. Seen as an excellent role model for young aviation trainees, Koga was sent home to work as an instructor in early 1938, but was subsequently killed in a flying accident in September of that same year (*K Osuo*)

PO2/c Saburo Sakai smiles for the camera in his Type 96 'Claude' at Hankow airfield, in China, in September 1939. As can be gauged from this view, the open cockpit of the Mitsubishi fighter afforded the pilot excellent all-round visibility. A month after this photo was taken, Sakai became a national hero when, on 3 October 1939, he single-handedly pursued 12 DB-3 bombers for over 150 miles before finally shooting one down (*S Sakai*)

As a member of the 13th AG, Koga was stationed in Shanghai for about a month after the outbreak of the China War, and he enjoyed his first aerial successes during his first encounter with the CAF on 19 September 1937 – two Curtiss Hawks fell to his guns over Nanking. Three days later, Koga downed a further pair of Hawks. On 24 November, he became an ace according to Western standards when he downed an I-16 over Nanking, and he continued his scoring run into December with a bomber (on the 2nd) and three I-16s (on the 9th) over Nanchang.

For distinguished service in the air war over China, Adm Kiyoshi Hasegawa awarded Koga with a personal citation on 31 December 1937, noting his destruction of 11 fighters and two bombers. At the same time, the honouree was promoted to warrant officer.

A veteran of many aerial engagements, WO Kiyoto Koga died on 16 September 1938 from injuries received during a crash 24 hours earlier whilst conducting night training exercises with the Yokosuka AG.

His score of 13 victories was officially recognised.

Warrant Officer Kanichi Kashimura

During the height of every armed conflict, a need arises to promote an outstanding individual as a role model for the rank and file. Kanichi Kashimura served this purpose in China, becoming known as 'the pilot who returned on one wing'.

Born in Kagawa Prefecture, Japan, in July 1913, he joined the Navy and graduated from flight training in July 1934. In October 1937, Kashimura was transferred to the 13th AG, where he saw combat for the first time on 22 November and downed two aircraft over Nanking.

On 9 December PO3/c Kashimura fought Curtiss Hawks over Nanchang, destroying one and then colliding with another aircraft (an unknown type that could have been either Japanese or Chinese), tearing off a third of his left wing. Through superb piloting, the calm aviator brought his crippled 'Claude' back to base, and after four landing attempts, the aircraft somersaulted on touching the ground on its fourth approach and lost its tail in the subsequent crash. Astoundingly, the pilot walked away from the wreckage unharmed. Local news reporters quickly sent the story back to Japan, where Kashimura gained instant fame.

PO3/c Kanichi Kashimura collided with an unidentified aircraft during aerial combat on 9 December 1937 and returned with a third of his left wing missing. News reports of his heroic struggle to make it back to base quickly spread throughout Japan, and his example of tenacity and fighting spirit was later used to inspire a new generation of naval fighter pilots (*K Osuo*)

Kashimura's Type 96 (No 4-115) was photographed from the ground as he made several landing attempts at an airfield in Shanghai. Although the aircraft violently somersaulted onto its back upon making contact with the ground, the pilot walked away without as much as a scratch (*K Osuo*)

After achieving eight victories over China, Kashimura was reassigned to the Yokosuka AG in March 1938. Once back in Japan, 'Kashimura, The Pilot Who Returned On One Wing' served as a living role model for future generation of naval aviators. Back in China for his second tour of duty by the end of 1939, he found that activity by the CAF had all but ceased, and he returned to instructional duties at Yokosuka without having scored further kills.

Kashimura was promoted to warrant officer in October 1942, and in December of that year was posted to the 582nd AG and left for service in New Guinea. Once in-theatre he was quickly back in combat, this time testing his skills against a far more formidable enemy. On 6 March 1943 WO Kashimura failed to return from a mission that had seem him escorting 'Val' dive-bombers on a raid on the Russell Islands. P-39s from the USAAF's 67th Fighter Squadron (FS) concentrated their attacks on the 'Vals' and therefore claimed no Zeroes. However, two A6Ms did fail to return, although only a single claim against a Zero was recorded on this date – Marine SBD gunner S/Sgt Robert H Banner of VMSB-132 claimed to have shot down an A6M 15 miles south-east of the Russells. Kashimura may have been his victim.

WO Kanichi Kashimura achieved 12 recognised aerial victories.

Lieutenant(jg) Matsuo Hagiri

Having completed his tour with the *Soryu* Fighter Squadron (see photo on page seven), Matsuo 'Mustachio' Hagiri joined the Zero-equipped 12th AG and went on to became a popular and daring fighter pilot over China – where he gained most of his victories. However, his greatest contribution to the JNAF would come during the final years of World War 2 when he was pressed into the role of test pilot (*M Hagiri*)

Matsuo Hagiri contributed to the JNAF's war effort both as a fighter and test pilot. Born in Shizuoka Prefecture in November 1913, he worked as a fireman before joining the navy, graduating from flight training in August 1935.

Exactly five years later Hagiri – as a member of the 12th AG – participated in the first combat mission in which the new Zero fighter was flown. This historic sortie took place on 19 August when Lt Tomotsu Yokoyama led a dozen A6Ms on a bomber escort mission to Chunking. Although no aerial combat took place, the mission did establish a new distance record for a single-engined fighter of over 1000 nautical miles.

As detailed earlier, the Zero's famous dogfighting debut on 13 September 1940 gave such a tremendous boost to the confidence of its pilots that some (like Hagiri) became very cocky with their new mounts. A perfect example of this occurred on 4 October when Hagiri participated in a highly publicised stunt that saw him and three comrades land on the enemy airfield of Taipingsze, at Chengtu, and attempt to vandalise parked aircraft and set the base command post alight! Escaping in a hail of small arms fire, but still not content with his part in the escapade, Hagiri then single-handedly attacked three fighters and downed two of them.

Following the introduction of the Zero, CAF pilots wisely chose to avoid combat with it at all costs, leaving Hagiri with little opportunity to increase his score, which stood at seven by the time he returned to Japan.

In July 1943 WO Hagiri was assigned to the 204th AG and sent to the Solomons, where his main opposition comprised F4U Corsairs and P-38s. Because of his experience, he often flew as flight leader.

On 23 September 1943 the 204th sortied 27 Zeroes to thwart an Allied raid on their anti-aircraft positions south-west of Kahili Airfield. Two squadrons of Marine Corsairs (VMF-213 and -214) attacked the airfield while Australian P-40s escorted the slower-moving SBDs and TBFs. WO Hagiri claimed two F4Us, but was in turn so severely wounded that he had to be sent back to Japan for further treatment.

As the war situation deteriorated for the Japanese, Hagiri was pressed into service as a test pilot, and when B-29s started to raid the Tokyo region he once again flew combat missions. In April 1945 he was wounded by Superfortress gunners and never flew again.

In a distinguished career, Lt(jg) Matsuo Hagiri shot down 13 enemy aircraft. He passed away on 15 January 1997.

Lieutenant(jg) Tetsuzo Iwamoto

The top ace of the JNAF in both the China and Pacific Wars was Tetsuzo Iwamoto, whose amazing seven-year career was revealed postwar both through his combat diary and by eyewitnesses.

A cunning pilot who favoured 'hit and run' tactics, Iwamoto was born in June 1916 as the third son in a family of three boys and a girl fathered by a Hokkaido Prefecture policeman. As a student of the Masuda Agricultural and Forestry High School, young Tetsu developed into a very opinionated individual, whose stubborn and righteous views caused consternation with his teachers and, eventually, with his military superiors.

With no aspirations of becoming a farmer, Iwamoto secretly enlisted in the navy in June 1934 after telling his parents that he was off to take the college entrance examinations – his parents were left extremely disappointed as they were counting on him to help on the family farm.

Iwamoto elected to become a fighter pilot rather than remaining a common seaman for aviators enjoyed special privileges. He took the difficult entrance examination and passed, being accepted into flight training and graduating in December 1936.

The future 'ace-of-aces' showed his ability right from the start. As a member of the 12th AG, his baptism of fire came on 25 February 1938 over Nanchang, China, when A1/c Iwamoto's flight was jumped by enemy I-15 and I-16 fighters whilst on a bomber escort mission. In the wild melee that followed, the young 22-year-old claimed four fighters shot down and one probable. Iwamoto repeated this performance on 29 April

Tetsuzo Iwamoto (shown here in 1945 as an ensign) became not only the top JNAF ace of the China War, but also World War 2. Immune to life-threatening (in a fighter pilot at least) traits like blind spirit and bravado, he favoured 'hit and run' tactics, and knew when to fight and when to run (*Y Izawa*)

over Hankow, when he again downed four fighters and was duly rewarded a citation from his CO for being the top pilot of the day.

In September 1938 Iwamoto was ordered back to Japan, where he became a member of the Saiki AG. With 14 kills in China, 'Tetsu' was the top JNAF ace of the conflict.

PO1/c Iwamoto was subsequently posted to the carrier *Zuikaku*, and on the opening day of the Pacific War he flew protective cover over the strike force as they launched their aircraft against Pearl Harbor. Iwamoto returned to Japan on 24 December, and later participated in battles over the Indian Ocean and Coral Sea. In August 1942 he was pressed into service as an instructor, as the disaster at Midway necessitated the mass training of replacement pilots.

Whilst Iwamoto feverishly trained new naval aviators, the Japanese bastion at Rabaul, New Britain, had been bearing the brunt of a massive US bombing campaign. Aircraft from the US Fifth and Thirteenth Air Forces had worn down the number of Zero fighters, and accompanying pilots, to a dangerous level, and as part of the reinforcement CPO Iwamoto was ordered to lead a formation of 15 replacement Zeroes to Rabaul in November. Once in-theatre, he became a member of the 253rd AG, and he and his men engaged the Americans on a daily basis.

On 17 November Iwamoto encountered the F4U Corsair for the first time during a strike on Torokina, his opponents being part of VF-17 'Jolly Rogers' (see *Aircraft of the Aces 8 - Corsair Aces of World War 2* for further details). Although the Japanese attack on Torokina was unsuccessful, Iwamoto claimed two of the navy Corsairs.

The New Year brought more American attacks, and following the huge carrier air strike against Truk Island on 16-17 February, the JNAF was forced to withdraw all serviceable aircraft from Rabaul. As part of the exodus, Iwamoto flew to Truk with the remnants of the 253rd, the unit

Also a veteran of the *Soryu* Fighter Squadron, PO1/c Hideo Oishi adds two victory markings to the impressive tail scoreboard of his 12th AG Zero No 3-173 at Hankow airfield – he had downed two enemy aircraft with this combat-seasoned A6M2 on 14 March 1941 over Chengtu. PO3/c Hatsumasa Yamatani had started the aircraft's scoring run by claiming four victories on 13 September 1940 during the type's 'baptism of fire'. Others who contributed to the tally included PO2/c Miyakuni Kamidaira and PO3/c Seiji Hiramoto (*K Osuo*)

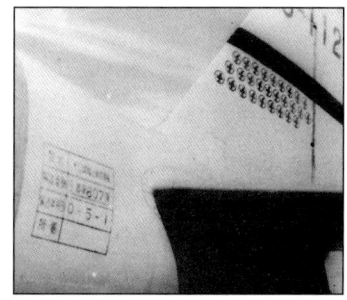

Another veteran A6M2 Zero of the 12th AG, this aircraft wears 28 kill markings on its tail. Having survived many months in combat, the aircraft was finally taken out of frontline service in June 1941 and donated to the Naval Academy at Etajima for display purposes (*K Osuo*)

This 14th AG A6M2 Zero Model 11 (serial No 9-182) was photographed over southern China in the autumn of 1940. The aircraft later participated in a vicious combat with enemy I-15/-16s and Curtiss Hawks over Kunming on 14 July 1941, after which the Zero pilots claimed to have destroyed 13 aircraft in just 15 minutes without loss (*via Phil Jarrett*)

immediately being thrust into action against B-24s which bombed the island on a near-daily basis.

Iwamoto returned to Japan in June 1944, but in October he was sent to fight over Formosa and the Philippines. By that stage the war situation had grown so desperate that he flew solo missions strafing beach landings and airfields at night – achieving very little, he was eventually sent home.

In early 1945 Iwamoto was transferred to the 203rd AG and fought against B-29s and carrier fighters attacking Kyushu, as well as seeing action over Okinawa. He spent the remaining months of the war training young flyers for the final *kamikaze* suicide attack at Iwakuni Airfield.

Totally disillusioned at his country's surrender, Iwamoto could not adjust to postwar Japan. He did various jobs but was never content, turning instead to alcohol, which caused many personal problems. The great ace died in 1955 aged just 38 due to septicaemia caused by a series of surgical operations on his back for a war wound.

Iwamoto kept an elaborate diary during his career, and by his own reckoning he had claimed some of the following – seven F4Fs, four P-38s, 48 F4Us, two P-39s, one P-40, 29 F6Fs, one P-47, one P-51, four Spitfires, 48 SBDs (plus another 30 by aerial burst bombs) and eight B-25s. Whilst flying from Rabaul he claimed 142 aerial victories out of a final tally of 202 destroyed, 26 shared, 22 unconfirmed, two damaged and two destroyed on the ground. Postwar Japanese historians have listed Iwamoto with 'just' 80 victories, but the true figure will never be known.

Lieutenant(jg) Watari Handa

Watari Handa was a famous veteran of the China War whose brilliant skills were not fully realised in World War 2 due to a combination of bad luck and health problems. Born in Fukuoka Prefecture in August 1912, he joined the navy in 1928, and after graduation from flight training in 1933, served both on the carrier *Ryujo* and with various land-based units.

Shortly after the start of the China War in August 1937, Handa saw action flying from the *Kaga* over Shanghai, duly recording his first aerial victory (a Hawk) on 9 September – 11 days later he destroyed three more aircraft over Nanking. In June of the following year Handa was transferred to the 15th AG and returned to action, this time over Nanchang. By the time he had finished his tour of duty in November his tally had risen to 15 (six officially recognised), and upon returning to Japan he was promoted to warrant officer. Handa's next assignment saw him instructing new flight trainees at Tsuchiura Air Base.

When the ace was posted to the Tainan AG in February 1942 he was already 30 years of age, which was considered to be somewhat old for an operational fighter pilot. Nevertheless, he brought his fame and a wealth of combat experience to the unit, and his presence was most welcome.

However, an incident on 13 May 1942 demoralised WO Handa and ended his flying career. He requested the loan of fellow ace Saburo Sakai's wingman, PO3/c Toshiaki Honda, for a recce mission over the enemy airfield at Port Moresby. Despite Honda's protest, Sakai ordered him to go, and when the three Zeroes were subsequently ambushed by P-39s over Seven Mile Strip, he was killed. Broken in spirit and blaming himself for Honda's loss, Handa was never able to regain his old touch, and upon

Lt(jg) Watari Handa became a great ace in China, but a flying incident in 1942 broke his spirit and ruined his career (*Y Izawa*)

being diagnosed with tuberculosis, he returned to Japan in late 1942.

Lt(jg) Watari Handa scored 15+ kills (13 officially) and died in 1948. On his deathbed he told his wife, 'I have fought bravely all my life, but I could never forgive myself for having lost Sakai's wingman at Lae'.

Warrant Officer Toshio Kuroiwa

Toshio Kuroiwa made his mark in JNAF history by claiming a share in the navy's first aerial kill. Born in Fukuoka Prefecture in 1908, he enlisted in 1926 and graduated from flight training two years later.

Tension between Japan and China led to the first Shanghai Incident of 1932, which saw the boycotting of Japanese goods result in riots in Shanghai. Shots were exchanged and the Japanese overreacted by sending an armed expeditionary force to protect their interests – Toshio Kuroiwa was part of that force aboard the carrier *Kaga*.

The first air-to-air combat between Chinese and Japanese fighters occurred on 22 February 1932 over the Souchow Railroad Station when three B1M3 carrier bombers and three A1N2 Type 3 biplane fighters were attacked by a lone Boeing P-12, flown by American mercenary Robert Short. Unaware of the escorts, Short attacked and shot down a bomber, but almost immediately Lt Nokiji Ikuta, Leading Seaman Kazuo Takeo and PO3/c Toshio Kuroiwa pounced on the brash American, sending him to a fiery death. The three men were officially credited with the Japanese military's first aerial kill and received citations.

During the China War, Kuroiwa was attached to the 12th AG and saw considerable action in 1938. With his wild antics in the air, he cultivated a 'bad boy' image, which his superiors tolerated because of his skill. Having turned 31 by the time his tour of duty ended in 1939, Kuroiwa was considered to be to old for further frontline flying, so he left active duty and gained employment flying airliners instead.

Toshio Kuroiwa disappeared off the Malay Peninsula on 26 August 1944 during a transport flight. His score of 13 was officially recognised.

PO Kuroiwa was one of the oldest fighter pilots of the China War, having first seen action in 1932 as one of a trio of men credited with Japan's premier aerial victory (*Y Izawa*)

A6M2 Model 11s of the 12th AG fly over the cloud-shrouded Chinese mainland on 26 May 1941. The aircraft marked with the double stripe was the personal mount of China veteran Lt Minoru Suzuki, whilst the second fighter was being flown by PO3/c Kunimori Nakakariya, who survived the war with 16 kills (*via Aerospace Publishing*)

EARLY MONTHS OF THE PACIFIC WAR

When Japan unleashed the might of its military forces against the Americans at Pearl Harbor and in the Philippines, it did so with the most modern aircraft and highly-trained pilots that it possessed at any time in its history. While some units in the JNAF were still flying Type 96 'Claudes', all of the fighter aircraft committed to the Pearl Harbor and Philippines missions were A6M2 Zeroes, many of which were flown by veterans of the China War.

The conflict in the Pacific grew out of economic and political discontent felt in Japan against 'Western Imperialists' – namely the United States and Britain. Japan's successful forays into Manchuria and China had allowed its military to test and perfect its arsenal of offensive weapons, especially its fighters and bombers. It also allowed JNAF and JAAF aircrew to perfect tactics that would give them the advantage over the air arms of the Western powers in the first critical months of war.

Success on the Chinese mainland throughout the 1930s led Japan's military leaders to grow overconfident in their forces' ability to wage war on a much larger scale in Asia, this overconfidence manifesting itself in the dramatic upsurge of fanatical nationalism that swept the nation.

By the summer of 1941 Japanese leaders knew that conflict was inevitable, and so ordered their forces to prepare for war whilst the politicians still it carried out diplomatic negotiations in Washington DC. Adm

Lt Saburo Shindo, flying AI-102, starts his take-off run alomg the deck of the *Akagi* as part of the second wave attack on Pearl Harbor. Shindo served as division officer within the carrier squadron at this time, and was one of the few Pearl Harbor veterans to survive the war (*via Aerospace Publishing*)

Isoroku Yamamoto, C-in-C of the Combined Forces, was given orders to undertake an all-out assault on US forces at Pearl Harbor, in the Hawaiian Islands. The date of the strike was set for 8 December 1941, and his force was comprised of 23 warships, including six fleet aircraft carriers, and 350+ aircraft.

By the time political negotiations failed, the carriers had already positioned themselves some 200 nautical miles north of Pearl Harbor. At 0130 (Tokyo time) bombers began roaring off the flightdecks.

Zero pilots played a key role in assuring the success of the surprise assault. In order to prevent the vulnerable torpedo- and dive-bombers being molested as they manoeuvred into position to make their runs, A6Ms strafed parked aircraft and shot down any that managed to launch. Not all of the Americans who sortied were 'easy pickings', however.

Lt Iyozoh Fujita found himself under attack as he led his men toward Wheeler Field, and in the wild dogfight that ensued, Japanese aviators were taken aback by the aggressiveness of their American counterparts – their opponents could have been 2Lts George Welch and Ken Taylor of the 47th Pursuit Squadron (PS), flying P-40Bs. Fujita poured fire into an aircraft below him, which smoked but escaped. Not wishing to push his luck any further, Fujita signalled to his men to withdraw and head

PO3/c Shimpei Sano clears *Akagi*'s island in A6M2 Zero 21 AI-111 as he too launches with the second wave attackers bound for Pearl Harbor. Sano was later killed during the Battle of Midway (*Maru*)

A6M2s of *Shokaku*'s fighter squadron run up as the carrier sails into wind for a dawn launch north-east of Hawaii. Six Zeroes from this unit participated in the first wave attack, strafing Kaneohe and Bellows airfields (*via Aerospace Publishing*)

Sporting ten cherry blossoms, the tail of Zero X-183 reveals the score of PO2/c Yoshiro Hashiguchi, who saw action with the 3rd AG over the Dutch East Indies at the start of the Pacific War. He later enjoyed further success over Darwin, Rabaul, and Guadalcanal. Attaining the rank of chief petty officer, Hashiguchi was finally posted missing in action on 25 October 1944 when his carrier was sunk. He achieved over ten victories (*K Osuo*)

Two great aces are seen as student pilots in this May 1941 class photo. Takeo Tanimizu (standing, second from right) and Shoichi Sugita (standing to Tanimizu's left) were classmates at Tsukuba Air Base, where they flew the Type 93 Intermediate Trainer, seen here as a backdrop. Their class graduated in March 1942 – prior to the Midway disaster. Subsequent training was notably inferior as the JNAF rushed to graduate pilots to make good the Midway losses (*T Tanimizu*)

towards the rendezvous area.

The attacking force suffered casualties amounting to 55 officers and enlisted men during the Pearl Harbor raid, with remarkably few of this number being fighter pilots – just nine Zeroes were lost to all causes (three in the first strike and six in the second). There was no wild jubilation or celebration at their success, however, the weary aviators simply being relieved that they had survived their first day of war. They also grieved for their comrades who had not returned.

The Pearl Harbor attack had been a spectacular success, for the US fleet in the western Pacific had been crippled with one bold stroke and the enlisted men and officers of the JNAF now considered themselves invincible. However, senior men at Naval GHQ (including Adm Yamamoto himself) were far from elated, for they had failed to catch their primary targets at anchor – aircraft carriers. They would come back to hurt them.

Japanese Navy Academy graduates were open-minded and worldly wise, differing greatly from their army counterparts. In their cruises to the West as midshipmen, they saw firsthand the industrial might and capabilities of the great economic superpowers, leading some to secretly believe that Japan could never win this new war.

Coinciding with the strike at Pearl Harbor, Japanese forces launched an all-out attack in the Philippines, Hong Kong and the Dutch East Indies – with very little in the way of natural resources, Japan need the oil reserves, rubber and mineral wealth of the Dutch East Indies to fuel its war effort.

From their base in Formosa, the Tainan and 3rd AGs raided Clark and Iba airfields in the Philippines in advance of the bombers, thus neutralising any fighter opposition. Despite the warnings radioed to their forces in the Philippines during the Pearl Harbor attack, the Americans were once again caught unprepared, resulting in the USAAC losing half of it aircraft destroyed or damaged in one raid.

Veteran fighter pilots like POs Kuniyoshi Tanaka, Saburo Sakai, Kaneyoshi Muto and WO Sadaaki Akamatsu tangled with P-40s in

lopsided dogfights, although the majority of American aircraft were destroyed on the ground. With another raid on 10 December, US air power in the Philippines was decisively crushed.

The success of these lightning strikes further boosted the morale of the JNAF, the missions setting a new distance record for the Zero. The entire round-trip distance from Formosa to the Philippines covered more than 1000 miles, and it was such an incredible distance for a single-engined aircraft that the Americans believed that they had flown from carriers – strict flight formation and fuel conservation training had paid off handsomely.

With the Philippines neutralised, the JNAF directed their attention to the Dutch East Indies. Attempting to defend the latter was the RAF, the Netherlands East Indies Army Air Force and surviving elements of the USAAC, and although they fought to near annihilation to thwart the invasion, they were overwhelmed by a superior enemy. Dutch F2A Buffaloes and Hawks, in particular, proved to be little more than 'cannon fodder' for the A6M2s, as Saburo Sakai later noted, 'The Buffaloes were rough, inferior, aircraft. They never stood a chance against our Zeroes.'

RAF Hurricanes and P-40s of the USAAC's 20th PS faired a little better than the Buffaloes, but the destruction of their airfields (and critical supplies and aircraft) allied with the total confusion and panic on the ground prevented them from effectively mounting an organised counterattack. The Java campaign concluded in the first week of March 1942 when organised resistance ceased, and thousands of Allied soldiers surrendered. Once again air support had proven to be pivotal in the Japanese *blitzkrieg* of the early months of the Pacific War. Now the JNAF turned their attention to New Guinea and Australia.

PO2/c Yoshiro Hashiguchi is seen seated in his A6M2 Zero X-183 whilst part of the 3rd AG in late 1941. The aircraft's rudimentary ring-bead gunsight is just visible in this photograph (*via Aerospace Publishing*)

The last sight that many an Allied pilot glimpsed in his rear-vision mirror prior to being shot down during the early months of the Pacific War. This particular Zero is a clipped-wing A6M3 Model 32, examples of which reached the frontline just in time for the Japanese foray across the Asia-Pacific rim (*via Aerospace Publishing*)

MIDWAY

Fought on 4-5 June 1942, the Battle of Midway marked the turning point in the Pacific War, as at last the Allies defeated the might of the Japanese fleet. When the engagement was over, the JNAF had lost four carriers and more than ten per cent of its veteran fighter pilots.

Emboldened by its dramatic victories at Pearl Harbor and in the Philippines and the Dutch East Indies, the Japanese High Command decided to capture the strategically crucial island of Midway in order to further threaten American Pacific Forces in Hawaii. Its capture would consolidate their hold on the Solomons, and help isolate Australia from the USA.

Adm Isoroku Yamamoto, Commander-in-Chief of the Combined Fleet, devised an elaborate plan to take Midway. He sent two small expeditions to attack targets in the Aleutians, thus hoping to divert the American Pacific Fleet to the north – the capture of the Aleutians would also prevent the Americans from attacking Japan. Meanwhile, the main body of the First Carrier Strike Force (led by VAdm Chuichi Nagumo), consisting of the carriers *Akagi*, *Kaga*, *Soryu* and *Hiryu*, supported by battleships, cruisers, and over 250 aircraft, steamed toward their target.

The Japanese plan was doomed to failure, however, for unbeknown to them, American cryptographers had succeeded in breaking the Japanese naval codes. Therefore, although commanding a numerically inferior force, Adm Chester Nimitz held the crucial advantage of surprise. He would be further aided by a series of incredible tactical blunders by the Japanese, which added greatly their catastrophe.

The battle commenced in the early hours of 4 June when 36 Zeroes sortied as escorts for 72 torpedo- and dive-bombers sent to attack Midway airfield. The large strike force was quickly detected by radar, and every available aircraft on the island was airborne within ten minutes to oppose the raiders. At 0620, combat was joined when Maj Floyd B Parks led VMF-221 (comprised of seven Buffaloes and five Wildcats) against the invaders – a further 11 Buffaloes and a single Wildcat provided backup.

In the ensuing dogfight, the Marine pilots were overwhelmed as they attempted to out turn their Japanese opponents in their nimble Zeroes. Thirteen brave Buffalo pilots paid with their lives as only ten of the twenty-five aircraft that sortied returned – most in damaged condition.

The Americans also sent out torpedo-bombers to attack the carriers, but they too were decimated before a single torpedo could strike home. Lt Iyozoh Fujita made a name for himself during this engagement, for he downed no fewer than ten enemy aircraft as the Americans swarmed toward the carriers. However, a second strike force would turn the tide of battle, for as the Zeroes tore into the torpedo-bombers, SBD Dauntless dive-bombers from the *Yorktown* pushed through unmolested to deliver fatal blows to the carriers *Akagi*, *Kaga* and *Soryu*.

The Japanese swiftly retaliated by despatching 'Val' dive-bombers from the surviving carrier *Hiryu* to attack the *Yorktown*. By the time the 'Vals' had completed their attacks the American carrier was well ablaze, but although 'Kate' torpedo-bombers followed up the dive-bombers' good work by striking the vessel twice with torpedoes, the stubborn carrier refused to die – on 6 June a third torpedo from a Japanese submarine finally sent *Yorktown* to the bottom.

The battle was not quite over, however, for aircraft from the *Enterprise* located the surviving Japanese carrier *Hiryu* and quickly reduced her to a gutted hulk. She was scuttled by her crew the following morning.

The loss of four fleet carriers, experienced pilots and aircrew and entire squadrons in a single engagement stunned the Japanese. In the subsequent scramble to make good their aviation losses, the JNAF recalled many veteran pilots from land-based units across the occupied territories back to Japan to serve as instructors. The mass training of pilots quickly began in earnest, but in order return units to their previous strengths, the entrance requirements were lowered and the flight training syllabus shortened – these factors combined to produce pilots ill-equipped for frontline flying. The JNAF would pay dearly for Midway.

Lieutenant Commander Iyozoh Fujita

Iyozoh Fujita was one of two naval aviators who was recognised as having shot down ten enemy aircraft in one day. The son of a doctor and a midwife, he was born in Shantung Province, China, in November 1917. He became interested in pursuing a naval career while attending high school, where his scholastic aptitude earned him entrance into the Naval Academy at Etajima in the Class of 1938. The young ensign completed flight training in June 1940.

When the Japanese attacked Pearl Harbor on 7 December 1941, Lt(jg) Fujita sortied from the carrier *Soryu* as a flight leader in the second wave fighter escort. He strafed ground targets and his Zero was hit by return fire, and as related in the previous chapter, while gathering the escorts for their return, his formation was jumped by either P-36s or P-40s and a wild dogfight ensued. Managing to disengage from the action in his damaged Zero, Fujita led his men back to the carrier where, upon landing, a piece of his engine broke off.

JNAF pilots entered 1942 in high spirits and with total confidence in the Zero. At the time a naval aviator needed to have completed between 50-100 hours' flying time and four-five landings to achieve carrier qualification, and even the youngest fleet pilot had at least 500 flight hours.

One of those pilots entering the Midway action buoyed by his previous success was Lt Iyozoh Fujita. He carried this confidence into action with him on 4 June when he intercepted a large number of torpedo-bombers during a combat air patrol over the carrier task force. Directed into position by shipboard radio vectoring, Fujita chose the previously untried tactic of diving headlong into the formation rather than attacking the group from the rear. Sweeping through with his guns continuously blazing, he was stunned to see two or three aircraft falling away smoking.

'This is the method!' Fujita exclaimed as he continued his attacks, subsequently shooting down four torpedo-bombers (three jointly) and three fighters (two jointly). Unfortunately, his aircraft was then hit by friendly fire and he had to ditch in the sea. Bobbing up and down in high waves with no hope of rescue, he resigned himself to death, but fortunately his was picked up after just four hours in the water by a destroyer.

Lt Iyozoh Fujita found his shooting eye during the Battle of Midway, becoming a double ace in just one day. He is one of just a handful of Pearl Harbor Zero pilots to have survived the war (*Maru*)

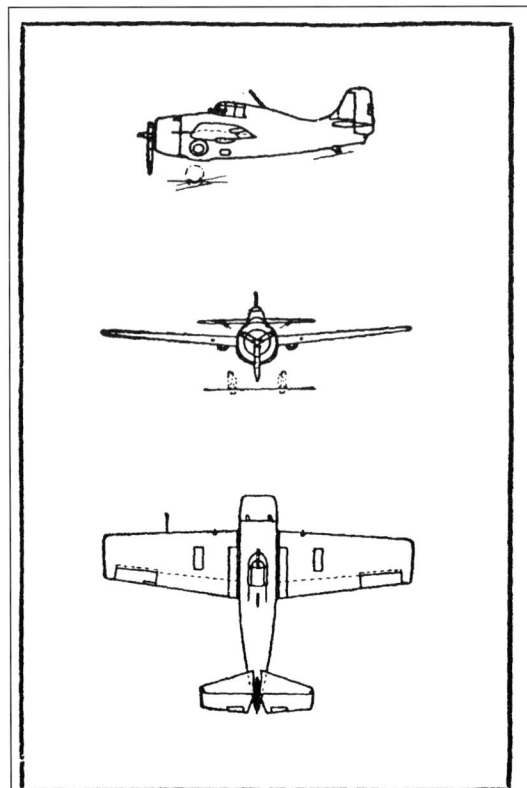

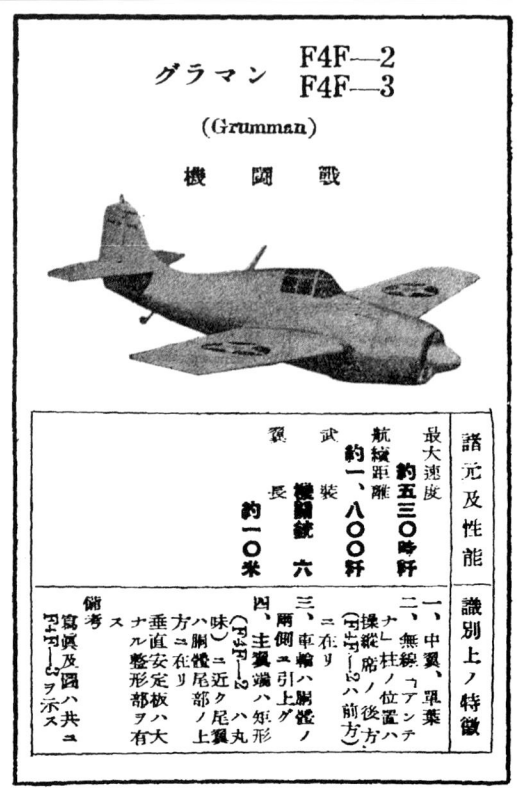

グラマン F4F—2
F4F—3

(Grumman)

機 闘 戦

'After Midway, many surviving pilots were pulled out to become instructors', lamented Fujita. 'Removing veteran pilots from frontline units caused us to loose fighting strength. In the end, it was a tremendous burden for our pilots. I think about ten per cent of our veteran pilots were lost at Midway.'

The next assignment for Lt Fujita was as division officer on the carrier *Hiyo*. He saw combat in the Solomons and at Guadalcanal, and in November 1943 was appointed group leader of the 301st AG, under the command of Cdr Katsutoshi Yagi.

As an experienced frontline pilot, Lt Fujita made repeated requests for better armament and gunsights, and although manufacturers listened to his recommendations, few if any improvements came forth.

Prior to the end of the war, Lt Fujita fought in the battles at Iwo Jima, Formosa and in defence of the home islands. He ended the war at Fukuchiyama airfield, waiting for the final all-out attack against the invading Americans which never materialised.

Lt Cdr Fujita's final kill total is unclear, as according to historians he achieved 11 victories, whilst other sources place his score at 42. 'I shot at that many, and my bullets did hit them, but how many went down, I don't know', says this modest gentleman. The number of recognised destroyed was seven.

Postwar, Iyozoh Fujita flew as a pilot for Japan Air Lines before retiring in 1978. The past president of the Zero Fighter Pilots Association, he was a guest panelist at the Battle of Midway Symposium held at NAS Pensacola in 1988. He currently resides in Tokyo.

These documents formed part of the official JNAF wartime recognition publication used by all units to instruct pilots on the shape and performance of their foes

NEW GUINEA, RABAUL AND THE SOLOMONS

In January 1942, Japanese forces invaded the South-east Pacific islands of New Britain and New Ireland after carrier pilots from VAdm Chuichi Nagumo's task force had quickly overwhelmed the defenders at Rabaul, on New Britain, and Kavieng, on New Ireland. They also destroyed the enemy's air defenses at Lae and Salamaua, along the north-eastern coast of New Guinea.

In order to isolate Australia from the USA, it was also necessary to conquer the Australian garrison at Port Moresby, so the JNAF poured aircraft into Rabaul, whilst advance contingents of fighters and bombers were positioned even closer to the target at forward bases at Lae and Salamaua.

Spearheading the aerial assault against Port Moresby (commencing on 24 February 1942) was the 4th AG, which was joined in March by the Tainan AG at Rabaul – the latter group moved the following month to Lae, and from then on aerial action was brisk as many young neophytes who had participated in the one-sided actions over the Philippines and the Dutch East Indies became hardened veterans fighting the Australians and the Americans. And while pilots from both sides claimed an extraordinary number of kills, loss records painted a more conservative picture.

Bravery and skill were exhibited by pilots on both sides, and victories were hard won. Saburo Sakai, who was the senior enlisted pilot in the Sasai Squadron of the Tainan AG, later spoke of their difficulties in-theatre; 'Our 20 mm cannons were big, heavy and slow firing. It was extremely hard to hit a moving target. Shooting down an enemy aircraft

This panoramic view illustrates just how rudimentary the facilities were at Rabaul for the Tainan AG in 1942. An important staging area for JNAF aircraft in the Solomons, the airfield at Rabaul was used as a central base for satellite strips at Lae (New Guinea) and Buin (Bougainville) (*Sakaida*)

Mechanics labour over a Zero 21 at Lakunai airfield as Mt Hanabuki belches smoke in the background – the active volcano being a familiar landmark for pilots approaching Rabaul. Field modifications performed on the Zero included sawing off the radio mast and removing the useless radio to in order to save weight (*Maru*)

was like hitting a dragonfly with a rifle! It was never easy to score . . .our opponents were tough!'

The Japanese force, set to invade Port Moresby was turned back during the Battle of the Coral Sea on 7 May, its defeat allowing the defenders to quickly reinforce their ranks. Jungle warfare raged on while both sides incessantly attacked each other's airfields and supply depots. The nature of the jungle terrain and myriad tropical diseases also inflicted casualties on both sides.

On 7 August the 1st Marine Division landed on Guadalcanal, this audacious attack stunning the Japanese at Rabaul. To counter the threat, missions previously flown against targets in New Guinea were quickly redirected to Guadalcanal, resulting in Zero pilots at Rabaul flying their longest missions to date – a round-trip of over 1100 miles. The Japanese counterattack proved unsuccessful, however, with the Americans pouring enough men and equipment into the region to overwhelm the defenders on Guadalcanal. In the skies overhead, US Navy and Marine Corps F4Fs exacted a heavy toll on Japanese units, with even modestly damaged aircraft seldom making it back to Rabaul. By February 1943 Guadalcanal had fallen.

As the Allied Forces moved quickly up 'The Slot', so the Japanese retreated to Bougainville. In the wake of the defeat Naval GHQ ceded the defence of New Guinea to the army, JAAF units duly leaving Rabaul so as to provide aerial support for their forces at Wewak and other bases.

On 18 April 1943 the navy suffered a further crippling blow when P-38s from Guadalcanal ambushed a flight of two 'Betty' bombers and six Zero escorts over Bougainville (see Osprey *Aircraft of the Aces 14 - P-38 Lightning Aces of the Pacific and CBI* for further details). In one of the bombers was Adm Yamamoto, C-in-C of the Combined Fleet. News of the admiral's death was greeted with shock in Japan, and it severely rocked the morale of the men in the frontline.

Although the 204th AG continued to oppose Allied intrusions up the Solomons chain, it too was decimated during long-range missions to Guadalcanal. Whilst attempting to defend their bases at their bases at Buin and Kahili from marauding B-24s, JNAF pilots were quickly set upon by overwhelming numbers of escorting P-38s, P-40s and F4Us. To add to their already desperate plight, many veteran Zero pilots were badly weakened by malaria and other tropical ailments, allowing them to be easily shot out of the sky by their relatively novice opponents.

In October 1943 the 201st and 204th AGs were pulled out of Bougainville and sent to Rabaul. During the last few days of that month reinforcement aircraft from New Ireland, Japan and aircraft carriers flooded into the airfields.

The beginning of the end for the JNAF on Rabaul commenced on 12

October when the USAAF's Fifth Air Force sent a force of over 350 aircraft to bomb the great stronghold into submission. Low flying B-25s and Beaufighters strafed the airfields, B-24 'heavies' bombed shipping in Simpson Harbour and P-38s roamed the skies looking for enemy fighters. A series of heavy raids in October and November further reduced Japanese aircraft stocks on Rabaul, and shattered the defenders' morale.

CPO Tetsuzo Iwamoto – the top scoring ace at Rabaul – remarked; 'Prior to the beginning of 1943, we still had hope and fought fiercely. But now, we fought to uphold our honour. We didn't want to become cowards . . . We believed that we were expendable, that we were all going to die. There was no hope of survival – no one cared anymore.'

The harsh tropical environment added to the decline of the JNAF at Rabaul, for unlike their Allied counterparts, the Japanese failed to control the mosquito problem which devastated whole units with malaria. The Allies, on the other hand, sprayed and dusted their bases frequently with the insecticide DDT, which was unavailable to the Japanese. The latter also lacked quinine (the anti-malaria medicine) and its synthetic substitute Atebin. Even if these had been available, Allied submarines and aircraft greatly reduced the number of cargo ships bringing medical supplies to Rabaul. So bad was the malaria problem that many veteran Zero pilots claimed that ill health was the leading cause of casualties at Rabaul.

Carrier pilots, who were not exposed to these health problems at sea, adopted a slightly more positive attitude, which often helped them to survive. PO Takeo Tanimizu explains; 'Fate determines at birth when and where you will die. Since there was nothing I could do about it, I didn't worry too much about dying, and concentrated on my duty.'

Those who survived their first encounters with US fighters over Rabaul quickly recognised the enemy's weaknesses. Tanimizu remembers;

'P-38s at low altitude were easy prey. They were not very fast, so they usually stayed at higher altitudes. Then, they'd swoop down on you, fire, and zoom up. You really had to be careful and keep looking up. Their weakest spot was their tail. A 20 mm hit and their tails would snap off. The only time you could shoot down a Sikorsky (F4U) was when it was fleeing. You had to shoot at it from a certain angle (from the rear, high position, into the cockpit). Otherwise the bullets would bounce off.'

Fellow carrier ace CPO Sadamu Komachi survived his battles with the

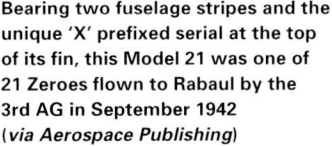

Bearing two fuselage stripes and the unique 'X' prefixed serial at the top of its fin, this Model 21 was one of 21 Zeroes flown to Rabaul by the 3rd AG in September 1942 (*via Aerospace Publishing*)

Grumman F6F Hellcat because he respected its fighting abilities; 'They were fast and manoeuvrable, and their pilots were good. They'd get on your tail and shower you with bullets! It was awful!'

Allied fighters slowly whittled down the JNAF at Rabaul to the point where the 20th AG had only one operational Zero left by 17 February 1944. When US carrier aircraft attacked the Japanese naval bastion at Truk and destroyed most of the island's fighters on the ground, orders were given to evacuate all airworthy machines immediately to Truk. By 25 February all that was left on Rabaul were a dozen 'junked' Zeroes which could not make the exodus and a few seaplanes. Rabaul would be bypassed by the Allied forces and allowed to 'wither on the vine'.

Warrant Officer Satoshi Yoshino

A beneficiary of high quality pre-war flight training, Satoshi Yoshino would make full use of this instruction during the Pacific War. Born in February 1918 in Chiba Prefecture, he was accepted into the naval flight reserve's enlisted pilot training course at 16 and graduated in August 1937. More tuition followed until March 1938, when Yoshino joined the first of several mainland air groups before being posted to the *Soryu* for active duty. He later became a member of the newly-organised Chitose AG, and in October 1941 advanced to the Marshall Islands with the group. Four months later Yoshino transferred to the 4th AG at Rabaul.

On 11 February 1942 he and three comrades in obsolete Type 96 'Claudes' caught three RAAF Hudsons over Gasmata, New Britain, and downed two – on the 13th he claimed another kill in the same area.

As part of the nucleus of veteran pilots in the 4th AG, Yoshino participated in heavy battles over Port Moresby and Horn Island, and by the time he joined the Tainan AG he had been promoted to warrant officer.

On 9 June 1942 Yoshino and his comrades scrambled to repel bombers heading for Lae. One group intercepted the 'heavies' while others engaged P-400s of the 39th FS, and it was one of the latter (flown by future P-38 ace 1/Lt Curran L Jones) which downed Yoshino near Cape Ward Hunt. The fallen ace duly received a posthumous promotion to ensign.

In 1988, Zero ace Saburo Sakai (Yoshino's comrade) met Curran 'Jack' Jones at a symposium in Fredericksburg, Texas, telling him, 'You must have been a great pilot yourself to have downed my comrade – Yoshino was one of our most outstanding pilots'.

According to Tainan AG records, Satoshi Yoshino achieved 15 kills.

Ensign Saburo Sakai

As Japan's most famous Zero fighter ace, Saburo Sakai claims that his greatest wartime success was not scoring 60+ kills, but having never lost a wingman in over 200 dogfights. Born to a poor farming family in Saga Prefecture in 1916, the son of a Samurai joined the navy in May 1933 in order to escape the shame of having failed at school.

While serving aboard the battleship *Kirishima* as a sailor, Sakai became fascinated with aircraft and decided to become a pilot. After failing the entrance examination twice, he passed on his third attempt and was

WO Satoshi Yoshino entered flight training as a 16-year-old, and although he only lasted five months in combat over Rabaul and New Guinea, he achieved 15 victories (*Y Izawa*)

The first long-range mission flown from Rabaul to Guadalcanal on 7 August 1942 nearly cost the life of CPO Saburo Sakai. Given up for dead, he is shown here just minutes after landing making his way to headquarters to give his report. Sakai received shrapnel wounds to his face (the wounds to his eyes were so severe that he eventually lost the sight in his right one), chest, left leg and elbow (*Sakai/Maru*)

accepted into flight training. In November 1937 Sakai graduated at the top of his class, being awarded the Emperor's silver watch.

As a member of the 12th AG, he saw action in the China War, achieving his first aerial victory on his first combat mission on 5 October 1938. Sakai was at the controls of one of fifteen 'Claudes' bounced by I-16s during a mission to Hankow, and in the subsequent engagement he broke almost every rule in the book and was nearly killed. Sakai eventually shot down an enemy aircraft by using up his entire ammunition supply, and upon his return to base the young neophyte was severely chastised, rather than congratulated, by his commander for his inferior performance.

By 3 October 1939 PO2/c Sakai had become a seasoned pilot, and on this date he proved it by chasing down 12 DB-3 bombers that had raided Hankow Airfield in a surprise attack. Although slightly wounded, Sakai jumped into his 'Claude' and took off alone in hot pursuit. The running gunfight ranged over 150 miles, and culminated in the demise of one of the bombers. News of his daring assault preceded him back to Japan, and Sakai returned home to a hero's welcome.

In June 1941 PO1/c Sakai was posted to the Tainan AG, with whom he participated in the raid on Clark Field, in the Philippines, on the first day of the Pacific War. He destroyed two B-17s on the ground and claimed

Lt(jg) Junichi Sasai wore this silver belt buckle for good luck. It was made by his father and presented to him when he went off to war. Japanese legend says that the tiger will roam over a thousand miles on its hunt, but will always return home safely. Sasai presented this to the wounded Saburo Sakai, who was being shipped home for hospitalisation. About two weeks later Sasai failed to return from a mission to Guadalcanal (*Sakaida*)

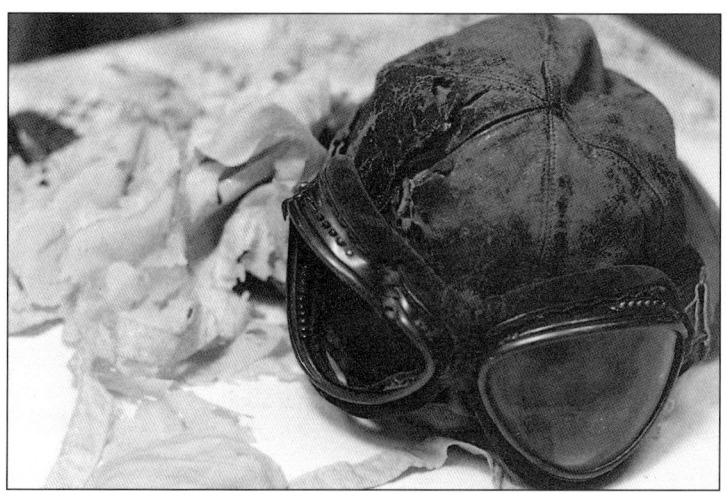

Sakai's torn leather helmet and silk scarf bears testimony to his fierce encounter with SBD gunners on 7 August 1942. A .30 cal tracer bullet missed his right eye by inches, leaving its mark on the goggles, whilst bullet fragments shattered the lens and left him permanently blind in that eye. Sakai stuffed his silk scarf under his flying helmet to stop the bleeding (*Sakaida*)

one P-40 shot down, although the latter type, flown by Sam Grashio, managed escaped with a big cannon hole in its wing.

On 10 December Sakai engaged a B-17C of the 14th Bombardment Squadron in the air for the first time, which he duly downed, the Japanese pilot being both shocked by the sheer size of the Flying Fortress.

With the Philippines captured, the Tainan AG commenced operations in the Dutch East Indies, where Sakai once again battled the B-17;

'There was no weakest area of the B-17. Every time was a close call. A particular incident I remember was in February 1942 over Balikpapan, Borneo, before I developed any method of attacking the bomber. There were two Zeroes and seven B-17s. I did everything I could to kill this aircraft but was not successful. Nothing worked!'

On 28 February 1942 Sakai encountered a DC-3 transport while on a lone patrol mission east of Surabaya, Java. Pacing the aircraft, when he pulled alongside to inspect it before shooting it down he noticed a blonde-haired woman and a small child peering at him through a fuselage window – Sakai spared the transport, letting it go on its way.

In April 1942 the Tainan AG was transferred to Rabaul, Zero pilots rotating between here and Lae during the fight with American and Australian units based at Port Moresby.

Sakai also conducted a personal war against the officer class, who regarded the enlisted pilots as expendable. As a result, his men were fed monotonous meals and denied tobacco, so he ordered his wingman to steal from the officers' mess and gave his approval for his men to smoke in direct violation of orders. Faced with discipline and morale problems, the CO of the group eventually ordered that improvements be made.

As the senior pilot in the Sasai Squadron, Sakai tutored his comrades (including the unit's CO, Lt(jg) Junichi Sasai) in the art of dogfighting. Many of his pupils went on to become aces.

On 22 July 1942 eight Zeroes intercepted a lone RAAF Hudson (A16-201 of No 32 Sqn) whilst flying a fighter cover mission over Buna. Anticipating an easy kill, Sakai chased after the twin-engined bomber, whose pilot, Plt Off Warren F Cowan, whipped his aircraft around and made a head-on attack at Sakai. Outnumbered eight-to-one, Cowan remained on the offensive, scattering the Zeroes into wild disorder, before Sakai eventually shot him down. As the only living eyewitness to this action, Sakai wrote a testimonial to the Australian Defence Minister in 1997, requesting that Cowan and his crew be cited for bravery. It was denied.

On 7 August 1942, during the first long-range mission to Guadalcanal, PO1/c Sakai shot down a Wildcat flown by future ace Lt J J Southerland (see Osprey *Aircraft of the Aces 3 - Wildcat Aces of World War 2* for further details) of VF-5, who parachuted to safety. As Sakai rejoined his flight, he was ambushed by a lone SBD flown by Lt Dudley H Adams of VS-71, the American pilot succeeding in firing a bullet through the cockpit of the Zero, which just missed the startled pilot's head by inches. Stung into action, Sakai downed the Dauntless, killing tail-gunner Harry E Elliot in the process. Lt Adams managed to parachute to safety, however, and was subsequently awarded the Navy Cross.

Having despatched two aircraft already on this mission, Sakai spotted what he thought were eight Wildcats in the distance – they were, in fact, SBD dive-bombers of VB-6, led by Lt Carl Horenburger. Unaware that he had been spotted, Sakai raced in for the kill, only to find himself in a trap as the tail-gunners opened up with their twin .30 guns, severely wounding the JNAF ace. In an epic four-and-a-half hour flight, Sakai returned to base after having been given up for dead. Permanently blinded in one eye, he sent back to Japan for further hospitalisation.

Upon recovery, Sakai frustratingly found himself in the role of instructor, teaching an ever-shrinking training syllabus to larger and larger classes of increasingly more youthful pilots.

In June 1944, he was at last thrust back into frontline flying, being ordered to Iwo Jima to join the Yokosuka AG. On 24 June he engaged in a wild combat with Hellcats of VF-1, -2 and -50, claiming three destroyed. However, his unit lost a staggering 23 Zeroes in reply.

With no hope of turning the tide against the invading Americans, the Yokosuka AG was ordered to resort to *kamikaze* suicide attacks. On 5 July Sakai duly set out with two wingmen on a one-way mission, nine Zeroes escorting eight torpedo-bombers on a futile sortie. Before they could reach the target, they were bounced by Hellcats, and disobeying orders to refuse combat and stay with the bombers, Sakai fought back and downed a Hellcat. Despite the efforts of the escorts, all the torpedo-bombers were swiftly destroyed. leaving Sakai and his two charges to battle darkness, bad weather and low fuel states in their struggle to return to base.

Twenty-four hours later Sakai and the remaining Zero pilots evacuated back to Japan, where he returned to instructing due to his lack of a further combat assignment. Transferred to the 343rd AG in December 1944, Sakai trained pilots destined for the new Shiden-Kai 'George'.

The great ace's last combat occurred on 17 August 1945 when (two days after the surrender announcement) he sortied with other pilots of the Yokosuka AG against a B-32 Dominator sent to photo-recce Tokyo. By his reckoning, he destroyed or damaged over 60 aircraft during his career.

In 1982 Saburo Sakai shook hands with Harold L Jones, one of the SBD gunners who wounded him. A resident of Tokyo, he occasionally gives motivational lectures, and continues to write books. Although blind in his right eye, Sakai has achieved three 'holes-in-one' playing golf!

Chief Petty Officer Sadao Uehara

Sadao Uehara was one of Saburo Sakai's original wingmen from the early days of the war. He entered flight training in June 1938 and graduated in October 1941, being immediately posted to the Tainan AG.

The opening day of the Pacific War saw Uehara flying against airfield targets at Luzon, in the Philippines, and on 19 February 1942 the young novice claimed his first victory when he shot down a P-40 of the 17th PS.

Uehara was one of the few original Tainan AG pilots to survive through to November 1942, when the unit was reorganised. By the time he returned to Japan, the following victories were recorded in his logbook; three P-40s, four F4Fs and a single P-39, TBF and B-25 (unconfirmed) – he also shared in the destruction of two B-17s, a PBY a C-47 and a Spitfire. After the disaster at Midway, many veteran pilots were pulled out of frontline duty to become instructors, Uehara included, and and like most of those affected by this decision, he hated his new assignment.

In September 1944, in anticipation of the American invasion of the

Pilots of the Tainan AG pose for the newspapers back home on 9 June 1942. In the front row, from left to right, are ; PO3/c Sadao Uehara, unidentified, Seaman 1/c Kenichiro Yamamoto and PO3/c Keisaku Yoshimura. Standing, left to right, are; PO1/c Saburo Sakai, PO3/c Seiji Ishikawa, war correspondent Hajime Yoshida and unidentified. Seconds after this photo was taken an air raid alarm sounded and the pilots scurried off into action (*Maru*)

Tainan AG 2nd Squadron pilots are seen at Rabaul in 1942. In the front row, from left to right, are; PO3/c Yoshizo Ohashi, PO3/c Seiji Ishikawa (5 victories), PO3/c Kenichi Kumagai (2 victories), Seaman 1/c Kenichiro Yamamoto and PO2/c Shin Nakano. In the second row, left to right, are; PO2/c Toshio Ota (34 victories), PO1/c Saburo Sakai (60+ victories), Seaman 1/c Masayoshi Yonekawa (6 victories) and PO3/c Unichi Miya. Standing, from left to right, are; PO1/c Hiroyoshi Nishizawa (86 victories), PO3/c Daizo Fukumori, PO3/c Yutaka Kimura, PO3/c Masuaki Endo (14 victories), PO1/c Katsumi Kobayashi and PO3/c Takeichi Kokubu. Of the pilots featured in these two group photographs, only Sakai, Uehara and Ishikawa survived the war (*Sakaida*)

Lt Hideki Shingo sorties from the carrier *Shokaku* in October 1942 during the Battle of Santa Cruz. He was the squadron leader of the carrier's Zero fighters, and a most capable leader who had seen action during both the China War and the early campaigns of the Pacific War. Shingo eventually rose to lieutenant commander rank (*via Aerospace Publishing*)

A6M2-N floatplane fighters are seen under inspection by mechanics aboard the seaplane tender *Kamikawa Maru* in August 1942 – the ship was en route from Yokosuka to the Shortland Islands, in the Solomons. On 13 September WO Kawamura became the first pilot within the unit to score a victory when he engaged an SBD dive-bomber preparing to land at Henderson Field, on Guadalcanal. The 'Rufes' also frequently engaged B-17s over the Solomons (*Maru*)

Two 'Rufes' are seen on a training flight off the Japanese coastline in late 1942. The floatplanes initially entered service in the standard Zero fighter light grey scheme, although this was soon replaced by the drab green seen on the aircraft in the background

Philippines, the newly-reformed 201st AG (II) was activated at Davao. By this stage in the war the need for veteran pilots had reached such an acute level that even instructors were brought back for active combat duty, Sadao Uehara being duly transferred to the 306th Sqn of the 201st AG. He claimed his last victory (a F6F Hellcat) within days of joining the unit, but soon fell seriously ill in the tropical environment and was sent

back to Japan in December. CPO Uehara ended the war as an instructor.

By his own reckoning, he destroyed over 13 aircraft during the war. About three years after VJ-Day, he told his old flight leader, Saburo Sakai, 'I hated you for being so severe to me in the early days. But thanks to you, I survived the war!' Uehara became an accomplished helicopter pilot after the war. He was killed in a helicopter accident on 27 August 1988.

Warrant Officer Sadamu Komachi

Standing over six feet tall, Sadamu Komachi was one of the tallest Zero pilots in the JNAF, his daredevil skills and exploits being frequently chronicled in his prefecture's newspapers, which made him famous.

He was born in Ishikawa Prefecture in April 1920, and enlisted in the navy after turning 18. Komachi commenced his career as a fighter pilot

Mitsubishi F1M 'Pete' observation seaplanes are seen moored at their coastal base on Shortland Islands. The F1M was extremely manoeuvrable, and carried two forward firing 7.7 mm machine-guns plus a flexible weapon of the same calibre for the observer. The 'Pete' could also be armed with two 60 kg bombs under the wings (*Maru*)

A pair of F1Ms carry out a coastal patrol. The heavy weathering of the aircraft's central float indicates just how much use this 'Pete' has seen (*via Phil Jarrett*)

after graduating from flight school in June 1940, his first assignment seeing him serve aboard the carrier *Shokaku*. On the opening day of the Pacific War he flew as protective cover over the Pearl Harbor attack fleet.

During the Battle of the Coral Sea in May 1942, Komachi recorded his first victories when he claimed two F4F Wildcats (one shared) and a dive-bomber. It was a Wildcat which also came close to nearly killing him on 24 August when he fought against F4Fs of VF-6 over Guadalcanal during the Battle of the Eastern Solomons. Spotting his prey below him, he dived down to make his kill. However, another Wildcat flown by Lt Albert Vorse quickly latched onto Komachi's tail and opened fire. Caught by surprise, the JNAF pilot feigned death by putting his Zero into a wild uncontrollable spin for 6000 ft. Vorse was so convinced by this desperate manoeuvre that he claimed a victory (his fifth out of an eventual tally of 11.5) and Komachi managed to cheat death.

During this combat much precious fuel had been consumed, and on his way back to base Komachi tanks ran dry and he was forced to ditch. He resigned himself to death while clinging to a floating drop tank, but a destroyer plucked him from the water at night using searchlights.

Rabaul – known as the 'Graveyard of Fighter Pilots' – was Komachi's next battle assignment, flying briefly with the 204th AG before transferring to the 253rd at Tobera airfield. Whilst here he became a specialist in the use of the aerial burst bomb (Ta-Dan) against formations of B-24s.

On the night of 18/19 February 1944, Rabaul and neighbouring areas were attacked by five American destroyers (*Farenholt, Buchanan, Landsdowne, Lardner* and *Woodworth)* of DesRon (Destroyer Squadron) 12. In column formation, they shelled various targets and launched 15 torpedoes against ships docked in Keravia Bay. Rabaul's coastal guns, designed for short distance firing only in anticipation of enemy landing attempts, remained silent, so PO1/c Komachi, livid with anger at their inability to fight back, volunteered to attack the enemy.

A single Zero, armed with two 60 kg bombs, roared off into the night. Purple flashes off the coast pinpointed the American destroyer convoy, whilst fires started by the vessels' shelling could be seen up and down the coast. Off Kokopo, the daring Zero pilot commenced his strafing attacks, which remained unchallenged by the ships. It was only when Komachi dropped his bombs (which missed) did the destroyers' anti-aircraft batteries responded fiercely. Komachi made repeated strafing attacks, then headed for home after exhausting his ammunition supply. He made the following report, 'I attacked the destroyers and set small to medium fires on three of them. I chased them out of the bay'. In reality the vessels had suffered very little damage, for the fires he had seen on the destroyers were actually the canvas gun covers burning away – in their haste to fire back, the ships' gunners had simply fired through the 'tarps'!

When the main element of the 253rd AG was withdrawn north to Truk on 19 February 1944, Komachi went with them and continued his struggle against the B-24s using aerial burst bombs from the island base. At this time he received the rare honour of a commendation from his superiors for his technical skills.

On 19 June 1944 15 Zeroes under the command of Lt Cdr Harutoshi Okamoto left Truk for Guam, in the Marianas. Unknown to the Zero pilots, who were running short of fuel, the airfield at Orote had just been

PO3/c Sadamu Komachi poses aboard the carrier *Shokaku* in early 1942. His exploits were well publicised in his home prefecture newspapers, and he gained a reputation for being a daring pilot (*K Osuo*)

raided by US carrier aircraft. The incoming flight of Zeroes was seen by the departing F6Fs, which quickly turned around and attacked at low altitude. In a head-on encounter with Ens Wendell Twelves of VF-15 at less than 200 ft, Komachi was caught off guard and his Zero took hits in the engine. Skilfully ditching his burning aircraft into the sea, he suffered serious burns to his face and body, but managed to swim ashore and eventually return to Japan by submarine – Komachi's Zero was one of two shot down Ens Twelves, these being his first kills. The Hellcat pilot would go one to score a further 11 victories (see Osprey *Aircraft of the Aces 10 - Hellcat Aces of World War 2* for further details).

Back in Japan, Komachi served with the Yokosuka AG until the end of the war . . . and a few days beyond. On 18 August 1945 he participated in the second interception of B-32 Dominators of the 386th Bomb Squadron over Tokyo, damaging the aircraft flown by Lt John R Anderson. Although the attack on the B-32s was legal under international law (Japan was still technically at war until the official surrender documents were signed on 2 September 1945), Komachi was fearful of Allied reprisals, and went 'underground' until US Occupation Forces left his country.

WO Sadamu Komachi flew around 2500 hours during World War 2, during which time he engaged in over 180 dogfights, force-landed twice and was shot down once. Attributed with over 40 kills by his peers, Komachi reckons that he scored 'perhaps half' of this total.

In 1994 he corresponded with Wendell Twelves of Springville, Utah, and they had plans to meet, but the pilot who downed Komachi during the 'Marianas Turkey Shoot' sadly passed away after a heart operation. Two years earlier the JNAF ace had been a guest panelist at the Battle of the Coral Sea Symposium at NAS Pensacola, Florida. He remarked, 'I'm just a lowly warrant officer, but I had admirals and captains saluting me and shaking my hand. This would never happen in Japan!'

Warrant Officer Gitaro Miyazaki

Gitaro Miyazaki was one of many Tainan AG aces who distinguished themselves over New Guinea in 1942. Born in June 1917 in Kochi Prefecture, he entered navy flight training in May 1933 and graduated in May 1937. Miyazaki subsequently served with the Saiki and Takao AGs.

In September 1938 (whilst flying with the 12th AG) Miyazaki was posted to the China War, although by the time he arrived in-theatre Chinese aerial opposition had begun to waver, and it wasn't until 5 October that he achieved his first victory – an I-16 over Hankow. He returned to Japan in June 1939 and joined the Yokosuka AG, although he was posted back to China for a second tour of duty with the 12th AG in 1941. Miyazaki claimed another victory on 11 August over Chengtu.

Following the organisation of the Tainan AG on the island of Formosa in October 1941, Miyazaki was posted to the unit as a newly-promoted warrant officer. On the opening day of the Pacific War, he was a flight leader in the 3rd Squadron which attacked Clark Field, in the Philippines, claiming one victory during the course of the mission.

Still with the Tainan AG, Miyazaki sortied over the Dutch East Indies before arriving at Rabaul in April 1942. From here He flew combat patrol missions against the enemy airfield at Port Moresby. On 1 June 24 P-39s

WO Gitaro Miyazaki's devotion to duty cost him his life, comrade Saburo Sakai, who witnessed his demise, blaming his death on ill health and a lack of teamwork (*Y Izawa*)

and P-400s of the USAAF 35th and 36th FSs (on the last day of their combat tours) scrambled to oppose an incoming flight of 24 'Betty' bombers escorted by a dozen Zeroes. The Americans tore into the bombers while the fighter escorts tried desperately to repel their attacks, and as the bombers completed their runs and turned for home, Miyazaki, who was below the 'Bettys', was viciously attack by an enemy aircraft that had dived straight through the formation at him. Hit repeatedly by cannon and machine gun fire, the Zero exploded in mid-air, killing its pilot.

Miyazaki was awarded a rare posthumous double rank promotion to lieutenant (junior grade) after his death. His tally of 13 kills was officially recognised, and the Naval All Units Proclamation No 3 stated that he had flown 37 missions and his flight had accounted for 44 aircraft destroyed, six burned on the ground and 30+ damaged. Miyazaki was the third of ten Tainan AG pilots honoured with posthumous double promotions.

Petty Officer Third Class Toshiaki Honda

Saburo Sakai's faithful wingman, Toshiaki Honda was also a character within the Tainan AG when out of the cockpit, his antics bringing comic relief to his comrades in the miserable environment of the tropics. He was born in Fukuoka Prefecture in 1919, and prior to his enlistment in the navy, he had worked as a ticket collector on a city tram.

Honda was accepted for flight training and graduated in June 1940. He became a member of the Tainan AG and flew his first combat mission during the attack against Clark Field on 8 December 1941 as the third man in the flight of Saburo Sakai and Ichio Yokogawa. Tangling with P-40s of the 21st Pursuit Squadron over the airfield, Honda failed to score.

After the assault on the Philippines, the Tainan AG ranged over the Dutch East Indies, then proceeded to the forward base at Rabaul. Once here, the group alternated between Rabaul and Lae. While at the latter airfield pilot morale sharply declined due to both the poor quality of meals and inequities between officers and enlisted pilots. Honda, who had a reputation as a scrounger, was duly ordered by Sakai to pillage the officers' mess kitchen for food to bring back to his squadronmates. Success in his task soon led to carelessness, as Honda was caught and beaten by an irate officer, who only stopped when Sakai fired his pistol at him – a court martial offence. Summoned before Cdr Yasuna Kozono, Sakai explained his actions and his mens' complaint, and astonishingly the incident was 'forgotten about' and the cuisine dramatically improved!

While Honda was not a gifted pilot, he was quite aggressive, and on 17 April 1942 he claimed three P-40s shot down over Port Moresby. He always told others, 'As long as I fly with Sakai, I'll never be shot down!'

On 13 May newcomer to the unit WO Watari Handa (see China War chapter) requested the loan of Honda from Sakai for a sweep over the airfield at Port Moresby. Despite Honda's protestation, Sakai ordered his wingman to go, and the Zero flight was duly bounced by seven P-39s of the 36th FS over the target. Capt Paul G Brown and 1Lt Elmer F Ghram caught Honda in a crossfire and the Zero exploded, killing the pilot.

Due to his fighting spirit, Toshiaki Honda was given a rare two rank posthumous promotion to petty officer first class, his citation stating that he had flown 47 missions, achieved five personal kills and 18 assists.

PO3/c Toshiaki Honda was the best wingman Saburo Sakai ever had, and also the most mischievous – Sakai grew suspicious of his wingman's endless supply of clean underwear, only to discover that Honda was stealing his! When confronted by Sakai, Honda admitted to the dastardly deed. The former later ordered him to steal food from the officer's mess (*Maru*)

Petty Officer First Class Masuaki Endo

For those Zero pilots who fought through the tough combats over New Guinea and Guadalcanal in 1942, the invaluable experience gained in battle only served to make them better pilots. Masuaki Endo was one of the few veterans from the Tainan AG to have survived these epic battles.

Born in Fukushima Prefecture in December 1920, Endo enlisted in the navy and graduated from flight training in October 1941. In February of the following year he was posted to the Tainan AG, advancing with it to Rabaul and Lae. A consistent scorer throughout the early months of war, Endo seemingly led a charmed life as his comrades fell one by one.

On 7 August 1942 the group flew the first long-range mission to Guadalcanal from its base at Rabaul – a one-way distance of over 560 miles. Seventeen Zeroes escorted twenty-seven 'Betty' bombers to counterattack the American landings on Guadalcanal, PO2/c Endo flying as second wingman to Lt(jg) Junichi Sasai. In his first combat with carrier fighters, the 21-year-old ace claimed an F4F and a pair of SBDs.

Subsequent missions to Guadalcanal took a heavy toll of veteran pilots, but Endo still cheated death through a combination of his flying skill and luck. In November 1942 the few surviving pilots were ordered back to Japan while the unit was reorganised as the 251st AG.

In May 1943 Endo returned to Rabaul as a member of the 251st, but failed to survive his first month back in action. On 7 June, the Japanese sortied 81 Zeroes and clashed with over 100 American and New Zealand fighters over the Russells. PO2/c Endo reportedly downed a P-38 (none were lost) before his aircraft was set on fire following a head-on attack by a P-40 flown by Lt Henry E Matson of the 44th FS. Determined to take his foe with him, Endo rammed his flaming Zero into the Warhawk, Matson parachuted out at 18,000 ft with burns to his face, neck and hands, and a mouthful of powdered Plexiglas. Endo was killed. Subsequently rescued, Matson was duly credited with two A6Ms destroyed.

Masuaki Endo received official recognition for 14 victories.

Lieutenant(jg) Junichi Sasai

Junichi Sasai earned the title 'Richthofen of Rabaul', and despite seeing combat for only a short period of time, his legacy as a great fighter-leader lives on to this day.

Born on 13 February 1918 in Tokyo as the son of a naval captain, young Junichi was always destined join the service as an officer when he reached an appropriate age. His early childhood was marked by ill health, resulting in him often being absent from school and teasing by his classmates. A regime of hard physical exercise and diet improved the youngster's health, however, and by the time he enrolled in high school, Junichi was fit enough to earn his Blackbelt in Judo – his outstanding achievements in school won him acceptance to Etajima (Naval Academy).

Sasai graduated in 1939 and was commissioned an ensign. He entered flight training and completed the course in November 1941, his tenacious spirit earned him the nickname of 'Gamecock'. By the time Japan entered the Pacific War the following month, Sasai had joined the Tainan AG. He flew with the group on a raid to Luzon (in the Philippines) on 10

PO3/c Masuaki Endo on 4 August 1942 at Rabaul. He was one of the few Tainan AG pilots to survive its first combat tour, which ended in November 1942. He returned from Japan to the Solomons in May 1943, but lasted barely a month before being killed (*Y Izawa*)

December, but he experienced engine trouble and was forced to abort.

Following victory in the Philippines, the Tainan AG saw considerable action in the Dutch East Indies, where it provided air support for ground troops. Sasai's first victory was recorded on 2 February 1942 over Maospati, Java, when he destroyed a Dutch Buffalo. Sixteen days later he claimed a P-40E of the 17th PS with just 280 rounds of machine-gun fire.

The Tainan AG advanced to Rabaul in April 1942, being reorganised with new officers, equipment and pilots soon after its arrival. Lt(jg) Sasai was duly given command of the 2nd Squadron, and pilots alternated between Rabaul and their forward base at Lae.

Within 2nd Squadron ranks were many experienced enlisted pilots, including PO1/c Saburo Sakai. The latter was most impressed with his new commander, for he showed genuine compassion towards his men unlike other officers. To insure his survival, Sakai personally tutored the young lieutenant in the art of dogfighting, and once Sasai found his shooting eye, he blossomed into a first rate pilot.

On 4 May 1942 he demonstrated his marksmanship by bouncing a flight of three P-39s and shooting them all down in less than 20 seconds. Sasai continued to score multiple victories, achieving his personal best of five in one day on 7 August 1942 over Guadalcanal. This feat was tempered by the serious wounding of his mentor Saburo Sakai during the same mission, and before the latter was sent back to Japan, Sasai gave him a personal memento – his special tiger belt buckle – which he claimed would protect him from further harm.

On 26 August Sasai led a nine-aircraft formation tasked with protecting 'Betty' bombers sent to strike at Henderson Field, on Guadalcanal. They were attacked over the target by 12 Wildcats from VMF-223, led by Majs John L Smith and Rivers J Morrell. Sasai failed to return from the mission.

In a letter to his family prior to his death, Sasai claimed 54 victories, and stated that he hoped to break the record of German World War 1 ace, Baron Manfred von Richthofen (who achieved 80 kills). According to the Naval All Units Proclamation No36, Sasai flew 76 missions with the Tainan AG and attained 27 recognised victories. He was promoted two grades to lieutenant commander for distinguished service.

Petty Officer First Class Toshio Ota

Toshio Ota belonged to the 'Clean Up Trio' in the Tainan AG, which was the premier JNAF unit operating against the Allies in New Guinea. The remaining trio members were Saburo Sakai and Hiroyoshi Nishizawa, who were two of the top aces in the air group at the time.

Ota was born in March 1919 to a farming family in Nagasaki Prefecture, and as a youth he was enthused with aviation and joined the navy at Sasebo in 1936. He was accepted into flight training in January 1939 and graduated in September. The China War was by then in its second year, and the exploits of JNAF pilots had received considerable newspaper coverage at home. Anxious for action, Ota passed through the Omura and 12th Air Groups before heading to China in June 1941. However, by the time he arrived in-theatre the air action had diminished considerably and he saw no combat.

Dubbed the 'Richthofen of Rabaul', Lt(jg) Junichi Sasai was a compassionate officer who treated his enlisted men with respect, unlike most of the officer pilots at Rabaul (*S Sakai*)

PO1/c Toshio Ota was the leader of the scoring race within the Tainan AG in 1942. Popular within his squadron because of his congenial ways, Ota nevertheless exhibited tremendous fighting spirit once in the air (*Sakaida*)

With the outbreak of the Pacific War, Ota flew as a member in the 3rd Squadron of the Tainan AG in the aerial assault on Clark Field on 8 December 1941, claiming one aircraft shot down. After this action, he sortied to the Dutch East Indies, where he was wounded over Balikpapan, Borneo, in a running gunfight with a B-17 – Ota was subsequently grounded for a number of months because of his wounds.

The Tainan AG was ordered to their new base at Rabaul in April 1942, Ota being transferred to Lt(jg) Junichi Sasai's 2nd Squadron upon arrival. He soon made a name for himself by doggedly pursuing a lone B-17 for over an hour before finally bringing it down.

Ota's congenial personality and aggressive fighting spirit soon caught the attention of Saburo Sakai (the unit's top scorer), and as with Lt(jg) Sasai, Sakai also tutored the former in dogfighting techniques. His protégé caught on very quickly, and soon a scoring race had developed between himself, his instructor and Hiroyoshi Nishizawa. Ota proved his ability on the 7 August mission to Guadalcanal, when he claimed four Wildcats destroyed in his first encounter with American carrier fighters.

On 21 October PO1/c Toshio Ota participated in a bomber escort mission to Guadalcanal which encountered Wildcats of VMF-212 head-on at high altitude. Although Ota quickly downed Marine Gunner 'Tex' Hamilton (a seven-kill ace), who parachuted out but was never recovered, he in turn had 1Lt Frank C Drury (six kills) whip around onto his tail in a tight climbing turn as the Zero flashed before him. The Wildcat pilot's aim was deadly accurate, and Ota fell to his death – Drury claimed two A6Ms during this sortie.

Toshio Ota was given a posthumous promotion to the rank of warrant officer, and according to his air group's record, he had scored 34 victories.

Warrant Officer Hiroyoshi Nishizawa

It was only after his death that Hiroyoshi Nishizawa rose to fame, thanks to the memoir of his comrade Saburo Sakai. Indeed, he was at one time thought to have been the JNAF's top ace.

Born on 27 January 1920 in Nagano Prefecture, Nishizawa was the son of a saké brewery manager. He joined the navy in June 1936 as a result of seeing a JNAF recruiting poster, the youngster working in a thread mill at the time. His boyhood dream of becoming a pilot was realised when he completed flying training in March 1939.

When the Pacific War began, Nishizawa was flying Type 96 'Claudes' with the Chitose AG in the Marshall Islands, and he duly accompanied the group to Rabaul, where he joined the 4th AG in February 1942. Nishizawa recorded his first victory on 3 February 1942 over Rabaul whilst still flying the thoroughly obsolete 'Claude'.

When elements of the Tainan AG arrived at Rabaul from the Dutch East Indies in April, Nishizawa was transferred into the 2nd Squadron, where he found himself in the company of PO1/c Saburo Sakai. The latter tutored the gaunt and sickly loner, together with PO2/c Toshio Ota, and together the threesome became famous as the 'Cleanup Trio'.

Nishizawa quickly mastered the art of dogfighting, scoring his first victory (a P-39) with the Tainan AG on 1 May over Port Moresby. The following day two P-40s fell to his guns, the group's American opponents throughout the month of May being the USAAC's 35th and 36th FSs.

Nishizawa's most successful day came on 7 August 1942 when, during a long-range bomber escort mission to Guadalcanal, he claimed six VF-5 F4Fs in his first encounter with American carrier fighters. Although the great ace's A6M sustained some damage, he returned safely to base.

In November, surviving pilots of the Tainan AG were transferred to the 251st, with those few who had survived the combats over Guadalcanal being held in high esteem by the JNAF.

On 14 May 1943 33 Zeroes escorted 18 'Betty' bombers sent to strike at shipping in Oro Bay. Opposing them was the 49th FG, who scrambled up three squadrons of P-40s. In the huge dogfight which ensued, Nishizawa claimed one Warhawk shot down and two more as probables, plus recorded his first victory over a P-38 – the JNAF claimed 15 victories in total, but the only USAAF loss was a solitary P-38 (from the 9th FS).

It was inevitable that sooner or later Nishizawa would test his skills against the gull-winged F4U Corsair – arguably the best fighter on either side in the region. This contest occurred on 7 June 1943 over the Russells, when 81 Zeroes tangled with USMC and RNZAF fighters. Four Corsairs of VMF-112 were lost in this action, although three of the pilots were saved – Nishizawa's claims for the mission were one F4U and a New Zealand P-40 destroyed.

For the rest of the summer of 1943 he fought daily battles with Corsairs and P-40s in the areas of Rendova and Vella La Vella, the former fighter being his toughest opponent. Marines from VMF-121, -122, -123, -124 and -221 all traded fire with 'The Devil', but failed to bring him down, resulting in Nishizawa being awarded a coveted ceremonial sword from Adm Jinichi Kusaka, CO of the 11th Air Fleet.

In September the 251st AG was re-rolled as a nightfighter unit, and PO1/c Nishizawa was transferred to the 253rd AG, based at Tobera Airfield (Rabaul). He flew with his new unit for just a month, however, for he was ordered to return to Japan in October to serve as an instructor as part of the JNAF's efforts to cure their fighter pilot shortage. The following month he received promotion to warrant officer.

Nishizawa hated his new assignment likening it to baby-sitting. He had very little patience with his trainees, many of whom would have been rejected for flight training just three years earlier, and after repeated requests for a combat assignment, he was transferred to the 201st AG in the Philippines in time to participate in the counterattack against the American naval fleets.

The first successful *kamikaze* suicide attack occurred on 25 October 1944 when Lt Yukio Seki and four other pilots attacked US carriers in Leyte Gulf. WO Nishizawa had played a pivotal role in this mission by leading the four escort fighters which had cleared the path for Seki by downing two patrolling Hellcats. He subsequently told his comrades that he would die soon, and requested a *kamikaze* assignment, although this was swiftly turned down because of his value as a fighter pilot.

On 26 October Nishizawa boarded a bomber used by the Navy's 1021 Transport Group and left Cebu Island for Mabalacat (near Clark Field) to pick up some replacement Zeroes. A frantic SOS radio message was received from the transport, but it failed to arrive at its destination and nothing more was learned of its fate.

PO1/c Hiroyoshi Nishizawa is seen as an instructor in Japan in 1943. He was not well suited to this task as he had very little tolerence for his trainees, and thus hating his assignment. Nishizawa was simply a skilled fighter pilot who could not teach (*K Osuo*)

In 1982, the circumstances surrounding Nishizawa's death were finally resolved. The aircraft had been intercepted between Puerta Gallera and Calapan, on the northern tip of Mindoro Island, by two Hellcats from VF-14 that were in the process of returning to their carrier.

'I stayed below a thin stratus cloud layer and my wingman stayed on top', recalled F6F pilot Harold P Newell. 'The aircraft popped out of the clouds slightly to my right in a left hand turn. It was at close range and I opened fire. After several short bursts the port engine and inboard wing section were in flames. The aircraft went into an increasingly steep diving left turn and I continued firing until the fuselage started shedding pieces and the fire increased.'

Lt(jg) Harold P Newell received credit for shooting down the bomber, which he identified as a 'Helen' – a JAAF Ki-49 twin-engined bomber which, at this stage in the war, the JNAF sometimes used for transport duties. Nishizawa's aircraft was not a DC-3 as reported elsewhere.

Hiroyoshi Nishizawa was posthumously elevated two ranks to lieutenant junior grade and issued a citation. According to the Naval All Units Proclamation No 172, Nishizawa attained a personal tally of 36 victories and two damaged while serving with the 201st. Shortly before his death, Nishizawa had reportedly told his last CO, Cdr Harutoshi Okamoto, that he had achieved 86 kills – postwar, he has been linked with scores of 147 and 103, but both tallies are pure fiction.

In May 1982, Harold P Newell met and shook hands with Nishizawa's mentor, Saburo Sakai, at a reunion in California.

Petty Officer Second Class Enji Kakimoto

Enji Kakimoto was typical of the many nameless Zero aces who enjoyed a brief career before been killed in the wholesale destruction of the JNAF. Officially listed as missing in action in August 1942, it wasn't until 1985 that his fate was finally unearthed.

He was born in Oita Prefecture in April 1920, and when the China War broke out in July 1937, he was so imbued with national spirit that he left his family farm and enlisted in the navy at Sasebo. The exploits of Japanese aviators over China excited young Enji, who initially served as a sailor aboard the cruiser *Myoko* following his enlistment. Once back ashore, he found that performing guard duty at various air bases was just as monotonous as farm labour, so he applied for, and was accepted into, flight training. He graduated in the 47th term flight class in October 1939.

Kakimoto's biggest day in action came during the fierce dogfight over Guadalcanal on 7 August 1942 when, as PO1/c Saburo Sakai's wingman, he claimed an F4F Wildcat and an SBD over Tulagi.

Just 20 days later PO2/c Kakimoto was shot down while escorting 'Val' dive-bombers on a mission to Rabi, New Guinea, ditching his Zero into the sea and swimming ashore. Captured by 'friendly' natives soon after reaching land, the young aviator was eventually turned over to the Australians. When Kakimoto failed to return from the mission he was declared missing and presumed killed in action.

Unbeknown to his squadron mates, Kakimoto had been shipped back to Australia, where he was imprisoned at the huge Cowra PoW camp in New South Wales. He played dumb with his captors, submitting to their

PO2/c Enji Kakimoto (seen here on 4 August 1942) was one of just a handful of Zero pilots who became a PoW. He helped organise the mass breakout from Cowra PoW Camp, in Australia, in 1944 (*Sakaida*)

questions and giving them misleading information. His fellow comrades remembered him as a militant hothead, who helped organise a breakout in a gesture aimed at erasing the shame of having been captured.

On 5 August 1944, more than 1100 Japanese PoWs broke out of the camp, and over 230 were either killed attempting to do so, or committed suicide rather than be recaptured – within nine days, all escapees had been accounted for. Although one of the main conspirators in the 'Cowra Breakout', Kakimoto never actually left the confines of the camp, choosing instead to throw a rope over a rafter in his hut and hang himself.

PO2/c Enji Kakimoto scored over five victories in his short career and now lies buried in the Japanese War Cemetery at Cowra.

Ensign Kenji Okabe

Kenji Okabe is honoured in JNAF history as having been the pilot who initially set the record for the most number of victories achieved during one mission.

Born in Fukuoka Prefecture in May 1915, Kenji joined the Navy and entered flight training in the 38th term class along with fellow sailor Saburo Sakai. Upon graduation in November 1937, he was assigned to the 12th AG and went to the China War. However, there was very little enemy air activity to be found, and Okabe saw no combat. Unlike Sakai, he then became a carrier pilot and their careers took different paths.

When Japan attacked Pearl Harbor, PO1/c Okabe was assigned to the carrier *Shokaku*, although his part in the raid consisted of flying combat air patrols over the carrier task force. His baptism of fire finally came on 9 April 1942 when JNAF carrier pilots attacked the British naval base at Trincomalee, on the island of Ceylon (now Sri Lanka) – Okabe claimed the destruction two No 261 Sqn Hurricane IIs.

He subsequently made a name for himself during the Battle of the Coral Sea on 8 May 1942. During a combat air patrol over the *Shokaku*, Okabe attempted to thwart determined attack by SBDs against his carrier. Protecting the Dauntlesses were F4F Wildcats, which constantly interfered by drawing his flight into dogfights while the dive-bombers tried to deliver their bombs. SBD pilot Lt John J Powers managed to break through the fighter barrier to hit the carrier, causing extensive damage and put it out of action – he was killed in the process, however, later being posthumously awarded the Medal of Honor for his actions.

When the fighting ended Okabe claimed three SBDs and three F4Fs destroyed, with a further a pair of Wildcats as probables – a new JNAF record had been set. Despite his best efforts, Okabe's carrier had been so badly damaged that he was forced to ditch, from where he was rescued.

By July 1943 Okabe was back on his old ship, and in November the *Shokaku* Fighter Squadron flew to Rabaul to help shore up the flagging defense of the base in the face of relentless Allied air attacks. The Coral Sea veteran participated in a number of intercept missions whilst ashore, adding more victories to his tally.

Okabe's carrier fighter career ended when he transferred to the Omura AG in Japan. He fought briefly in the Philippines from October 1944 until he returned to Japan towards the end of the year, and then went on to see further action during aerial attacks over Okinawa in April 1945

PO3/c Kenji Okabe is seen in 1942 whilst serving aboard the *Shokaku*. He set a naval record of eight enemy aircraft destroyed in a day during the Battle of the Coral Sea (*Sakaida*)

with the 601st AG. After falling to halt the US invasion of Okinawa, Okabe's unit was all but grounded as it strove to conserve fuel and build up its aircraft inventory for the final battle which never came.

Ens Kenji Okabe claimed over 50 victories in his career.

Warrant Officer Kiyomi Katsuki

The JNAF produced just two floatplane aces during World War 2, with Kiyomi Katsuki being one of them. Born in Fukuoka Prefecture in April 1919, he joined the navy in June 1938, and by May 1941 had graduated from flight training for the seaplane reconnaissance role – assignments to various units followed.

When the Pacific War started, Katsuki was flying from the seaplane tender *Chitose*, and he completed a number of reconnaissance and patrol missions over the Philippines and the Dutch East Indies in an F1M 'Pete' biplane scout. On 11 January 1942 the Japanese sent a convoy of special landing force marines to Kema, in the Northern Celebes, which was opposed by Seven Dutch and American PBYs off Menado. Katsuki and his squadronmates attacked the flying boats in their 'Petes', the former downing a Dutch PBY (No Y-58 of GVT-17) for his first victory.

In September 1942 Katsuki was transferred to a forward seaplane base in the Shortland Islands to undertake patrol missions to Guadalcanal. On 4 October, while flying combat air patrol over the fleet in his 'Pete', he spotted four enemy fighters and five B-17s. In order to prevent the the bombers from hitting the seaplane carrier *Nisshin,* Katsuki dove on the lead Flying Fortress – a B-17E of the 72nd BS, flown by Lt David C Everitt Jr – and commenced his attack. After completing his pass, he rammed the aircraft from below, tearing the right main wing and the vertical stabiliser off the bomber and damaging his own right wing. The gutsy pilot and his observer quickly baled out of their 'Pete' and were rescued by the destroyer *Akizuki.* The crew of the B-17 all perished.

For the actions of 4 October, in which Katsuki thwarted the bombing of the *Nisshin,* he received the following rare personal citation from Capt Tamotsu Furukawa, CO of the *Chitose,* which stated in part;

'Kiyomi Katsuki found four American fighters and five B-17s coming over the *Nisshin.* He started attacking the lead B-17; the return gunfire was very severe. But he had to stop this aircraft at all costs, so he decided to ram it. He approached from 50 metres under the B-17 and then turned just before contact, and tore off the main wing of the enemy bomber. His aircraft was broken up and he parachuted. Because of his attack, the enemy stopped attacking the fleet . . . In front of the enemy, you stayed calm and decided on the right method and did it. Your deed is most admirable. To attack the enemies at the risk of your own life is our Navy tradition . . . You are hereby awarded a special award of a gold chevron.'

Katsuki later returned to Japan and began conversion training from seaplane scout ('Pete') to seaplane fighter ('Rufe') at Yokusuka Air Base. He was then assigned to the 452nd AG and posted to their base at Shumshu, in the Aleutians, around July 1943. Soon after his arrival USAAF Eleventh Air Force B-25s and B-24s started pounding the Japanese on Paramushiru Island, in the frigid Kuriles, and eventually recaptured Attu Island in May. Between August and October Katsuki claimed a B-25.

PO1/c Kiyomi Katsuki became the second ranking JNAF floatplane ace of World War 2. He also saved the seaplane carrier *Nisshin* from certain destruction by destroying a B-17 in a ramming attack (*K Osuo*)

The three hatchets displayed over the unit code N1-118 on this A6M2-N seaplane fighter denote victories scored by the aircraft in the Solomons in 1942. Lt Keizo Yamazaki flew this aircraft with the 802nd AG, claiming a P-39 probable on 13 February 1943 (*K Osuo*)

On 12 September Maj Frank T Cash of the 404th BS led a flight of B-24s to attack a troop staging area on Paramushiru Island. Ten seaplanes teamed with JAAF 'Oscars' of the 54th Sentai to attack the Liberators, and Katsuki and four comrades duly claimed two B-24s destroyed – one of these was flown by Maj Cash.

PO3/c Katsuki and the few surviving members of his seaplane unit left the area when their seaplane base finally froze over, returning to Japan on board the submarine I-36. Upon arriving back at Yokosuka, he commenced conversion onto the new Kawanishi N1K Kyofu 'Rex' seaplane fighter. Upon completing his training, Katsuki was assigned to the 934th AG, moving with the group to Ambon Island in the south-west Pacific area of Indonesia. In January 1944 he used a 'Rex' to destroy a B-24, which was the type's first success, although this victory was one of the few

A mix of green and grey 'Rufes' of the 802nd AG are seen lined up at their Imieji base in the Marshall Islands on 27 May 1943. The second aircraft from the left is N1-118 (seen on the previous page in detail), flown by Lt Keizo Yamazaki. Seaplanes could make a base in any area of calm water, with tents providing shelter for pilots and mechanics alike (*Maru*)

Pilots and mechanics stand to attention awaiting inspection, again on the Marshall Islands (*via Robert C Mikesh*)

A6M3a Zero 22s of the 251st AG are seen in a rare air-to-air photograph heading out on a patrol from Rabaul in 1943. The tail code of this fighter was originally UI-105, but at various times the prefix 'UI' was painted out with the hastily applied green daubed over the remainder of the aircraft's previously grey fuselage. This particular fighter was one of many flown by veteran ace Hiroyoshi Nishizawa, and it seen here carrying a 330 l (72.6 Imp gal) drop tank (*via Aerospace Publishing*)

high points for the group, which was disbanded shortly afterwards. The veteran seaplane pilot then undertook further conversion training to learn to fly the Zero fighter from land, and was subsequently posted to the 381st AG. He later flew in the defence of the Balikpapan oilfields, before downing a further two enemy aircraft over Singapore.

In February 1945, Katsuki returned to Japan and was based at Omura airfield, where he flew Raidens on home defence sorties until the surrender. His final tally of at least 16 kills included seven scored in seaplanes.

Warrant Officer Kenji Yanagiya

Kenji Yanagiya would have been considered an 'average' Zero pilot but

VAdm Jinichi Kusaka (in the dark cap) was CO of the JNAF at Rabaul. He had previously headed the Naval Academy at Etajima prior to his appointment to the 11th Air Fleet in the South-east Pacific. Kusaka instituted the unofficial awarding of ceremonial swords to pilots for distinguished service, and he served at Rabaul from 1942 until the end of the war (*Maru*)

for fate, as he was the sole surviving escort pilot of the disastrous Adm Yamamoto mission.

Yanagiya was born in March 1919, and he enlisted in the navy as a seaman recruit in January 1940 at Yokosuka Naval Station. Subsequently plucked out of the ranks for flight training, he completed his course at Oita Air Base in March 1942 and was then assigned to the 6th AG.

In October 1942 Yanagiya was sent to Rabaul to serve with the 204th AG, and he recorded his first victory with the group on 5 January 1943 during an attack on Buin, on Bougainville, by P-38s (from the 339th FS) and B-17s. Although Yanagiya claimed a twin-engined Grumman XF5F-1 Skyrocket as his victim, this was an experimental fighter which never saw service – two P-38s were lost on this mission.

On 18 April Yanagiya, and five other pilots, was assigned to escort two 'Betty' bombers conducting an inspection tour of the frontlines – the lead bomber carried Adm Isoroku Yamamoto, Commander in Chief of the Combined Fleet. Sixteen P-38s from Guadalcanal intercepted the Japanese flight off the south-west coast of Bougainville, and Adm Yamamoto's bomber was shot down by 1Lt Rex Barber before the Japanese could take any effective action. The other 'Betty' was also destroyed.

In the ensuing dogfight, Yanagiya claimed one P-38, but it was to be a hollow victory. Having failed to protect their leader, yet having all returned to base unscathed, the escort pilots were given every opportunity to redeem themselves through glorious death – within three months four were dead.

On 8 June 1943 Yanagiya was severely wounded in combat while on a mission to Guadalcanal. His right arm was amputated and he was sent home to Japan for further hospitalisation.

By October of 1944 Yanagiya had recovered enough to become an instructor, but he never saw combat again. He ended the war with at least eight victories and married the nurse who had taken care of him.

In April 1988, Yanagiya shook hands with Rex Barber and the surviving P-38 veterans from the Yamamoto Mission at the Adm Nimitz Museum in Fredericksburg, Texas. He still lives in Tokyo today.

Warrant Officer Hiroshi Okano

Although a late starter in the Tainan AG, Hiroshi Okano had risen to

Kenji Yanagiya was the sole wartime survivor of the Zero escorts assigned to protect Adm Yamamoto during his fateful frontline tour in April 1943. He was amazed by the celebrity status accorded to him for his role in the mission by American historians and veteran P-38 pilots alike when he visited the USA in 1988 (*Sakaida*)

PO3/c Hiroshi Okano scored six victories with the Tainan AG and a dozen more with the 201st AG in the Solomons. Of the 21 pilots in his training class, only he and two others survived the war (*Sakaida*)

prominence by the end of the war. Born in Ibaragi Prefecture in May 1921, he enlisted in the navy in June 1938. The start of the Pacific War found Okano flying in the Marshall Islands with the Chitose AG, although he was posted to the Tainan AG at Rabaul in late May 1942.

On 25 June, the Tainan AG sortied 25 Zeroes from Lae to attack Port Moresby. Along the way, they intercepted six B-17s escorted by 24 escort fighters, and in the wild dogfight that ensued, Okano claimed his first kill.

In December 1942 he was transferred to the 201st AG and returned once again to the Marshall Islands. There was no enemy air activity to be found in this region, however, and Okano's unit spent most of its time training and conducting patrols. In February 1943, the group was recalled to Japan, where the pilots underwent more training.

As the air war over the Solomons intensified, the 201st AG was rushed to Buin in July 1943. The many months of training now paid off for PO1/c Okano for he quickly blossomed in combat, scoring around a dozen victories in this theatre of operations. In November now CPO Okano was transferred to the 331st AG, with whom he participated in combats over western New Guinea, before returning to the mainland.

WO Okano ended the war attached to the 701st Squadron of the 343rd AG – the so-called 'Squadron of Experts'. He achieved 19 victories.

Warrant Officer Sekizen Shibayama

Sekizen Shibayama was one of 'Rabaul's Last Eagles', a member of a guerrilla fighter squadron abandoned to its fate on New Britain.

Born in Saitama Prefecture in December 1923, he joined the navy and entered flight training in June 1940. After graduation in May 1942, Shibayama fulfilled the role of flight instructor at Yatabe airfield until posted to the 201st AG at Rabaul in September 1943 – he was subsequently transferred to the 253rd.

On 11 November Shibayama took off to intercept American carrier aircraft attacking Rabaul. As the novice pilot attempted to climb to altitude he experienced engine trouble, forcing him to unwittingly dive into a formation of eight Hellcats. In the resulting melee, future 10-kill ace Lt A B 'Chick' Smith of VF-9 clobbered Shibayama's Zero, sending it down in flames. The Japanese pilot glided his aircraft into Simpson Harbour and was later rescued – Smith claimed two A6Ms on this date.

Suffering from both a leg injury and malaria, Shibayama was grounded and saw no further action until the 253rd retreated to Truk Island where, as one of a handful of sick and injured pilots, he was left behind as the group continued its retreat northwards. A number of mechanics had also been abandoned on Truk, and they set about salvaging around a dozen Zero fighters from wrecks, thus creating a new squadron. Because of his combat experience, Shibayama and WO Shigeo Fukumoto were tasked with training half a dozen other pilots during the lull in fighting.

On 3 March 1944 seven Zeroes encountered F4Us of VMF-223 during a training flight over Tobera Airfield. In the short combat which ensued, the Japanese claimed five victories, including one to Shibayama (no F4Us were actually lost). Another scrap followed nine days later, this time involving F4Us from VMF-222. The Japanese claimed two, but again no Corsairs were lost – two Zeroes were, however, destroyed.

A happy PO Sekizen Shibayama is seen in the cockpit of a 'Claude' whilst serving as a flying instructor. Posted to Rabaul in late 1943, he flew as part of the 'Guerrilla Air Force' after the JNAF had officially departed the area. Shibayama, and a handful of other pilots and mechanics, performed a commendable job in an impossible situation (*S Shibayama*)

For the remainder of the war, Shibayama flew a number of patrol and bombing missions against American forces, and by August 1945 the unit was comprised of just two airworthy Zeroes. When Sekizen Shibayama was notified of the final surrender at at Kara (Buin) airfield, he was awaiting orders to make a solo suicide attack against approaching enemy warships. By his own reckoning he had attained 13 victories.

In August 1971 the veteran ace was reunited with his old Zero after it had been recovered from Simpson Harbour. The remarkable reunion took place in Bakersfield, California, and an examination of his seat revealed that a .50 cal 'slug' had missed his 'crown jewels' by inches. Today, Shibayama resides in Tokyo.

Chief Petty Officer Takeo Okumura

During the Pacific War few fighter pilots became a 'double ace-in-a-day', Takeo Okumura being one of those in this elite band – his claim of ten places him in the same league as top US Navy ace Cdr David McCampbell, who set the American record of nine destroyed and two damaged.

This extraordinary JNAF ace was born in Fukui Prefecture in February 1920. He enlisted in the navy at Kure in June 1935, and opting for a career in aviation, he was selected for flight training in February 1938. Okumura graduated in September of the same year.

Arriving in China just in time to participate in the final aerial actions of the conflict, Okumura was good from the very start. On 7 October 1940 seven A6M2 Zeroes of the 14th AG escorted 27 G3M 'Nell' bombers sent to raid Kunming. Whilst in the vicinity of the target CAF I-15 biplanes fighters attempted to intercept the 'Nells' but the Zeroes made short work of them, downing 13 in a matter of minutes – Okumura was credited with destroying four of them in what had been his first engagement.

As this mission clearly proved, the new Zero was vastly superior to anything the Chinese could boast in their arsenal, and fighter opposition all but ceased following the A6M2's introduction in August 1940. Indeed, Okamura's quartet of kills on 7 October were the 20-year-old pilot's only victories of the China War. Returning to Japan, he subsequently helped train pilots until July 1942, when he was assigned to the carrier *Ryujo*.

It was in the Solomons that Okumura became a master of dogfighting. On 24 August, he was escorting torpedo-bombers sent to attack American ships at Guadalcanal when they were intercepted by into Wildcats led by legendary ace Capt Marion Carl of VMF-223. A turbulent dogfight ensued, and Okumura became separated from his flight, who reported him lost upon returning to *Ryujo*, although he later returned alive – Carl claimed four kills (out of an eventual tally of 18.5) during this action.

When Okumura's first tour of duty in the Solomons ended, he had achieved 14 recognised aerial victories. He returned to Japan in December, but was posted back to the frontline in July 1943 as a member of the 201st AG, flying from their base at Buin.

Okumura's ten-kill haul came on 14 September during a massive Allied attack on Buin. The Japanese sortied over 200 Zeroes from the 201st and the 204th AGs in opposition, and in three separate missions during the course of the day, Okumura accounted for an F4U, a B-24 (shared), two P-40s, five F6F Hellcats and an SBD. After the battle, Adm Jinichi

CPO Takeo Okumura became a double ace-in-a-day when he downed ten aircraft during three missions on 14 September 1943. He received a coveted ceremonial sword from VAdm Jinichi Kusaka for his actions (*Y Izawa*)

Kusaka, CO of the 11th Air Fleet at Rabaul, presented the ace with a ceremonial sword for distinguished service. Frustratingly for Okumura, individual credits were no longer being recorded due to a naval directive issued in June 1943, although his claim was unofficially touted as being the highest one-day score ever achieved by a JNAF pilot in action.

Eight days later Okumura failed to return from a bomber escort mission against a convoy sighted near Cape Cretin, New Guinea, the 35 Zeroes sortied being attacked by P-38s (432nd FS) and P-40s (35th FG).

CPO Takeo Okumura was subsequently recommended for a double rank promotion due to his distinguished record, but this was never realised. Four of his victories from the China War were officially recognised, and it is said he achieved roughly 50 victories in the Solomons.

Warrant Officer Masaaki Shimakawa

Masaaki Shimakawa holds the distinction of being the top surviving JNAF ace of his native Tokushima Prefecture. Born in December 1921 as the youngest of five brothers, he joined the Sasebo Marines on 1 June 1939, thus realising his boyhood dream. This same dream quickly turned to harsh reality, however, for as a lowly enlisted man, Shimakawa was treated very poorly, being constantly hit. His contempt for officers grew.

Shimakawa decided to become an aviator, completing carrier fighter training in August 1940 and receiving an assignment to the Oita AG, followed in October 1941 by a posting the newly-formed Tainan AG.

On the opening day of the Pacific War, Shimakawa was the third wingman in the trio of Gitaro Miyazaki and Toshio Ota, both of whom went on to become distinguished aces. The Tainan and 3rd AGs combined to attack airfields in the Philippines, and during his baptism of fire, he claimed a P-35 over Del Carmen.

The Tainan AG then became involved in an 'air extermination' campaign over the Dutch East Indies, Shimakawa flying as wingman to Saburo Sakai. On 28 February 1942 he sortied with Sakai and witnessed his mentor shoot down a F2A Buffalo with miraculous skill, resolving at the same time to learn from this master. The young novice firmly believed that the export version of the Buffaloes (B-339Bs) were flown tenaciously by the Dutch, holding their own against the Zeroes of the Tainan AG.

When the group left for Rabaul in April 1942, Shimakawa was assigned to the 6th AG, boarding the carrier *Kaga*. During the Battle of Midway, he was thrown from the deck of his carrier into the sea as it sank, and while many of his comrades were sucked downed with the doomed vessel, he managed to survive – the 6th AG was virtually wiped out at Midway.

Reformed in Japan as part of the 204th AG, the survivors of the 6th were sent to the Solomons in August 1942. Flying from Bougainville, Shimakawa was involved in many fierce contests, as later recounted;

'The F4Fs at Guadalcanal were extremely tough fellows. We were confident in our skills and we were evenly matched. Our biggest enemies were long-range missions and bad weather. Many pilots lost their lives to stupid operational causes and not to enemy pilots.'

On 11 January 1943 Shimakawa and seven comrades attacked Wildcats of VMF-121 out of the sun over Guadalcanal, the Zero pilots overwhelming their counterparts in the F4Fs and forcing them into a

WO Nobuo Ogiya of the 204th AG was an expert marksman, and during one 18-day period he downed 13 enemy aircraft to set a naval record (*Y Izawa*)

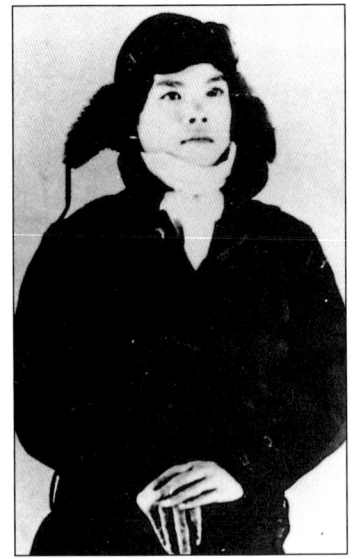

PO Masaaki Shimakawa survived the sinking of his carrier *Kaga* during the battle of Midway. Having dodged enemy bullets and shot down eight fighters, he then fell victim to a malaria-carrying mosquito (*Maru*)

protective Lufbery circle. Upon seeing his comrades in trouble, Marine Gunner Ed Zielinski joined the circle in the opposite direction, scattering the Zeroes, and saving his comrades' lives.

During this radical manoeuvre Zielinski's F4F was damaged, and he now found himself alone, trying to nurse his crippled fighter back to base. After thoroughly scanning his instrument panel to check on his engine's vital signs, he glanced back out of his cockpit and was horrified to see a Zero flying on his wing! Its pilot made no attempt to attack the American, although the latter was rather unnerved by his opponent's stare. As the American contemplated ramming the Zero in order to bring the uneven contest to a swift end, the A6M suddenly dove down, looped in front of the Wildcat and repositioned itself on the Marine's tail – but did not fire. The Zero repeated this manoeuvre and the American pressed his gun button as the fighter looped in front of him. The guns remained silent, however, as the Zero completed its roll and was last seen heading for Munda. When asked about this incident many years later, Shimakawa responded, 'It could have been me, but I don't remember it quite like that'.

In a classic example of overclaiming, in the wake of this memorable encounter, the Zero pilots were credited with 18 victories for just one loss, whilst the Marines claimed ten kills and one probable for a single Wildcat shot down – Shimakawa added two victories to his tally.

While at Bougainville, Shimakawa was stricken down with a severe case of malaria and subsequently sent back to Japan aboard a hospital ship in March 1943. After his recovery, he became an instructor with the Omura AG and served with various units until war's end.

Masaaki Shimakawa downed eight aircraft and assisted, or shared, in the destruction of another 12-13. He passed away on 25 September 1997.

Ensign Shigetoshi Kudo

Shigetoshi Kudo was a pioneer nightfighter pilot in the JNAF who helped formulate effective techniques to counter bombers in the South Pacific.

Born into a farming family in February 1920 in Oita Prefecture, he joined the navy in 1937. Kudo's path to becoming a premier fighter pilot was unspectacular, for his first role in the JNAF was as a mechanic. Switching to flying, he trained as a reconnaissance pilot and in October 1941 was assigned to the Tainan AG, with whom he duly saw combat in both the Philippines and Dutch East Indies.

During the early morning of 29 August 1942, B-17s from Port Moresby raided Rabaul, and somehow Kudo managed to get above the the formation in his C5M Type 98 'Babs' recce aircraft and claim a bomber destroyed and a second as a probable thanks to the use of an aerial burst bomb. These night raids were designed to rob the Japanese defenders of much-needed sleep, rather than to destroy important targets (bombing accuracy was minimal). Allied bomber crews considered such sorties as 'milk runs', because anti-aircraft fire was inaccurate and there were no nightfighters in-theatre.

Rabaul's first effective nocturnal fighter was the J1N1 Gekko ('Irving') fast twin-engined long-range recce aircraft. It was equipped with a pair of upward and downward firing 20 mm cannon, which were initially deemed as being ridiculous by staff officers at Naval GHQ and fiercely

Rabaul's 'King of the Night', PO1/c Shigetoshi Kudo, poses with a ceremonial sword and citation from VAdm Jinichi Kusaka in July 1943. His pioneering efforts against four-engined bombers over Rabaul helped the JNAF formulate night-fighting tactics that were later flown against B-29s over Japan (*K Osuo*)

131

CPO Yoshimi Hidaka of the 204th AG was also an escort pilots on the Adm Yamamoto mission. He claimed one P-38 probable during this sortie and was subsequently killed on 7 June 1943 over the Russells. He had claimed 20 victories by the time of his death (*Maru*)

The 253rd AG personnel pose for a group shot at Tobera Airfield, Rabaul, in February 1944. Three of the JNAF's top aces are sitting in the second row, namely Sadamu Komachi (second from right), Shigeo Fukumoto (third from right) and Tetsuzo Iwamoto (fourth from right). The unit began pulling out to Truk soon after this photo was taken, beginning 20 February 1944. Disabled pilots, along with 12 unserviceable A6Ms, were left behind, leaving Rabaul to its fate (*Y Izawa*)

resisted. Cdr Yasuna Kozono, deputy commander of the Tainan AG and instigator of the weapons fitment, persisted with the arrangement, however, and when the first Gekko arrived at Rabaul on 10 May 1943, CPO Shigetoshi Kudo was ordered to go and test it in combat.

Eleven days later, at 0320, Kudo scored the first Gekko nightfighter victory over Rabaul after he and observer Lt(jg) Akira Sugawara encountered B-17E 41-9244 of the 64th BS, flown by Maj Paul Williams, at 0320. Slipping beneath the Flying Fortress undetected, Kudo raked the undersides of the bomber with devastating effect. 'I heard one dull explosion, then a series of smaller ones. The ship wrenched to the left and shuddered . . .' sole survivor M/Sgt Gordon Manuel later recalled.

More was yet to come before daybreak, however, for Kudo and Sugawara found another B-17 at 0408, although they failed to get into an effective firing position. Twenty minutes later, he manoeuvred his aircraft beneath a second 64th BS B-17 (41-9011) and sent it down in flames. CPO Kudo had expended 178 rounds in destroying two B-17s. Cdr Kozono's 'wild scheme' had been fully validated.

During the course of June, CPO Kudo destroyed a total of five B-17s at night, with a sortie on 26 June resulting in a double victory – the sole survivor from either crew was 2Lt Jose Holguin from B-17 (41-2430) of the 65th BS, who parachuted into Japanese territory and was made a PoW.

Kudo's last recognised night kill occurred on 7 July 1943 when he downed a Hudson over Buin airfield. The following month the 23-year-old 'night hawk' was awarded a coveted ceremonial sword by Adm Junichi Kusaka, commander of the 11th Air Fleet at Rabaul, in recognition of his distinguished service.

Initially, the Americans believed that their night losses were due to operational reasons, although it wasn't long before they realised that JNAF nightfighters were the culprits. Consequently, the USAAF changed from night to daylight attacks, thus putting the Gekkos out of business. Following this tactical change Kudo returned to Japan in February 1944 and was assigned to the Yokosuka AG. He was severely

PO3/c Hiroshi Shibagaki (centre, third row from bottom) of the 204th AG claimed his first victory on 7 November 1943 at Rabaul. By the time he was killed on 22 January 1944, he had achieved 13 officially recognised aerial victories. Shibagaki was one of the few pilots in this post-Midway flight training class to become an ace (*Y Izawa*)

injured in a landing accident in May 1945 whilst still flying with this group, his wounds effectively ending his war career – in 1960, Kudo died from complications resulting from his old landing injury.

Ens Shigetoshi Kudo achieved nine recognised aerial victories, earning him the moniker of 'King of the Night' for his nocturnal prowess.

Warrant Officer Hideo Watanabe

The Allied counter offensive in the Solomons began taking such a toll of Zero fighter units, and their irreplaceable commanders, that veteran enlisted men such as Hideo Watanabe were forced to step into positions of leadership – a role in which the young pilot performed admirably well.

Born into a farming family in Fukushima Prefecture in June 1920, Watanabe joined the navy at Yokosuka soon after turning 17 and completed his flight training in November 1941. As one of the last pilots trained prior to the outbreak of the pre-Pacific War, Watanabe was posted to the Marshalls-based Chitose AG in March 1942. About a year later he transferred to the 204th AG at Bougainville, seeing much action.

June 1943 proved to be a disastrous month for the 204th, for it lost a number of veteran flight leaders. On the 7th CPO Yoshimi Hidaka (20 victories) and PO1/c Yasuji Okazaki were both killed, whilst PO2/c Kenji

CPO Hideo Watanabe assumed a position of leadership within the 204th AG despite being an enlisted man. For his fighting spirit and distinguished service, he was awarded a ceremonial sword by VAdm Jinichi Kusaka

Veteran fighter pilot WO Shigeo Fukumoto led Rabaul's 'Guerrilla Air Force' of eight Zero fighters after the 253rd AG had retreated to Truk. Having survived the war with an impressive score of 72 victories, he was killed in a road accident in December 1945 (*K Osuo*)

Yanagiya was severely wounded – these three veterans had been a part of the escort for the ill-fated Adm Yamamoto mission. On 16 June another crippling blow was delivered when group leader, Lt Zenjiro Miyano, and Lt(jg) Takeshi Morizaki (squadron leader and Yamamoto mission escort pilot) failed to return. With a lack of qualified officer pilots and a shortage of warrant officers, CPO Watanabe assumed command of the squadron and flew as formation leader.

Watanabe plunged into the enemy formations with as much vigour as his predecessors had done, trying to lead his demoralised pilots through example. This tactic almost cost him his life, however. In the late afternoon of 26 August he single-handedly attacked a B-24 which had raided Buin, quickly shooting it down – he also claimed a Wildcat (none were involved in this combat). Escorting the Liberators on this day were F4U Corsairs from VMF-214 and -215, these aircraft engaging the Zeroes soon after Watanabe's audacious attack. The JNAF ace was hit hard by a Corsair that manoeuvred in behind him, a fragment from a .50 cal round striking him in the back of the head and exiting through his right eye.

In order to shake of his assailant, the wounded pilot violently threw his Zero into a dive, only pulling up at wave top height. Despite his injuries Watanabe somehow made it back to base and carried out a safe landing. While recovering in the hospital at Rabaul, Adm Junichi Kusaka, CO of the 11th Air Fleet, honoured the young aviator with a ceremonial sword for distinguished service. He duly returned to Japan by ship for further hospitalisation, and in June 1945 he was posted to the 1081st Transport Group.

Hideo Watanabe was officially credited with 16 victories. He now resides in Fukushima Prefecture.

Japan's Asahi Newspaper sent a reporter to Rabaul in January 1944 to interview pilots, but his articles were heavily exaggerated so as to minimise the tremendous losses being suffered by the JNAF. The pilots in this view are, from left to right, Takashi Kaneko, Masajiro Kawato, the reporter and Yoshinobu Ikeda (*Y Ikeda*)

Warrant Officer Ryoji Ohara

Ryoji Ohara gained considerable combat experience in the Solomons fighting F4U Corsairs – and lived to tell the tale. Born in Miyagi Prefecture in February 1921, he joined the navy as soon as he was old enough, and subsequently graduated from flight training in July 1942.

Ohara was sent to the 6th AG base at Buin in October as a replacement pilot, recording his first victory on 23 October 1942 when his unit fought ten Wildcats of VMF-212 over Guadalcanal (no US aircraft were lost).

On 13 May 1943 Ohara was flying as wingman to air group leader Lt Zenjiro Miyano when a combined force of 54 Zeroes attacked Marine F4Us over the Russel Islands. Diving out of the sun from 24,000 ft, the JNAF pilots bounced the flight of five VMF-124 Corsairs, which were circling at 20,000 ft. Ohara managed to shoot down the Marine's leader, Maj William Gise, on his first pass before a wild dogfight ensued.

Upon disengaging from the battle, Ohara became separated from his flight, and was set upon by two Corsairs. One of his opponents was 1Lt William Cannon, who chased Ohara half way to New Georgia Island, before the Japanese pilot chose to fight for his survival. On a desperate counterattacking manoeuvre, Ohara fired on his pursuers and claimed one destroyed – Cannon's Corsair was holed three times by 20 mm rounds but still made it home. Having seen off his attackers, Ohara was forced to make an emergency landing at Kolombangara Island, where he counted 38 bullet holes in his Zero.

Ohara fought with distinction with the 204th AG before returning to Japan and joining the Yokosuka AG. He subsequently flew home defence missions until 17 August 1945, his last sortie seeing him engage photo-recce B-32 Dominators over Tokyo.

Dubbed the 'Killer of Rabaul', WO Ryoji Ohara claimed 48 kills. After the war he joined the Japanese Self-Defence Air Force, before running a simulator school for airline pilots. Now fully retired, he lives in Tokyo.

Lieutenant Zenjiro Miyano

Zenjiro Miyano was the great leader of the 204th AG whose innovative ideas – he was the first JNAF pilot to adopt the effective 'fighter four' formation – and leadership skills remain revered to this day.

He was born in Osaka and entered the Navy Academy with the 65th Class, graduating from flight training in April 1940.

As a member of the 12th AG, Miyano was posted to the China War, but arrived too late to see combat. He subsequently became a division officer in the 3rd AG and participated in the raid on Luzon on the first day of the Pacific War. During this sortie he claimed his first aerial victory.

When the 3rd AG moved into the Dutch East Indies, Miyano continued to fly combat air patrols. On 3 March 1942 he led his Zeroes on a long-range attack against the Western Australian port town of Broome, destroying 22 aircraft (predominantly flying boats full of Dutch evacuees) and numerous installations and vehicles.

While returning to base with his two wingmen, Miyano encountered a Dutch DC-3 flown by Capt Ivan Smirnoff, Russia's second highest scoring ace (with 12 victories) of World War 1. The Dakota was packed with military personnel, and their families, fleeing Bandung, on Java, for the safety of Australia. The three Zeroes fired repeatedly at the transport, and although Smirnoff was wounded in the attack, he still managed to crash land the damaged aircraft on a beach. Prior to take-off, Smirnoff had been entrusted with a small sealed box containing a fortune in jewels, and this was accidentally lost in the water during the evacuation of the aircraft. Some of its contents was later recovered over the next few years.

The following month the 6th AG was organised, with Lt Miyano as its division officer. Embarked on the carrier *Junyo*, Miyano and his men headed for the Aleutians, with plans to assault Midway after the completion of their initial task. On 3 June Miyano led a six-Zero escort for 'Val' dive-bombers as part of a multi-carrier attack force sent to strike at Dutch Harbor. The following day at around 1800 hours, Miyano led his Zeroes back to the target, although this time P-40Es from the USAAF 11th FS opposed the strike. The Japanese were credited with six Warhawks destroyed while the Americans claimed a Zero and three 'Vals'. The *Junyo*

WO Ryoji Ohara was known to his comrades as the 'Killer of Rabaul'. He held his own against the dreaded F4U Corsairs in wild dogfights across the Solomons, one of his early victims being Maj William Gise, CO of VMF-124 (*Maru*)

Lt Zenjiro Miyano was the first JNAF pilot to adopt the effective four-fighter flight formation used by the Americans. Under his leadership, his unit claimed over 200 victories (*Maru*)

failed to participate in the Battle of Midway, surviving the disaster to return to port on 24 June.

Due to the fierce counterattack by Allied forces in the Solomons, an immediate need for both fighters and pilots was conveyed to the Naval High Command, and on 7 October 1942 Lt Miyano led 27 Zeroes (along with equipment and ground personnel) aboard the carrier *Zuiho*, bound for Rabaul. Once fully assembled on land, the unit moved to their forward base at Buin, where the 6th AG was reorganised into the 204th AG.

Once in the frontline, Lt Miyano immediately set about analysing American fighter tactics and devising his own countering manoeuvres, which included copying the USAAC's successful four-aircraft flight formation and developing new fighter-bombing tactics. In March 1943 Miyano became group leader, and while most officers were inexperienced and relied on enlisted men to insure their survival, he was always in the lead, setting an example to others (claiming many kills in the process).

On 16 June 1943 Miyano's luck ran out, for he was shot down and killed while escorting dive-bombers sent to attack enemy positions at Lunga. His score stood at 16 at the time of his death.

The Naval All Units Proclamation No 72, issued in conjunction with a posthumous double promotion to the rank of commander, stated that Lt Miyano's unit had destroyed 228 aircraft in the air and damaged 76.

Lieutenant Chitoshi Isozaki

Chitoshi Isozaki was one of the 'grand old men' of the navy's fighter force, having seen frontline service for over 13 years. Widely respected throughout the ranks, he had the rare distinction of attaining officer status from his humble beginnings as a seaman recruit.

Isozaki was born on 12 January 1913 in Aichi Prefecture, and after graduation from middle school, he joined the navy. Entered flight training in October 1932, he graduated in March of the following year and then served as a flight instructor. One of his pupils during this tuitional phase in his career was the renowned ace Saburo Sakai.

When the China War erupted in 1937, Isozaki flew combat missions from the carrier *Ryujo* and *Kaga*. At the end of 1939, he was posted to the 12th AG and engaged in further combats, but scored no victories.

In October 1941, now WO Isozaki was transferred to the Tainan AG and served in the Dutch East Indies, before returning to Japan to serve as an instructor once more at Omura airfield when his former unit was posted to Rabaul.

In April 1943 Isozaki was promoted to the rank of ensign after more than ten years of service. It was rare for enlisted men to reach officer status, and Isozaki's promotion was a testament to his skill and leadership. In the same month, he was ordered to join the 251st AG at Rabaul.

On 16 June 1943 Ens Isozaki recorded his first kill when he fought US and New Zealand fighters over the Russells. By the time he was sent home to Japan in March 1944, he had served with both the 204th and 201st AGs at Bougainville and Rabaul, and achieved close to a dozen victories.

In Japan, Isozaki served briefly with the 302nd AG at Atsugi alongside fellow old timer Ens Sadaaki Akamatsu – they both trained pilots hard, and several veterans credit their survival to these two 'old masters'.

Although Lt Chitoshi Isozaki saw service during the China War, he failed to score his first victory until June 1943. Despite being over-whelmed by the Americans, Isozaki was still able to achieve more than a dozen victories by war's end (*Y Izawa*)

In May 1945 Lt(jg) Isozaki joined the elite 343rd AG, which was equipped exclusively with the Shiden-Kai ('George') fighter. As a division officer in the 301st Squadron, he saw very little combat in the remaining months of the war.

Chitoshi Isozaki logged more than 4000 flight hours during his career. This modest gentleman stated that he never knew exactly what his tally was, but 12+ victories seems to be accurate. As a respected senior member of the 343rd AG and Zero Fighter Pilots Association, he ran a small noodle shop in Matsuyama City until he passed away on 20 June 1993.

This early model A6M2 was abandoned by the Tainan AG at Rabaul in late 1942 after suffering battle damage (*via Aerospace Publishing*)

A single A6M2 (in the foreground) and a quartet of A6M5s (in the background) are seen running up at Buin (Kahili airstrip) in late 1943. These aircraft are 582nd AG (ex-*Zuikaku* AG) aircraft (*via Robert C Mikesh*)

CENTRAL PACIFIC TO THE PHILIPPINES

By mid 1944 the fate of Japan's war effort was sealed as the American naval 'juggernaut' bypassed various enemy strongholds in the South Pacific in their race toward the Philippines. Allied submarines prowled the sea lanes while aircraft bombed and strafed airfields, shipping and supply depots.

As the Allied forces pounded Rabaul, Adm Chester Nimitz led his fleet through the Central Pacific. The pattern adopted by the Americans would see heavy naval bombardment firstly soften up Japanese defences, before Marines, followed by army infantry, stormed the islands. Using such tactics, the Gilbert Islands were under Allied control by the end of November 1943. In the immediate aftermath of invasion, US Navy engineers immediately created airstrips in the Gilberts to enable aircraft to attack the Marshall Islands. The latter subsequently proved difficult for the Japanese to defend, as hundreds of small coral atolls were scattered over 400,000 square miles.

Pilots prepare to climb into their fuelled and armed up A6M5cs somewhere in the Philippines in 1944 (*via Aerospace Publishing*)

With his Sakae 21 throbbing away in front of him, and his silk scarf ballooning out around his neck as the slipstream builds up with the increased acceleration of the fighter, an anonymous A6M5 pilot takes off to do battle with superior Allied forces perhaps for the last time (*via Aerospace Publishing*)

The 252nd AG had been providing a modicum of air defence for the Marshalls from their bases on Roi and Wake Islands since February 1943, although they had seen very little action until September when B-24s began to raid their airfields. On 5 October 1943, US carrier aircraft attacked Wake Island, with Hellcats from the carriers *Cowpens*, *Essex*, *Lexington* and *Yorktown* overwhelming the 26 Zeroes sent up to oppose the strike – 16 A6Ms failed to return.

When the alarm sounded at Roi, Lt Yuzo Tsukamoto mustered six Zeroes as escorts for seven 'Betty' bombers sent to bolster Wake's defences. Rather than help defend the island, the formation simply became more Hellcat 'fodder' as it was intercepted by navy fighters some 30 miles short of their destination. Only three aircraft, including Tsukamoto's, eventually landed on Wake.

With few aircraft remaining, the 252nd AG tried to counterattack, but were detected by Allied radar and intercepted every time. Although about 30 Zeroes remained on Taroa by December, carrier air raids on the island destroyed most of the fighters on the ground, while the rest were shot down in one-sided dogfights. Their last combat occurred on 29 January, and like most of the preceding engagements, achieved nothing.

The path was now wide open for an assault on the Marianas Islands. Should they fall, Allied forces would then be centrally placed for a direct attack on Japan, the Philippines and New Guinea. JNAF land- and carrier-based aircraft assembled to defend against the anticipated onslaught, and on 11 June 1944 the bombardment of Guam commenced.

On 19 June, Adm Marc Mischer's US Task Force 58 – composed of 18 carriers and over 475 Hellcats – engaged VAdm Jisaburo Ozawa's carrier armada of nine carriers and over 450 aircraft. The Battle of the Philippine Sea was the last time the Imperial Navy possessed enough strength to challenge the US Pacific Fleet. Although strong in numbers, JNAF squadrons were hampered by a lack of co-ordinated battle tactics and well-trained pilots. The end result was the total overwhelming of Japanese formations by swarms of marauding Hellcats, who cut them to ribbons – the aerial massacre was so one-sided that it was dubbed the 'Marianas Turkey Shoot' by participating F6F pilots. The 343rd AG was literally destroyed in this action, being forced to disband on 10 July.

When the smoke had finally cleared from the two-day battle, the Japanese had lost the carriers *Shokaku*, *Taiho* and *Hiyo*, and suffered crippling damage to the *Zuikaku* and *Chiyoda*. Also lost were over 300 aircraft and veteran pilots and aircrews. This was Japan's worst military disaster to date, and it effectively 'broke the back' of the JNAF in the Pacific.

RAdm Joseph Clark, commanding TF58.1, now headed for another show down at Iwo Jima.

This underside view of an A6M5 Zeke 52 reveals the staple JNAF fighter in near-perfect planform. The Model 52 was the most prolific of all Zero variants, with over 6000 being built (*via Aerospace Publishing*)

His pilots had scored heavily on 15 June over the island, and they now wanted an encore – the 'Marianas Turkey Shoot' had simply whetted their voracious appetite. Although Iwo Jima was just a tiny volcanic island, its strategic position made it a highly-valued prize, for Zero fighters based there posed a serious threat to B-29s sent to bomb Japan.

The Yokosuka AG was ordered to Iwo Jima in June, arriving during a lull in the bombardment. On the 24th, in their first combat over the island, pilots from the unit – as well as members of the 252nd and 301st AGs – were badly mauled by TF58.1 Hellcats. Over 80 Zeroes had sortied, and only around half had returned.

The second and third combats for Iwo Jima's Zeroes occurred on 3-4 July when, despite heroic efforts by the defenders, the Yokosuka AG lost 22 veteran pilots, including their leader, Lt Sadao Yamaguchi (an accomplished ace with 12 victories). American warships later destroyed many aircraft on the airfields with their 'big guns', leaving the distinguished Yokosuka AG to become a unit without aircraft. The survivors were evacuated back to the mainland, and the island was abandoned to its fate.

As the US Task Force swept through the Central Pacific, the Japanese prepared for the onslaught by ordering the 1st Air Fleet at Davao, in the Philippines, to stop the Allied advance. This was an impossible task, however, for the fleet's units lacked trained pilots, fuel and aircraft. The VAdm Ozawa's humiliating defeat at the Battle of the Philippine Sea forced the JNAF to adopt desperate measures in their fight with the Allies.

The invasion of the Philippines commenced on 23 October 1944 with troop landings on Leyte. The subsequent naval clash, christened the Battle of Leyte Gulf, saw the demise of Japan's two greatest battleships, the *Yamato* and *Musashi*.

With events going from bad to worse for the Japanese, VAdm Takijiro Onishi – CO of the 1st Air Fleet – gave birth to the dreaded *Kamikaze* Suicide Corps, his radical idea being to equip a Zero fighter with a 250-kg bomb and have volunteers crash themselves into the decks of aircraft carriers. The few remaining 'fighter' Zeroes were to act as escorts to protect the *kamikazes* from prowling enemy aircraft, plus record their results.

'We had no criticism about the *kamikaze* operations because we thought we had to die inevitably', recalled former Zero pilot Masahiro Mitsuda. 'We thought nothing of whether it would be a futile effort or not'.

Even officer pilots like Lt Cdr Iyozoh Fujita (hero at Midway) echoed these sentiments; 'We had few planes and no fuel to train pilots, so we had no other choice'.

With no hope of survival, pilots volunteered in droves for a chance to strike back at the enemy in a wave of hyper patriotism. As a further incentive, those *kamikaze* who died were promised double rank promotions.

The first successful suicide attack occurred on 25 October when bomb-laden Zeroes from the 201st AG sank the escort carrier *St Lo* and damaged six others. The news of this initial success spread like wildfire, renewing the sagging morale of an entire nation.

Allied forces were quick to enact countermeasures, however, with combat air patrols and destroyer pickets serving to insulate the carriers in their first line of defence. Further success therefore became more and more elusive as hundreds sortied into oblivion – the 201st AG wrote their obitu-

Ens Isamu Miyazaki was a chivalrous pilot who spared the life of an opponent flying a badly damaged Hellcat. His unit was destroyed in the Marshall Islands, although he survived, ending the war with 13 victories (*I Miyazaki*)

ary in the Philippines campaign.

Whilst Allied land forces invaded Luzon and became bogged down in ground action, the naval units continued their advance toward Japan.

Ensign Isamu Miyazaki

Isamu Miyazaki once spared the life of an US fighter pilot, which was a chivalrous act totally foreign to the JNAF's philosophy of giving no quarter to the enemy.

Born in Kagawa Prefecture in October 1919, he enlisted in the navy in 1936 and served as a common sailor, before volunteering for fighter training. He completed the course in November 1941, and 12 months later he advanced to Rabaul with the 252nd AG

Ens Saburo Saito scored his first victory on 1 February 1943 – an F4F over Guadalcanal. Later fighting over Rabaul and Bougainville, he destroyed eight enemy aircraft during a one-week period. Saito claimed his final kill on 24 October 1944 east of Luzon, although he was seriously wounded during the same action when he force-landed on the shore of Lamon Bay. Repatriated to Japan, he ended the war with at least 18 victories (*Maru*)

Veteran pilots of the famous Yokosuka AG fought an overwhelming number of Hellcats over Iwo Jima during June and July 1944. The aces seen are; Ryoji Ohara (48 victories, front row, left), Masami Shiga (16 victories, back row, 2nd from left), Tomita Atake (10 victories, 3rd from left), and Kiyoshi Sekiya (11 victories, right) (*Y Izawa*)

Mabalacat Airfield, in the Philippines, is seen on 25 October 1944 as Lt Yukio Seki's *kamikaze* flight, with accompanying escorts, prepares to sortie in the first successful suicide attack carried out against US warships (*Maru*)

The caption for this official US Navy photograph reads, 'A Japanese *kamikaze* pilot taxying his bomb-laden "Zero" fighter to take-off position on a Philippine airfield during the Leyte operations in October-November 1944. His comrades cheer as the plane passes between them' (*via Aerospace Publishing*)

On 12 November Miyazaki was of 30 Zeroes escort 19 torpedo-equipped 'Betty' bombers sent to attack American transports off Lunga Point. Marine pilots of VMF-112 and -121, together with USAAF P-400s, intercepted the Japanese formation and a great dogfight ensued – Miyazaki's first action ended with the destruction of an F4F.

The 252nd AG flew sorties from Rabaul, Ballale (Bougainville), Lae and Munda, during which time Miyazaki gained considerable experience through hard fought battles over the Solomons.

On 1 February 1943 the 252nd was ordered to the Marshall Islands, where the level of combat lessened until the autumn, when American carrier fighters attacked the Gilbert Islands. Miyazaki subsequently fought B-24s which had come to soften up targets for the impending invasion.

On 30 January 1944 Miyazaki fought in his air group's last battle. In his

The great ace WO Hiroyoshi Nishizawa became a reluctant instructor in the mass training of Zero pilots, and he is shown here in 1944 with his trainees. Back in the frontline, he provided the escort on 25 October 1944 for Lt Yukio Seki's *kamikazes*. The following day Nishizawa was shot down and killed in a transport aircraft (*Sakaida*)

Ens Yoshinao Kodaira commenced his combat career in China, and later fought in the Battles of the Coral Sea and the eastern Solomons, and over Guadalcanal. During the Battle of Leyte Gulf he shot down a Hellcat, but on 8 November he was injured in a take-off accident and sent back to Japan. He ended the war with 11 victories (*Sakaida*)

WO Kazuo Sugino first entered combat on 2 November 1943 over Rabaul when he shot down two aircraft He later joined the 634th AG and saw considerable action over Formosa and the Philippines, before ending the war as an instructor for *kamikaze* pilots. In over 495 missions he claimed 32 victories (*Maru*)

A veteran of Rabaul, CPO Takeo Tanimizu (see next chapter for his biography) subsequently served in Formosa with the Tainan AG during the summer and winter of 1944, battling with USAAF B-24s and P-51s. On 3 November 1944 he was shot down by a P-51 over Amoy Harbour, China, and survived with critical burns. Upon his recovery he volunteered for the *kamikaze*s but was rejected (*T Tanimizu*)

This rare photograph shows a training camera attached to the top wing of a veteran A6M2 Zero 21 – this modification was used strictly for tuitional purposes only. Lt Masatake Hayasaki (right) was an instructor pilot in the 256th AG at Lunghwa Airfield, Shanghai, China (*Hayasaki Family*)

second sortie four Zeroes fought an uneven dogfight which saw three of them sustain damage, forcing them to withdraw. Now alone, Miyazaki chanced upon a solitary damaged Hellcat flying 30 metres above the sea, and he tailed the American until satisfied that his opponent could not fight. Flying alongside, he stared at the pilot, who 'had such a pitiful expression on his face', the ace later recalled, that "I didn't have the heart to shoot him down, so I let him go'. Ens Fletcher Jones of VF-10 eventually ditched his fighter, but was drowned.

With the destruction of the 252nd AG, Miyazaki returned to Japan in February as one of only three surviving pilots. In January 1945 he joined the elite 343rd AG, flying home defence sorties until the surrender.

Isamu Miyazaki achieved at least 13 victories.

Lieutenant Commander Ayao Shirane

When asked who were the greatest fighter-leaders of the JNAF, Ayao Shirane's name is always mentioned, along with Mochifumi Nango and several others. Shirane was born into a prominent family in Tokyo (1916), his father later becoming a cabinet secretary in the Japanese government. He graduated from the Naval Academy at Etajima in the 64th Class.

As a 'deck officer' graduate of the academy, Ens Shirane was given flight training and completed his course in March 1939, becoming a fighter pilot. Posted to the 12th AG in China, he participated in the raid on Chungking on 19 August 1940 when the new Zero fighter made its com-

Lt Ayao Shirane was a respected fighter-leader whose unit introduced the new 'George' fighter into combat against the Americans over the Philippines (*Y Izawa*)

bat debut – Lt Tamotso Yokoyama led a dozen Zeroes on a bomber escort mission, although no enemy fighters were encountered.

On 13 September Lt(jg) Shirane led the 2nd division (six fighters) of 13 Zeroes, commanded by Lt Saburo Shindo, in the Zero fighter's true baptism of fire. After escorting 'Nell' bombers to Hankow, Chinese fighters rose to challenge the Japanese, and in the ensuing one-sided dogfight, the 13 JNAF fighter pilots claimed the destruction of all 27 enemy fighters. Shirane himself accounted for one aircraft destroyed – his first aerial victory. Adm Shigetaro Shimada, CO of the China Area Fleet, later issued a special unit commendation to mark this historic event.

When the Pacific War broke out, Lt Shirane was serving on the carrier *Akagi* as a division officer. Although he did not fly on the Pearl Harbor raid, he did participate in the Battle of Midway in June 1942, when he led 18 'Val' dive-bombers and nine Zero escorts in an attack on Midway Island itself. Upon completion of their task, the Shirane group returned to their carrier to perform combat air patrols over their ship, although they could not prevent the *Akagi* from being attacked by US dive-bombers – the vessel sank that night.

Lt Shirane was then transferred to the carrier *Zuikaku* to assume duties as their division officer. He stayed on in this position, seeing action in the Battle of the Eastern Solomons and the Battle of Santa Cruz, until November 1942, when he was posted to the land-based Yokosuka AG.

In November 1943 Shirane was assigned to the newly-organised 341st AG, this unit having originally be formed to make use of the new Shiden ('George') fighter. However, deliveries were seriously delayed, and it wasn't until February 1944 that the first handful of aircraft arrived just in time for training exercises to commence. In July the air group was split into two squadrons, and Shirane became CO of the 401st. Despite intensive training, the unit experienced numerous setbacks due to the inexperience of its pilots and design defects which plagued the new fighter.

In October Lt Cdr Shirane took his unit to Mabalacat airfield, on Luzon, where they saw immediate action. Attacking enemy forces at Leyte , they suffered heavy casualties at the hands of numerically-superior USAAF fighter groups.

On 24 November 1944 Ayao Shirane was killed in aerial combat with P-38s from the 433rd FS near Ponson Island, on the western coast of Leyte Island. At the time of his death he had nine officially recognised aerial victories to his credit.

Lt Cdr Shirane's superb organisational skills, and his ability to lead the rank and file, endeared him to both his subordinates and superiors.

Ensign Minoru Honda

This young pilot had a miraculous career that even included returning from the 'dead'! Honda credited his wartime survival to the following three rules: 1) don't be over anxious for a kill; 2) know how and when to escape; and 3) keep nervous, be alert and spot the enemy first.

Minoru Honda was born in Kumamoto Prefecture in 1923, enlisting in the navy and entering flight training in October 1939. Whilst still under instruction he nearly killed himself when his aircraft became entangled with a target tow. He had vowed to hit his target at whatever cost due

Ens Minoru Honda suffered a great indignity at the hands of his superiors when he returned alive from a mission after being declared killed. He harboured a passionate hatred for the officer class, and also voiced his opposition to the *kamikaze* suicide attacks (*Y Izawa*)

to his prior inferior performance, and luckily for him, the target fell away at the last moment and his life was spared, although he subsequently received a severe reprimand from his superiors.

In April 1942 Honda was assigned to the Kanoya AG, his first combat occurring when he and his flight of eight intercepted nine RAF Buffaloes over Singapore. In his excitement at seeing the enemy, he failed to release his drop tank or fire his guns! In one of the worst displays of aerial combat discipline, Honda remembers, 'we all broke off individually and climbed and dove like wildmen. There wasn't a single kill on either side, and everyone escaped unharmed'. The 19-year-old neophyte with 95 hours of flight time in the Zero duly became separated from the rest during the aerial melee, and was the last to return to base. Another severe reprimand followed.

In September Honda advanced to Rabaul, where he fought in many aerial engagements over eastern New Guinea and the Solomons. During this period he was forced to make an emergency landing on Kolombangara Island, and when approached by a group of curious natives, Honda held up a bag of candy in one hand and a Browning automatic in the other. The natives were friendly, and tended to his needs for ten days until he was rescued.

In the meantime, PO1/c Honda had been written off for dead. For distinguished service, he had been given a rare posthumous double promotion, and expecting a hero's welcome on his return, he was once again chastised! His immediate superiors did not want to make a corrections in the casualty report for a lowly enlisted man, so for seven days straight, Honda was ordered to fly long-range combat missions alone into enemy territory in the hope that he would not return alive. Finally, when a senior officer learned of this matter, he was taken off the suicide missions, brought back to 'life', and stripped of his double promotion – such an increase in rank for a living enlisted man would have been unprecedented.

In April 1944 Honda was transferred to Fighter Squadron 407, and later fought in the Philippines. Here, he trained young novices for *kamikaze* attacks, which was a task that left him totally demoralised. Honda bitterly complained to his superiors about the stupidity of using his subordinates as human bombs.

His last assignment was with the elite 343rd AG flying home defence sorties against B-29s attacking southern Japan. Although a strict and unforgiving leader according to his surviving comrades, Honda owed his life to his tough training.

'One of our big problems was that we were educated that mind over might could win a war', Honda stated after the war. 'We fought by spirit while we were told that the Americans were lazy so-and-so's. This was not true. American pilots were very brave and extremely courageous. Yet unlike us, they would not take stupid chances. Our leadership wasn't as flexible as our enemy's. The Americans learned from their mistakes and developed better planes and battle techniques, while we clung religiously to the one-man Zero fighter "lone wolf" approach . . . what a mistake!'

Honda downed at least 17 enemy aircraft, although he estimates that he hit between 40 and 50 before he stopped counting. After the war, he became a test pilot and spent a lot of time in the USA flying the Mitsubishi MU-2.

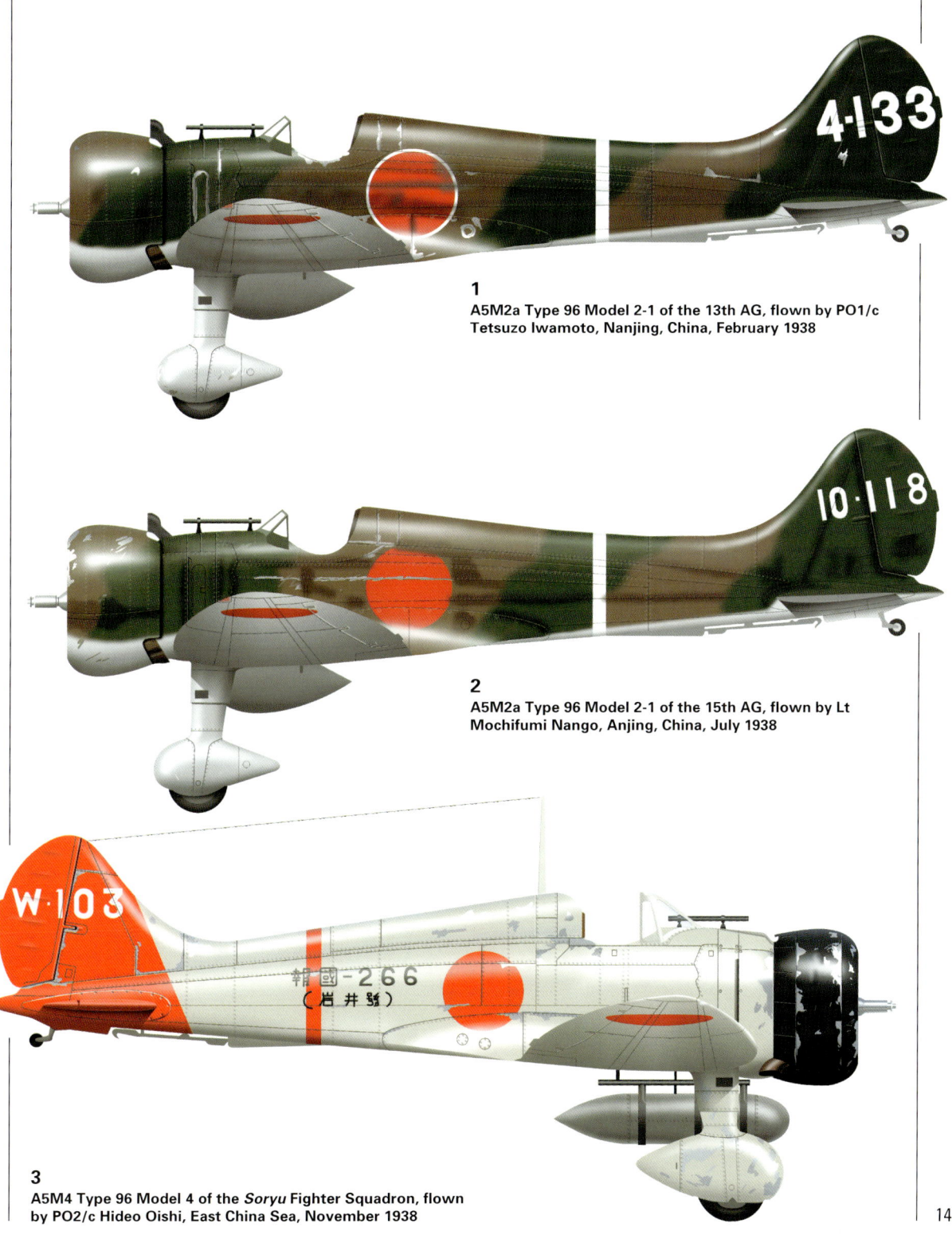

1
A5M2a Type 96 Model 2-1 of the 13th AG, flown by PO1/c
Tetsuzo Iwamoto, Nanjing, China, February 1938

2
A5M2a Type 96 Model 2-1 of the 15th AG, flown by Lt
Mochifumi Nango, Anjing, China, July 1938

3
A5M4 Type 96 Model 4 of the *Soryu* Fighter Squadron, flown
by PO2/c Hideo Oishi, East China Sea, November 1938

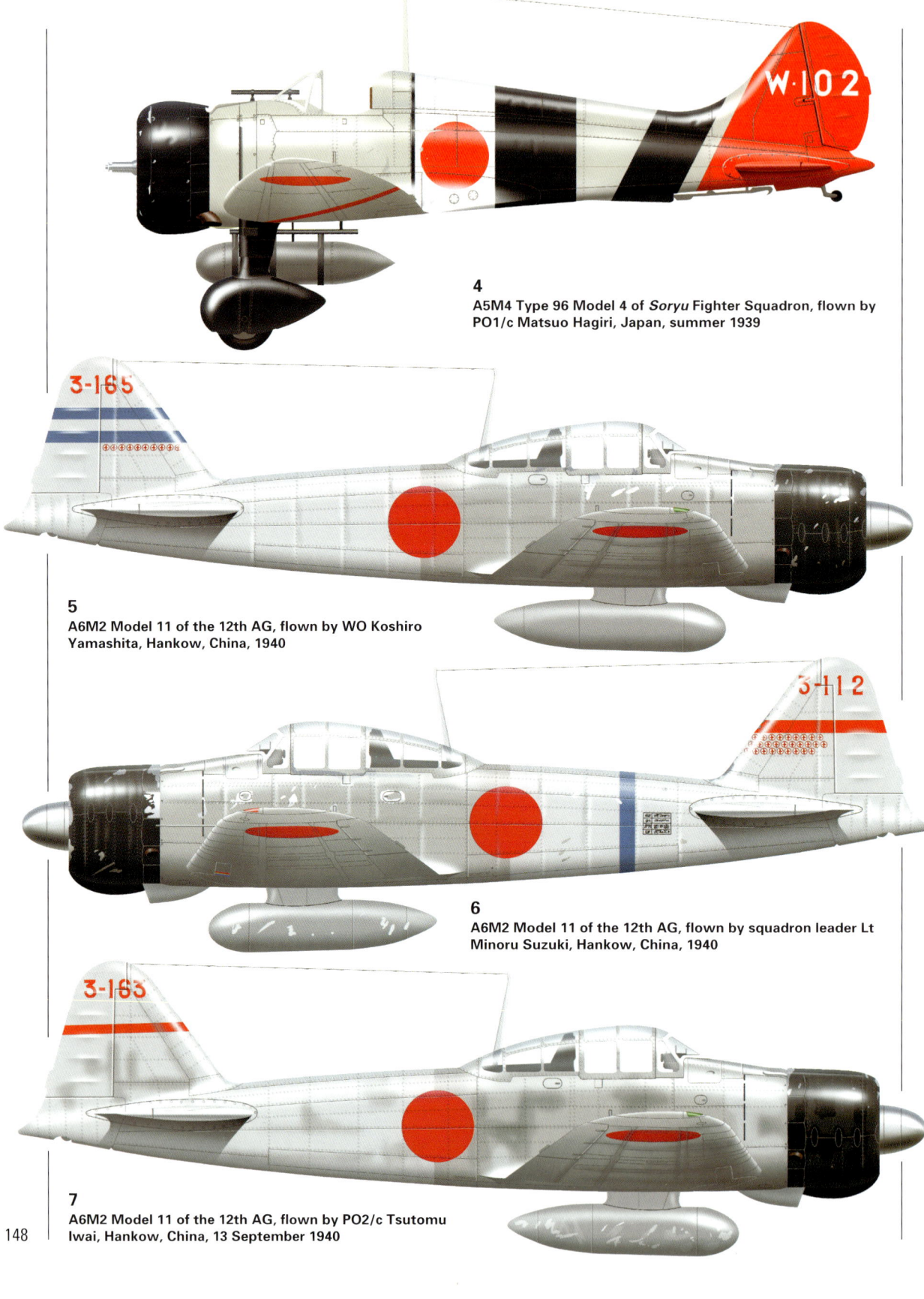

4
A5M4 Type 96 Model 4 of *Soryu* Fighter Squadron, flown by PO1/c Matsuo Hagiri, Japan, summer 1939

5
A6M2 Model 11 of the 12th AG, flown by WO Koshiro Yamashita, Hankow, China, 1940

6
A6M2 Model 11 of the 12th AG, flown by squadron leader Lt Minoru Suzuki, Hankow, China, 1940

7
A6M2 Model 11 of the 12th AG, flown by PO2/c Tsutomu Iwai, Hankow, China, 13 September 1940

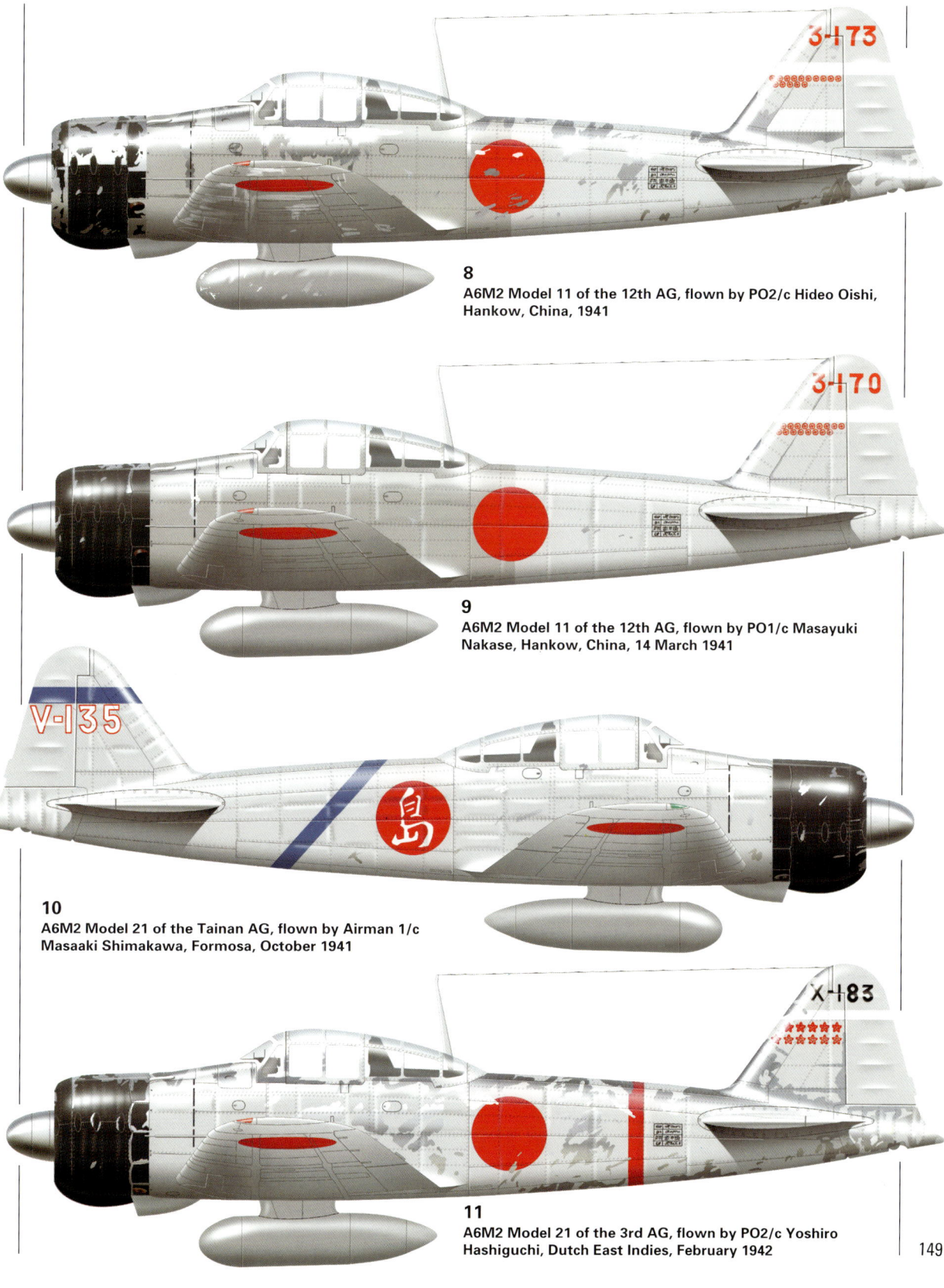

8
A6M2 Model 11 of the 12th AG, flown by PO2/c Hideo Oishi,
Hankow, China, 1941

9
A6M2 Model 11 of the 12th AG, flown by PO1/c Masayuki
Nakase, Hankow, China, 14 March 1941

10
A6M2 Model 21 of the Tainan AG, flown by Airman 1/c
Masaaki Shimakawa, Formosa, October 1941

11
A6M2 Model 21 of the 3rd AG, flown by PO2/c Yoshiro
Hashiguchi, Dutch East Indies, February 1942

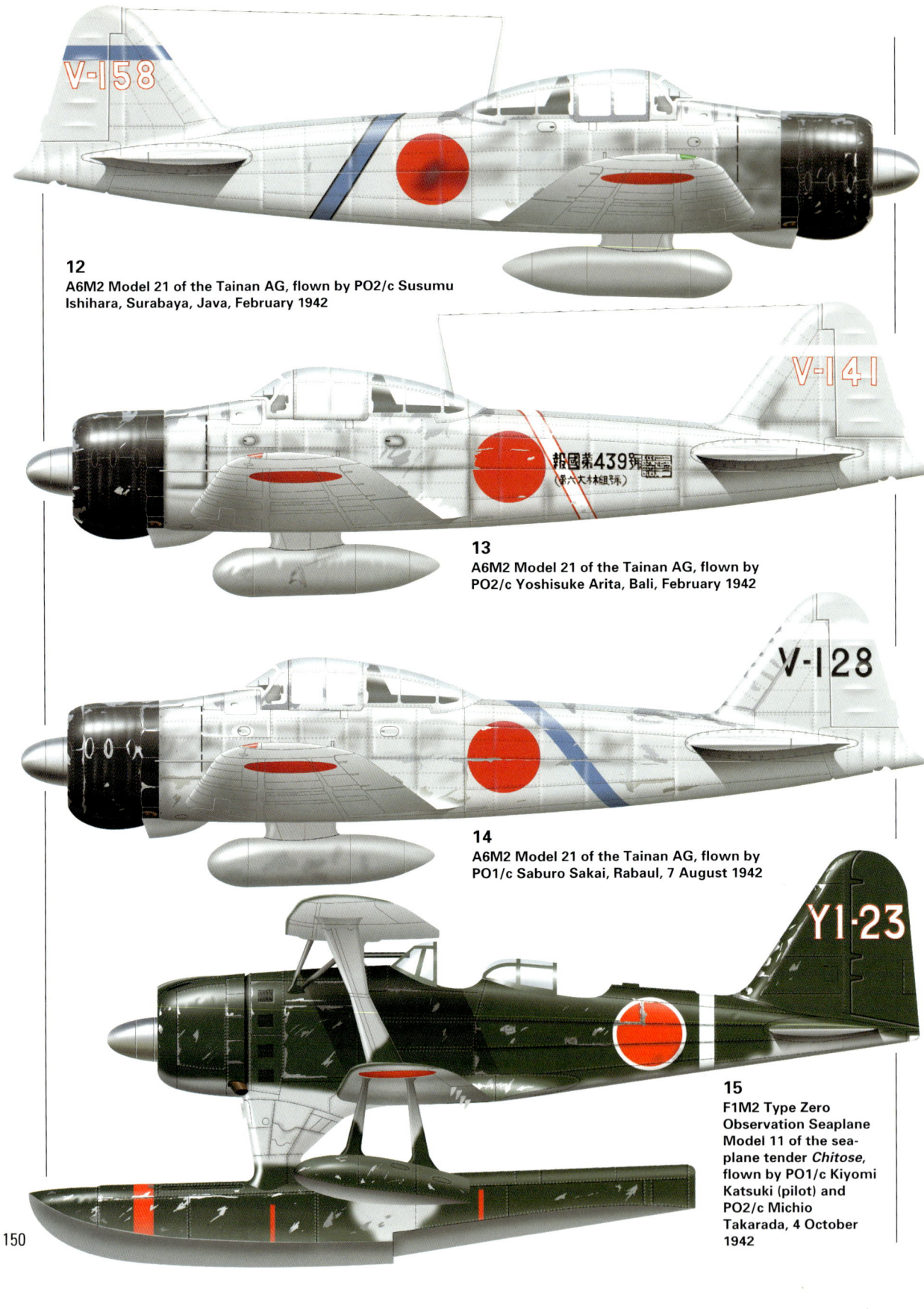

12
A6M2 Model 21 of the Tainan AG, flown by PO2/c Susumu Ishihara, Surabaya, Java, February 1942

13
A6M2 Model 21 of the Tainan AG, flown by PO2/c Yoshisuke Arita, Bali, February 1942

14
A6M2 Model 21 of the Tainan AG, flown by PO1/c Saburo Sakai, Rabaul, 7 August 1942

15
F1M2 Type Zero Observation Seaplane Model 11 of the seaplane tender *Chitose*, flown by PO1/c Kiyomi Katsuki (pilot) and PO2/c Michio Takarada, 4 October 1942

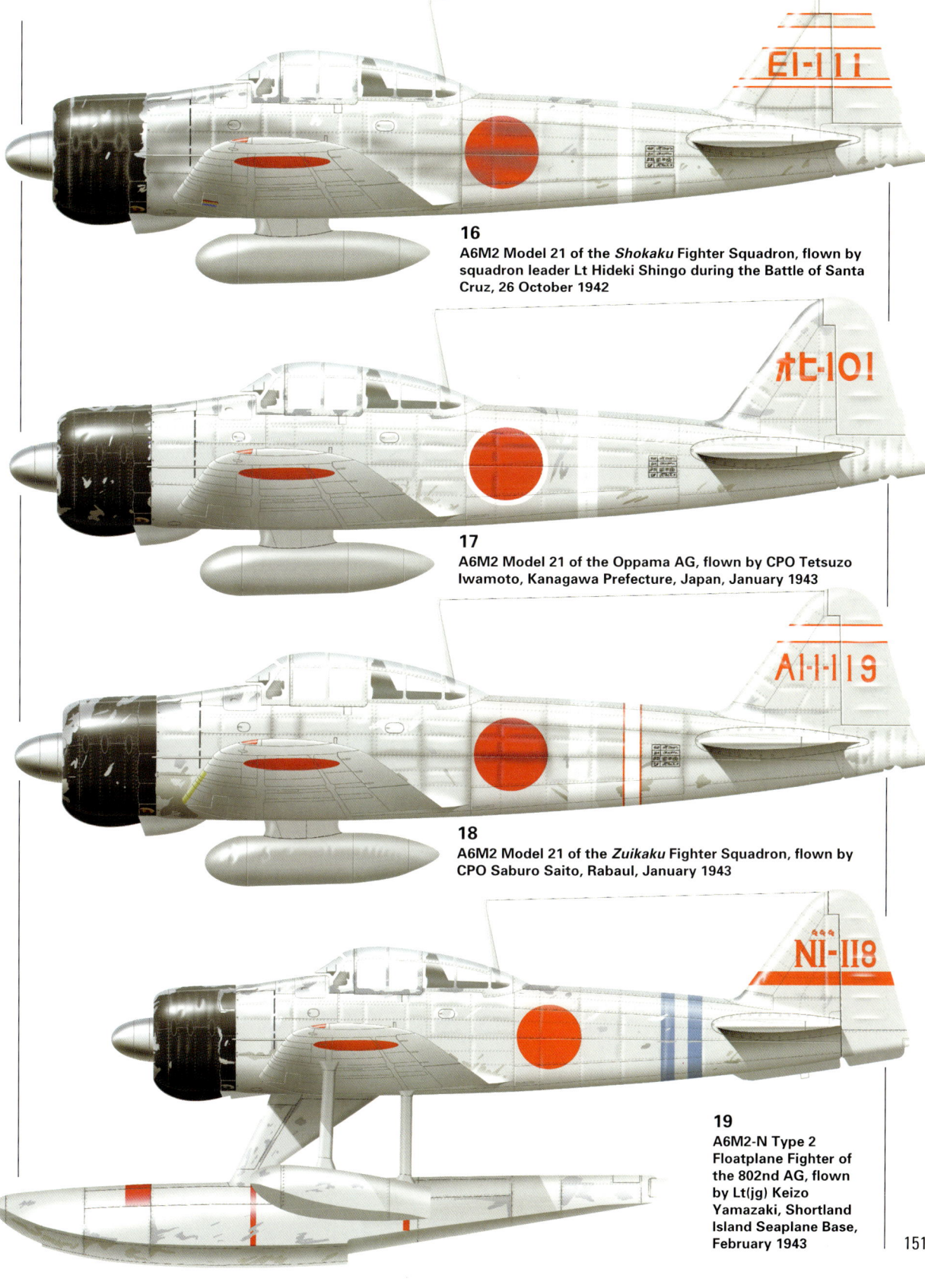

16
A6M2 Model 21 of the *Shokaku* Fighter Squadron, flown by squadron leader Lt Hideki Shingo during the Battle of Santa Cruz, 26 October 1942

17
A6M2 Model 21 of the Oppama AG, flown by CPO Tetsuzo Iwamoto, Kanagawa Prefecture, Japan, January 1943

18
A6M2 Model 21 of the *Zuikaku* Fighter Squadron, flown by CPO Saburo Saito, Rabaul, January 1943

19
A6M2-N Type 2 Floatplane Fighter of the 802nd AG, flown by Lt(jg) Keizo Yamazaki, Shortland Island Seaplane Base, February 1943

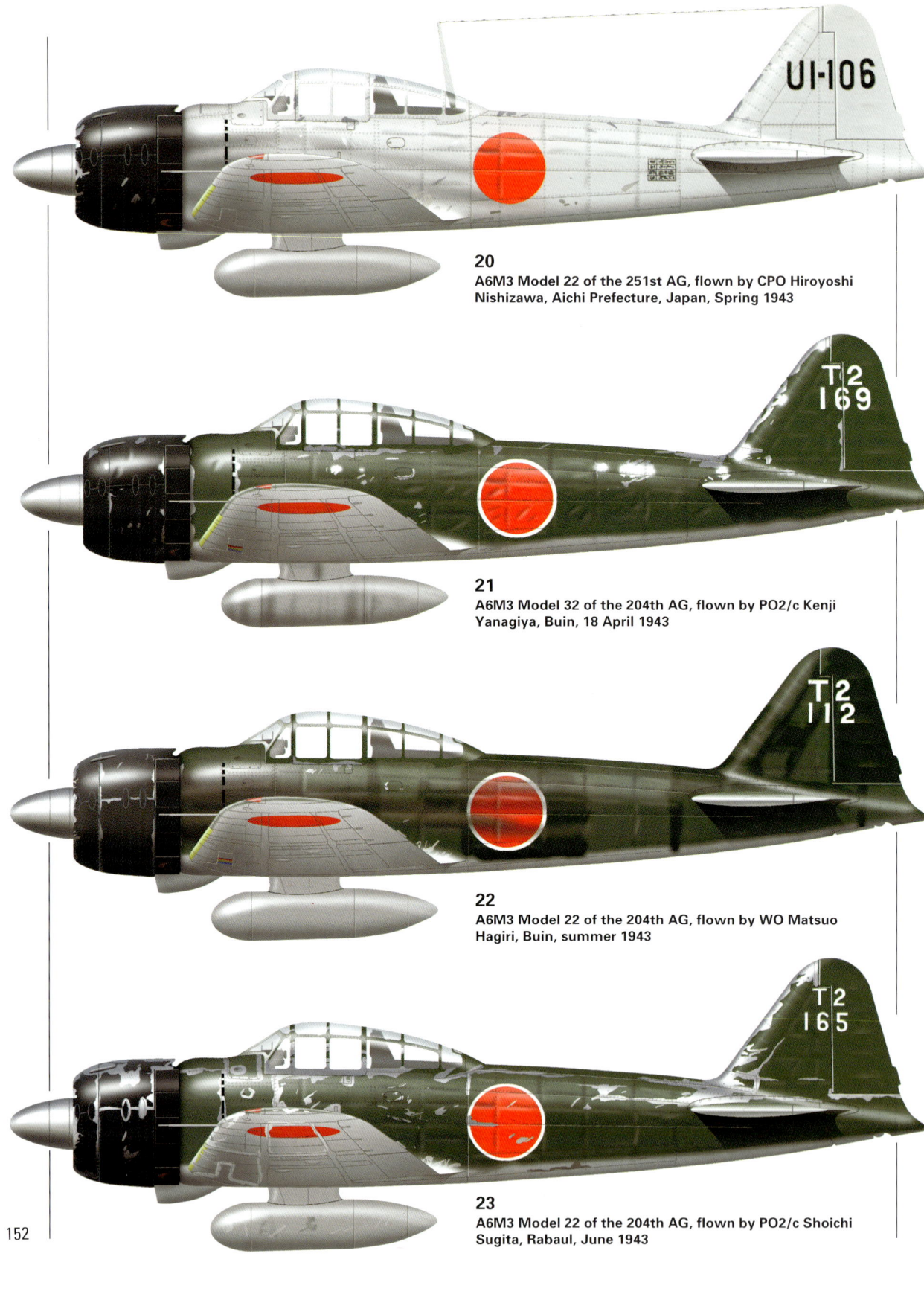

20
A6M3 Model 22 of the 251st AG, flown by CPO Hiroyoshi
Nishizawa, Aichi Prefecture, Japan, Spring 1943

21
A6M3 Model 32 of the 204th AG, flown by PO2/c Kenji
Yanagiya, Buin, 18 April 1943

22
A6M3 Model 22 of the 204th AG, flown by WO Matsuo
Hagiri, Buin, summer 1943

23
A6M3 Model 22 of the 204th AG, flown by PO2/c Shoichi
Sugita, Rabaul, June 1943

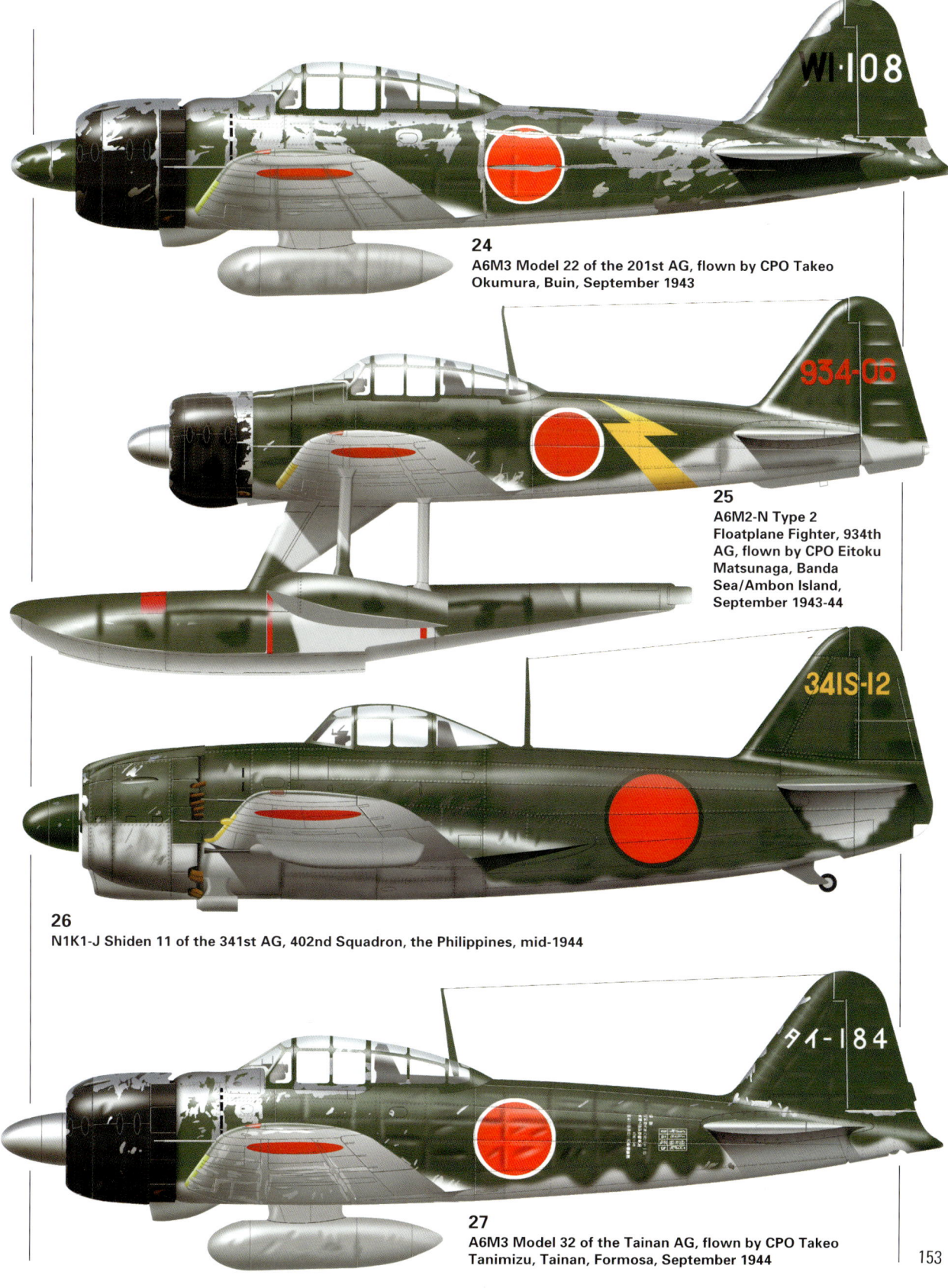

24
A6M3 Model 22 of the 201st AG, flown by CPO Takeo
Okumura, Buin, September 1943

25
A6M2-N Type 2
Floatplane Fighter, 934th
AG, flown by CPO Eitoku
Matsunaga, Banda
Sea/Ambon Island,
September 1943-44

26
N1K1-J Shiden 11 of the 341st AG, 402nd Squadron, the Philippines, mid-1944

27
A6M3 Model 32 of the Tainan AG, flown by CPO Takeo
Tanimizu, Tainan, Formosa, September 1944

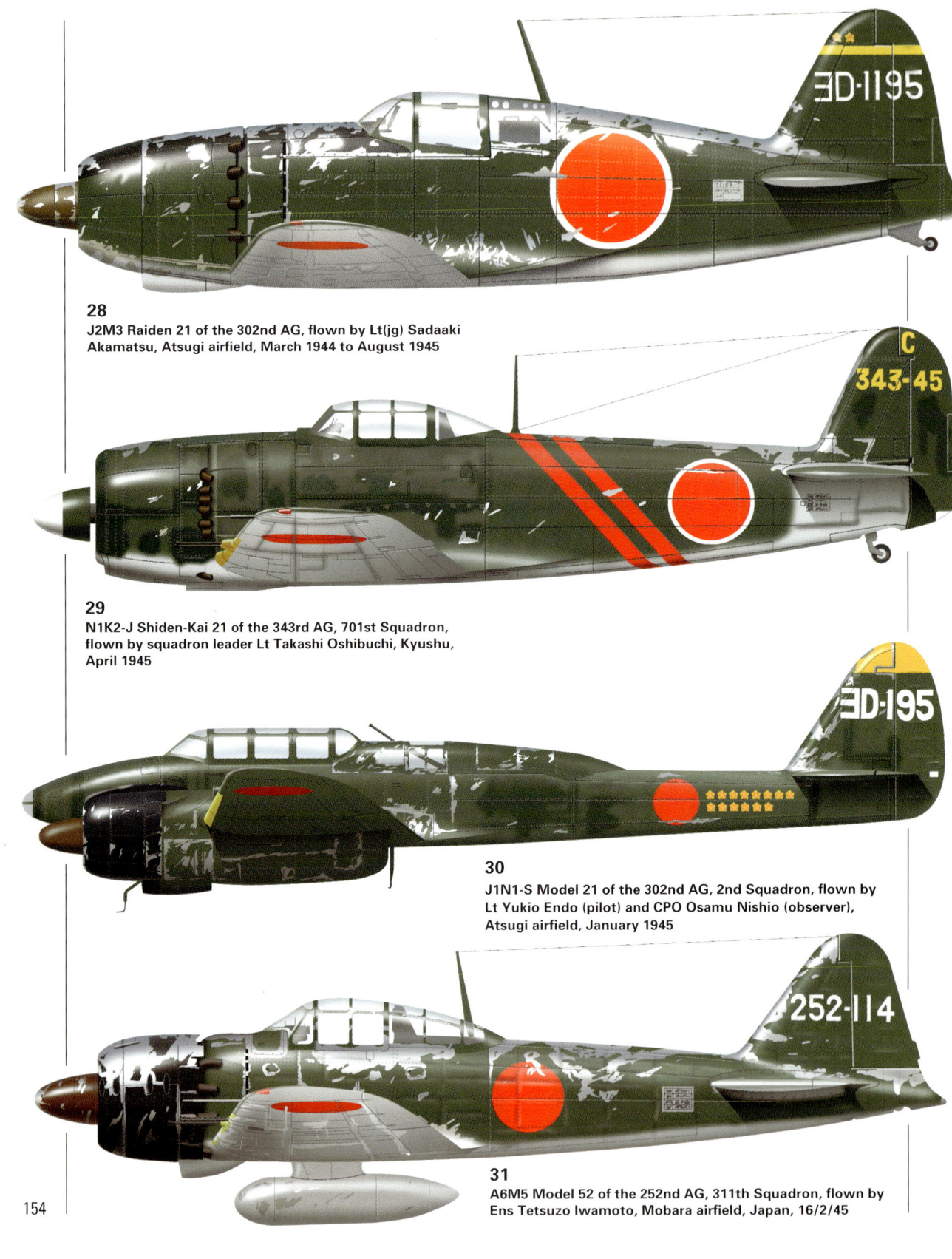

28
J2M3 Raiden 21 of the 302nd AG, flown by Lt(jg) Sadaaki
Akamatsu, Atsugi airfield, March 1944 to August 1945

29
N1K2-J Shiden-Kai 21 of the 343rd AG, 701st Squadron,
flown by squadron leader Lt Takashi Oshibuchi, Kyushu,
April 1945

30
J1N1-S Model 21 of the 302nd AG, 2nd Squadron, flown by
Lt Yukio Endo (pilot) and CPO Osamu Nishio (observer),
Atsugi airfield, January 1945

31
A6M5 Model 52 of the 252nd AG, 311th Squadron, flown by
Ens Tetsuzo Iwamoto, Mobara airfield, Japan, 16/2/45

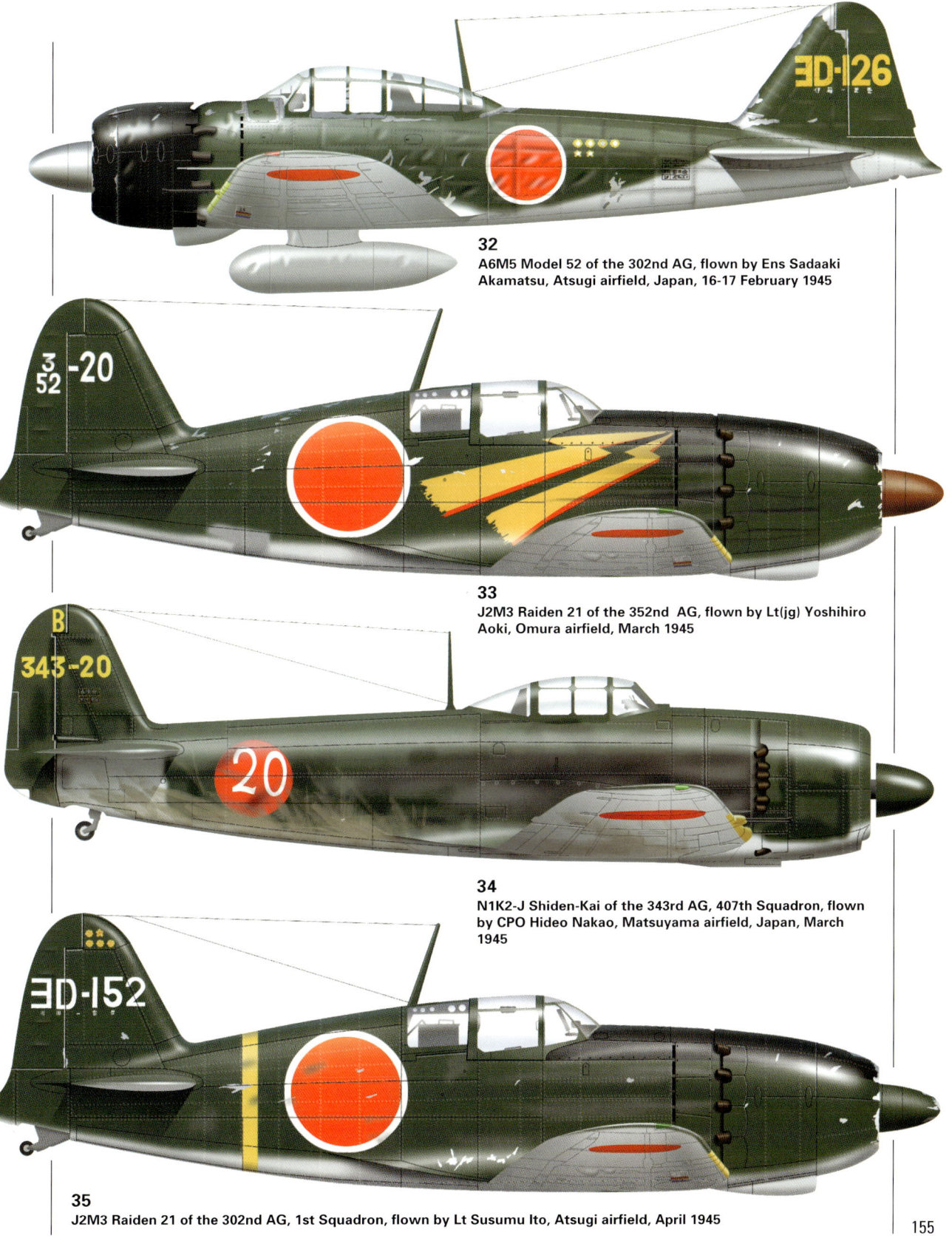

32
A6M5 Model 52 of the 302nd AG, flown by Ens Sadaaki
Akamatsu, Atsugi airfield, Japan, 16-17 February 1945

33
J2M3 Raiden 21 of the 352nd AG, flown by Lt(jg) Yoshihiro
Aoki, Omura airfield, March 1945

34
N1K2-J Shiden-Kai of the 343rd AG, 407th Squadron, flown
by CPO Hideo Nakao, Matsuyama airfield, Japan, March
1945

35
J2M3 Raiden 21 of the 302nd AG, 1st Squadron, flown by Lt Susumu Ito, Atsugi airfield, April 1945

36
N1K2-J Shiden-Kai 21 of the 343rd AG, 301st Squadron,
flown by CPO Katsue Kato, Matsuyama airfield, April 1945

37
J2M3 Raiden 21 of the 332nd AG's Tatsumaki Unit, flown
by WO Susumu Ishihara, Kanoya Air Base, 27 April 1945

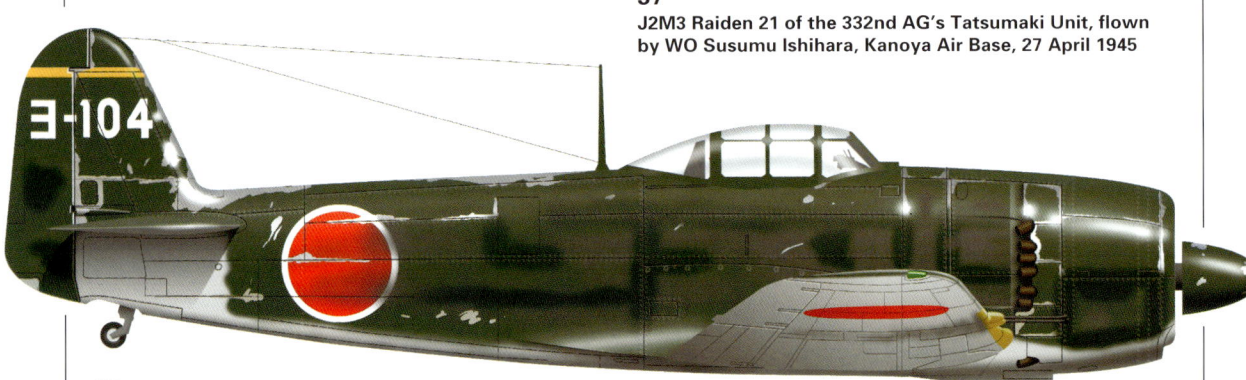

38
N1K2-J Shiden-Kai 21 of the Yokosuka AG, flown by Ens Kaneyoshi Muto, April 1945

39
N1K2-J Shiden-Kai 21 of the 343rd AG, 407th Squadron, flown by WO Isamu Miyazaki, Kyushu, April 1945

40
N1K2-J Shiden-Kai 21 of the 343rd AG, 301st Squadron, flown by squadron leader Lt Naoshi Kanno,
Matsuyama airfield, Japan, April 1945

41
J1N1-S Gekko Model 23 of the Yokosuka AG, 7th Squadron, flown by CPO Juzo Kuramoto (pilot) and Ens Shiro Kurotori
(observer), Yokosuka airfield, May 1945

42
A6M5 Model 52 of the 203rd AG, 303rd Squadron, flown by CPO Takeo Tanimizu, Kagoshima Prefecture, Japan, June
1945

43
A6M7 Model 63 of the 302nd AG, flown by squadron leader Lt Yutaka Morioka, Atsugi airfield, Japan, 3 August 1945

1
PO3/c Sadamu Komachi, serving
aboard *Shokaku* in 1941-42

2
Lt Yutaka Morioka of the 302nd AG at
Atsugi in early 1945

3
PO1/c Takeo Tanimizu, serving
aboard *Junyo* in May 1942

4
Lt(jg) Sadaaki Akamatsu of the 302nd
AG at Atsugi in early 1945

5
PO1/c Kaneyoshi Muto of the 12th
AG, formerly in China, in 1938

6
PO2/c Saburo Sakai of the 12th AG at
Nanchang, in southern China, in 1939

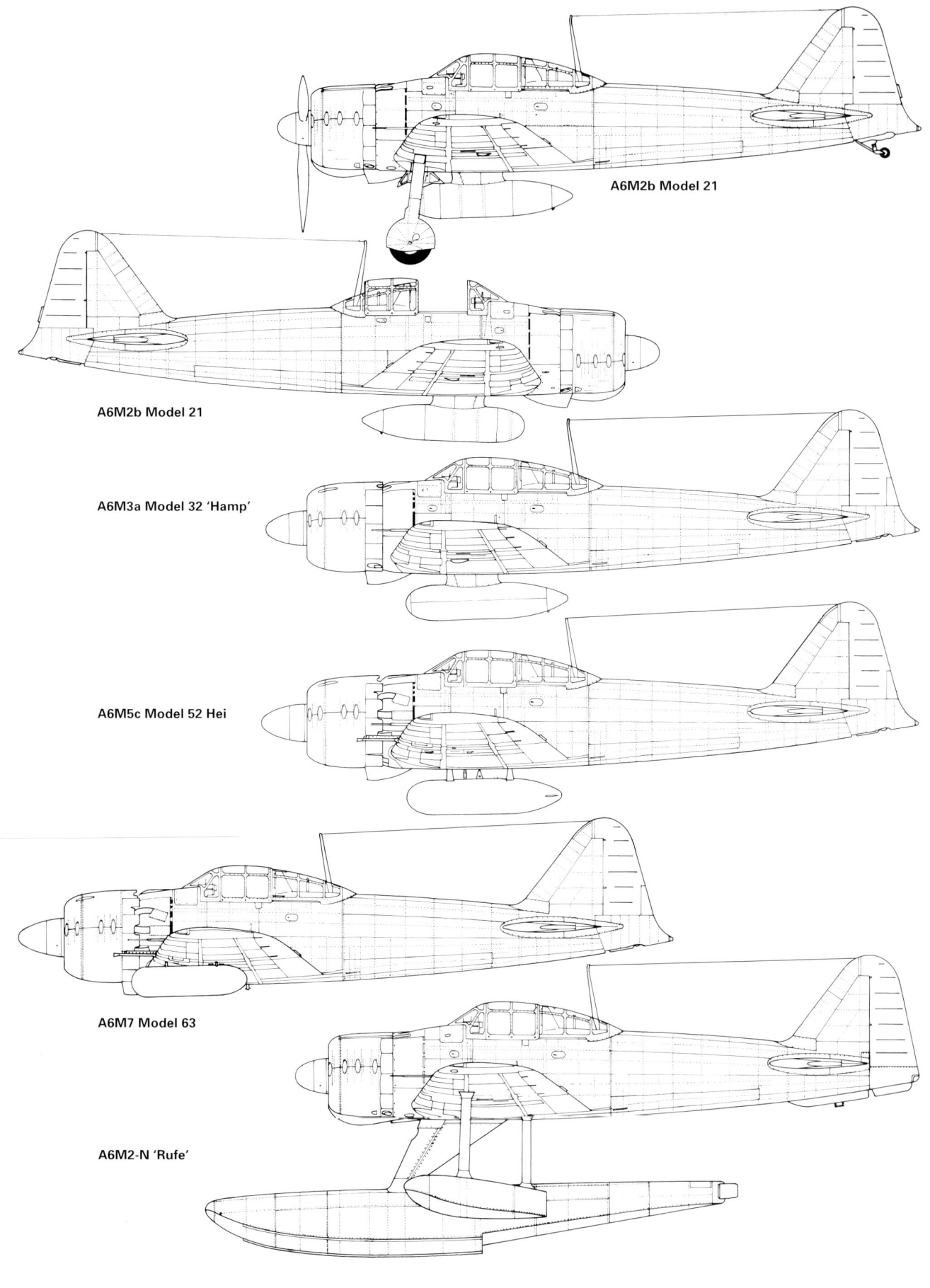

A6M2b Model 21

A6M2b Model 21

A6M3a Model 32 'Hamp'

A6M5c Model 52 Hei

A6M7 Model 63

A6M2-N 'Rufe'

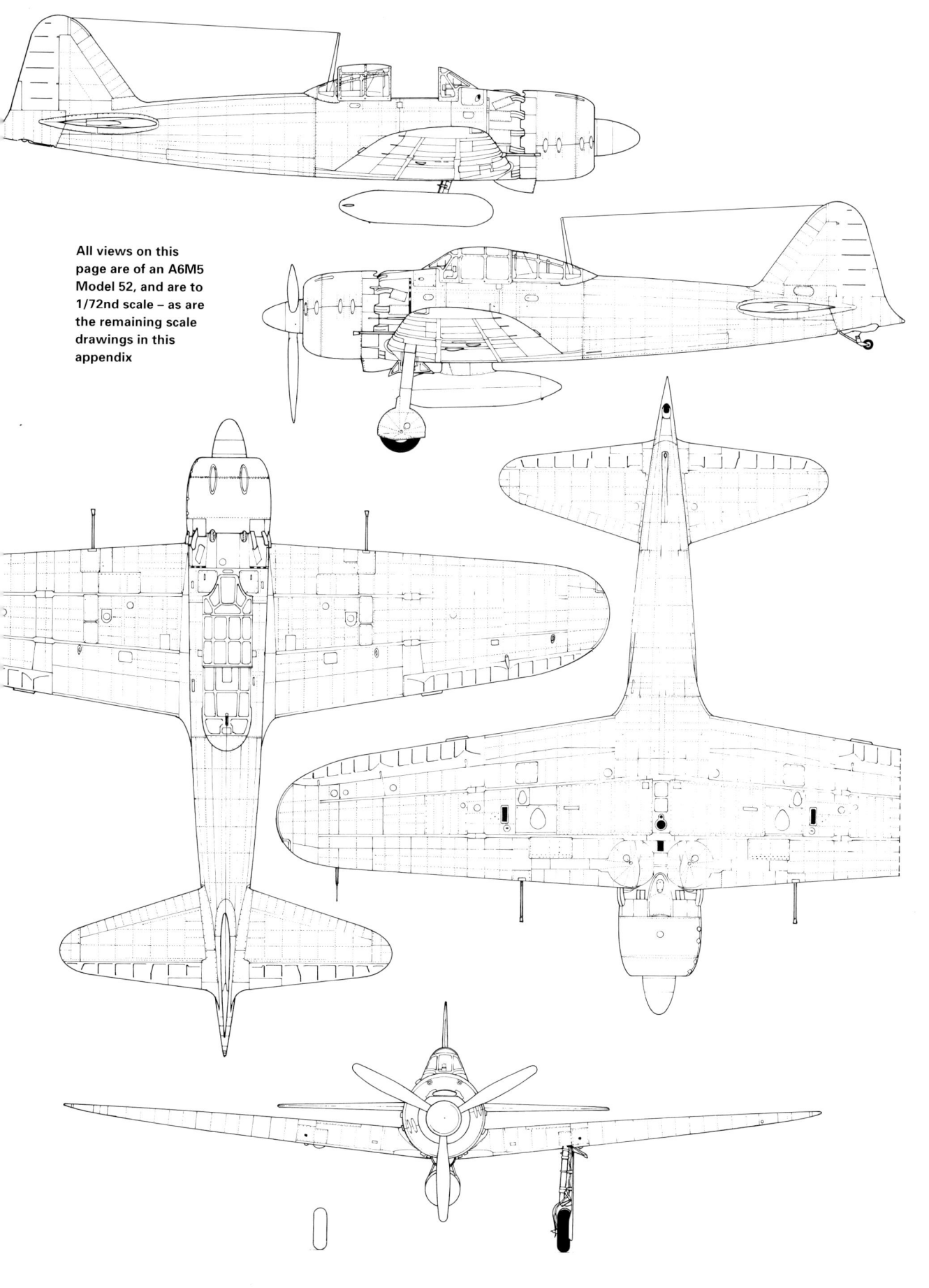

All views on this page are of an A6M5 Model 52, and are to 1/72nd scale – as are the remaining scale drawings in this appendix

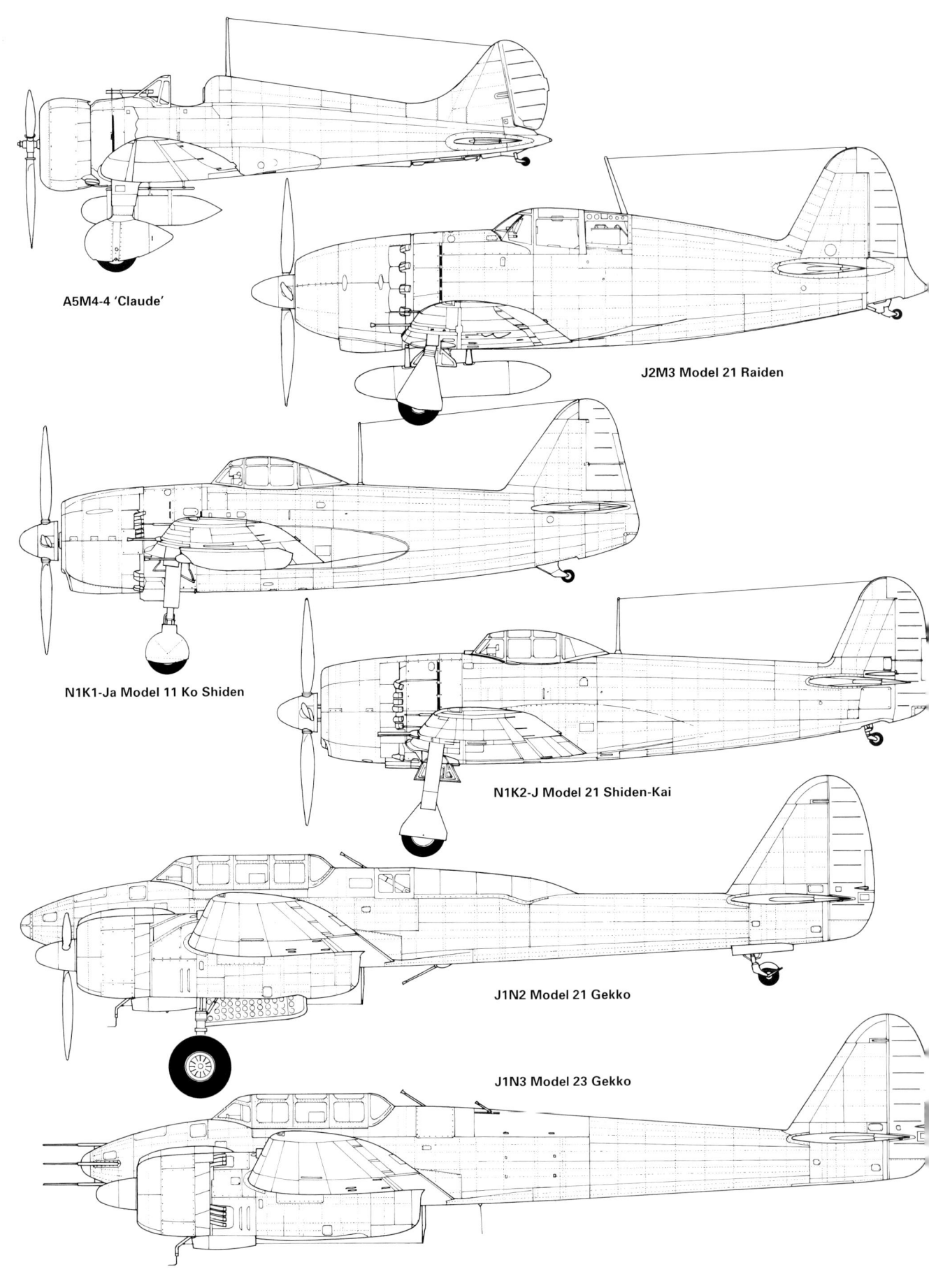

A5M4-4 'Claude'

J2M3 Model 21 Raiden

N1K1-Ja Model 11 Ko Shiden

N1K2-J Model 21 Shiden-Kai

J1N2 Model 21 Gekko

J1N3 Model 23 Gekko

1

A5M2a Type 96 Model 2-1 of the 13th AG, flown by PO1/c Tetsuzo Iwamoto, Nanjing, China, February 1938

The white unit marking '4' was used by the 13th AG between October 1937 and November 1940. Iwamoto noted in his diary that '4-133' was a distinguished aircraft which he flew from the first days of the China War, and in every major engagement he fought in. He also wrote that it had the most victories in the unit. This Type 96 was flown by many pilots.

2

A5M3a Type 96 Model 2-1 of the 15th AG, flown by Lt Mochifumi Nango, Anjing, China, July 1938

The white unit marking '10' was used by the 15th AG from June through to November 1938, whilst the white fuselage band indicates a flight leader. On 18 July 1938 Lt Nango was killed in this fighter when he collided with an I-15 over Lake Poyang during a bomber escort mission to Nachang.

3

A5M4 Type 96 Model 4 of the Soryu Fighter Sqn, flown by PO2/c Hideo Oishi, East China Sea, November 1938

The unit designation 'W' was used from the end of 1937 through to 1940. The inscription on the fuselage indicates that this fighter was presentation aircraft No 266, purchased by a Mr Iwai and donated to the navy – a common practice during the China War and the first months of the Pacific war.

4

A5M4 Type 96 Model 4 of Soryu Fighter Squadron, flown by PO1/c Matsuo Hagiri, Japan, summer 1939

With a maximum speed of 270 mph at 9845 ft. the Type 96 could fly circles around the new Zero fighter – in mock dog-fights, the '96 won every time. Matsuo Hagiri went on to enjoy a distinguished career during World War 2.

5

A6M2 Model 11 of the 12th AG, flown by WO Koshiro Yamashita, Hankow, China, 1940

The 12th AG used the number '3' as their unit designation, followed by the individual aircraft number, in 1940–41. The distinctive red swallow in a circle victory markings were fre-quently found on many of their Zeroes during this period.

6

A6M2 Model 11 of the 12th AG, flown by squadron leader Lt Minoru Suzuki, Hankow, China, 1940

This fighter was flown by numerous pilots (including Lt Suzuki), most of whom contributed to the 28 victories painted on its tail. This high-scoring Zero was returned to Japan and exhibited at the Naval Academy after its tour of China ended in late 1940. Lt Cdr Suzuki finished the war as a squadron leader in the 205th AG in Formosa, having scored eight kills.

7

A6M2 Model 11 of the 12th AG, flown by PO2/c Tsutomu Iwai, Hankow, China, 13 September 1940

During the famous engagement over Hankow on this date, 13 Zeroes destroyed 27 enemy fighters without suffering a single loss – Iwai downed two. He later served in almost every theatre of the Pacific War, including home defence, and lived to see the end of the conflict, having scored 11+ victories.

8

A6M2 Model 11 of the 12th AG, flown by PO2/c Hideo Oishi, Hankow, China, 1941

Although the radio equipment in the Zero was virtually useless from the word go due to static, there was no need for pilots to remove them (as in later years) in order to reduce weight. Oishi had achieved six victories before he was killed in aerial combat over the Philippines on 12 September 1944.

9

A6M2 Model 11 of the 12th AG, flown by PO1/c Masayuki Nakase, Hankow, China, 14 March 1941

On this date young novice Nakase downed six Soviet I-152s in his first action, becoming one of the early JNAF 'ace-in-a-day' pilots. His total ammunition expenditure amounted to just 110 rounds of 20 mm cannon shell and 575 7.7 mm machine-gun bullets – Nakase later gained another three victories in China. On 9 February 1942 he became one of the first JNAF aces killed during World War 2 when his aircraft was shot down by ground fire during a strafing attack on armoured cars in the Celebes. The 18-victory ace received a double posthumous promotion to the rank of ensign.

10

A6M2 Model 21 of the Tainan AG, flown by Airman 1/c Masaaki Shimakawa, Formosa, October 1941

The Tainan AG utilised both the 'V' unit designation (from October 1941 through to October 1942) and a diagonal fuselage stripe to marking their Zeroes. This aircraft was further personalised through the addition of the kanji character 'Shima' inside the red sun emblem on the fuselage – this was a temporary marking made from crushed chalk and water, and it served as aid to identifying the pilot during carrier landings (training) and long-range flights. Each pilot in the squadron painted the first kanji of his surname onto his aircraft.

11

A6M2 Model 21 of the 3rd AG, flown by PO2/c Yoshiro Hashiguchi, Dutch East Indies, February 1942

The 'X' unit designation was used by the 3rd AG from April 1941 through to October 1942. Various pilots flew 'X-183', adding their victories to its score, although most of the kills were achieved by Hashiguchi. He later fought in the Solomons and the Philippines, where he met his death on 25 October 1944 having scored over ten victories.

12
A6M2 Model 21 of the Tainan AG. flown by P02/c Susumu Ishihara, Surabaya, Java, February 1942
Ishihara flew this aircraft during the Dutch East Indies cam-paign, performing mostly ground attack and patrol roles. He later saw considerable action in the Solomons battles and ended the war with over 30 victories.

13
A6M2 Model 21 of the Tainan AG, flown by P02/c Yoshisuke Arita, Bali, February 1942
This presentation aircraft was flown by Arita prior to his death in aerial combat over Port Moresby on 1 May 1942.

14
A6M2 Model 21 of the Tainan AG, flown by P01/c Saburo Sakai, Rabaul, 7 August 1942
Wearing the white tail stripe of a flight leader, 'V-128' was the mount of CPO Sakai during his eventful long-range mission to Guadalcanal on 7 August. He claimed three kills during the sortie, but was also seriously wounded by SBD gunners from VB-6. Given up for dead, Sakai flew for nearly five hours before gliding his Zero into Rabaul's Lakunai airfield out of fuel.

15
F1M2 Type Zero Observation Seaplane Model 11 of the seaplane tender Chitose, flown by P01/c Kiyomi Katsuki (pilot) and P02/c Michio Takarada, 4 October 1942
Although the biplane fighter era ended with the introduction of the Type 96, the F1M2 (codenamed 'Pete') was nevertheless produced in quantity during World War 2. The team of Katsuki and Takarada were flying 'Y1-23' on 4 October 1942 when they rammed and destroyed a B-17 which was about to attack the seaplane carrier Nisshin.

16
A6M2 Model 21 of the Shokaku Fighter Squadron, flown by squadron leader Lt Hideki Shingo during the Battle of Santa Cruz, 26 October 1942
Lt Shingo led his Zeroes in the second wave attack on the US Task Force, during which they claimed five aircraft shot down. The tail code designation 'EI' was used from September 1941 through to October 1942. Shingo survived the war and later became a jet fighter pilot in the Japan Self Defense Air Force.

17
A6M2 Model 21 of the Oppama AG, flown by CPO Tetsuzo Iwamoto, Kanagawa Prefecture, Japan, 1/43
Following the loss of many veteran pilots at Midway, Iwamoto was pulled out of combat in August 1942 and sent home to become an instructor. In November of that same year a JNAF directive redesignated all named land-based units going overseas with numbers. The unit designation on this aircraft (written in Japanese phonetic characters and preceding its number '101') reads 0-Hee (Oppama Aviation).

18
A6M2 Model 21 of the Zuikaku Fighter Squadron, flown by CPO Saburo Saito, Rabaul, January 1943
The Zuikaku Fighter Squadron was reorganised following the carrier's return to Japan after the Battle of Santa Cruz (October 1942). The unit designation 'A1-1' replaced 'E11', and was used until November 1943. The squadron assisted in the evacuation of Guadalcanal, before being temporarily based ashore at Rabaul and Bum. Saito scored his first victory on 1 February 1943 when he jointly shot down a Wildcat of VMF-112 near Savo Island. He was wounded on 24 October 1944 near Luzon and never flew again, having scored over 18 victories and completed 2118 flying hours.

19
A6M2-N Type 2 Floatplane Fighter of the 802nd AG, flown by Lt(jg) Keizo Yamazaki, Shortland Island Seaplane Base, February 1943
Codenamed 'Rufe' by the Allies, this aircraft was one of two successful floatplane designs utilised by the JNAF, the great benefit of this type of fighter being its ability to be based almost anywhere along an island coastline – tents would provide housing for pilots and groundcrew. On 13 February 1943 Lt(jg) Yamazaki claimed a P-39 probable flying this fighter, whilst various other pilots also enjoyed success with it – these kills were marked with small red hatchets on the tail.

20
A6M3 Model 22 of the 251st AG, flown by CPO Hiroyoshi
Nishizawa, Aichi Prefecture, Japan, Spring 1943
The unit designation 'UI' was used from 1942 through toJune 1943, during which time Nishizawa flew this aircraft as an instructor.

21
A6M3 Model 32 of the 204th AG, flown by P02/c Kenji Yanagiya, Bum, 18 April 1943
Yanagiya flew 'T2-169' on the ill-fated Adm Yamamoto escortmission, during which he claimed a P-38 probable. Note that this aircraft lacks a radio mast, which has been cut off in order to save weight. Unshielded ignitions in the engine interfered with radio reception, rendering it virtually worthless – pilots also discarded the radio equipment too. Understanding commanders did nothing to stop the practice.

22

A6M3 Model 22 of the 204th AG, flown by WO Matsuo Hagiri, Buin, summer 1943

Hagiri had shot down six enemy aircraft during his two-month stay with this unit, before being wounded in aerial combat with F4U Corsairs and RNZAF P-40s on 23 September 1943 over Kahili. Prior to being hit he had claimed two victories. Hagiri subsequently returned to Japan for hospitalisation.

23

A6M3 Model 22 of the 204th AG, flown by P02/c Shoichi Sugita, Rabaul, June 1943

Even experienced pilots like Sugita did not have their own assigned aircraft, flying whatever fighter was available at the time. During the month of June he destroyed or damaged two F4Fs, three F4Us and three unspecified aircraft.

24

A6M3 Model 22 of the 201st AG. flown by CPO Takeo Okumura, Buin, September 1943

The unit designation 'WI' was used from June 1943 through to 1944, during which time CPO Okumura set the JNAF record for shooting down the most number of enemy aircraft in a single day – ten on 14 September 1943 over Buin.

25

A6M2-N Type 2 Floatplane Fighter, 934th AG, flown by CPO Eitoku Matsunaga, Banda Sea/Ambon Island, September 1943-44

Reputedly the top floatplane ace of the Pacific War with eight kills, Matsunaga survived the war and has since shunned publicity, thus relegating his career into historical obscurity.

26

N1K1-J Shiden 11 of the 341st AG, 402nd Squadron, the Philippines, mid-1944

The 341st AG was to be armed with the new Shiden fighter in 1943, but due to production delays it did not receive its first aircraft until February 1944. A modified and further developed land-based version of the 'Rex' floatplane, the Shiden was modified extensively, and finally gained acceptance into JNAF service. Despite the 'George's' highly-regarded automatic combat flap system, it was plagued by engine and undercar-riage problems, leading Lt Iyozoh Fujita, Midway air hero and division officer of the 402nd Squadron, to sum the much-tout-ed fighter up with just two words — 'No good'

27

A6M3 Model 32 of the Tainan AG, flown by CPO Takeo Tanimizu, Tainan, Formosa, September 1944

This aircraft belonged to an operational training unit, rather than the famous Tainan AG, which was active over New Guinea in 1942. The unit designation in phonetic characters read Tai, followed by the aircraft number '184'. Tanimizu was flying this aircraft on the night of 31 August 1944 when he downed B-24 44-40783 of the 425th BS/308th BG, flown by 1Lt Norman B Clendenen. The kanji inscriptions on the rear fuselage reads, 'Combat diary. 31 August 1944, participated in combat over Takao. 3 September, the same. Downed one B-24'. Pilots rarely had inscriptions painted on their aircraft, Tanimizu doing so to encourage his inexperienced comrades.

28

J2M3 Raiden 21 of the 302nd AG, flown by Lt(jg) Sadaaki Akamatsu, Atsugi airfield, March 1944 to August 1945

Akamatsu flew this aircraft both on training flights and in combat, the victory markings on its tail indicating that the Raiden had received the credit for these successes, not the pilot.

29

N1K2-J Shiden-Kai 21 of the 343rd AG, 701st Squadron, flown by squadron leader Lt Takashi Oshibuchi, Kyushu, April 1945

The letter 'C' on the tail of this 'George' denotes that it belongs to the 701st Squadron, whilst the double red diagonal fuselage stripes indicate a squadron leader's aircraft. On 16 April 1945 Oshibuchi led 32 'Georges' to Okinawa during the No 3 Kikusui Operation, the fighters subsequently claiming 20 F6Fs destroyed for the loss of nine N1K2-Js. Oshibuchi was killed on 24 July 1945 in '343-C-13' when he was downed by VF-49's Lt George M Williams over the Bungo Straits.

30

J1N1-S Model 21 of the 302nd AG, 2nd Squadron, flown by Lt Yukio Endo (pilot) and CPO Osamu Nishio (observer), Atsugi airfield, January 1945

This Gekko's victory markings consist of five double cherry blossoms (destroyed) and nine single blossoms, (probables), these successes having been achieved by Endo and Nishio. At the time of their deaths on 14 January 1945, the pair had been credited with at least eight B-29 victories.

31

A6M5 Model 52 of the 252nd AG, 311th Squadron, flown by Ens Tetsuzo Iwamoto, Mobara airfield, Japan, 16 February 1945

On this day US carrier aircraft raided the Tokyo region, Iwamoto leading eight Zeroes of his squadron in counterattack against F4U Corsairs. Before the day ended, he had claimed seven destroyed and one damaged.

32

A6MS Model 52 of the 302nd AG, flown by Ens Sadaaki Akamatsu, Atsugi airfield, Japan, 16-17 February 1945

Capable of speeds of up to 351 mph at 19,685 ft. the

Model 52 was rushed into combat during the autumn of 1943, and in the hands of veteran pilots proved to be a match for the F6F and F4U. During the two-day carrier attacks on Tokyo Akamatsu used this Zero to claim four Hellcats kills – as indicated by the chrysanthemum victory markings. The two cherry blossom markings indicate damaged claims.

33
J2M3 Raiden 21 of the 352nd AG, flown by Lt(jg) Yoshihiro Aoki, Omura airfield, March 1945
Formed in August 1944 to protect the Sasebo, Nagasaki and Omura areas, this unit was called Kusanagi (Heavenly Scythe), but it did not live up to its name. Reserve Lt(jg) Aoki served as a division officer within the 352nd AG, heading the Raiden unit in attacks on B-29s. Extraneous markings such as these lightning bolts were rare on JNAF aircraft.

34
N1K2-J Shiden-Kai of the 343rd AG, 407th Squadron, of CPO Hideo Nakao, Matsuyama airfield, Japan, 3/45
The number '20' in the red 'meatball' indicates that this aircraft was used for training prior to combat. The Shiden-Kai carried two 20 mm Type 99 Mark 4 cannon in each wing, with a rate of fire of over 490 rpm. Each cannon was belt-fed from a magazine which held 250 rounds, although pilots felt that the weapons' fired too slowly.

35
J2M3 Raiden 21 of the 302nd AG, 1st Squadron, flown by Lt Susumu Ito. Atsugi airfield, April 1945
The fuselage band indicates that this aircraft was flown by a flight leader, and the kill markings on the upper tail comprise four chrysanthemums (definite) and one cherry blossom (probable or damaged). The kanji characters beneath the 'Yo-D (for Yokosuka Defence) 152' read 'Maintenance P01/c Fukuda', who was its mechanic. Ito was the 2nd Division leader.

36
N1K2-J Shiden-Kai 21 of the 343rd AG, 301st Squadron, flown by CPO Katsue Kato, Matsuyama airfield, 4/45
The white '02' marking was a temporary number used for training purposes, this aircraft being flown by CPO Katsue Kato on 16 April 1945 from Matsuyama. This aircraft was one of 32 'Georges' sortied during the No 3 Kikusui Operation (special attack) to Okinawa, Kato being killed in this action.

37
J2M3 Raiden 21 of the 332nd AG's Tatsumaki Unit, flown by WO Susumu Ishihara, Kanoya Air Base, 27 April 1945
The '32' on the tail denotes the last two digits of the 332nd AG, this group being organised for the defence of Kure. Ishihara achieved 16 officially recognised kills

before individual credits were abolished – his score stood at 30+ by war's end.

38
N1K2-J Shiden-Kel 21 of the Yokosuka AG, flown by Ens Kaneyoshi Muto, April 1945
The backward 'E' on the tail is a Japanese phonetic katakana (writing), pronounced 'Yo' (for Yokosuka Defence). The unit had several such aircraft for test and evaluation purposes.

39
N1K2-J Shiden-Kai 21 of the 343rd AG, 407th Squadron, flown by WO Isamu Miyazaki, Kyushu, April 1945
The letter 'B' denotes the 407th Squadron, whilst the white diagonal stripe shows that this aircraft was flown by a flight leader. The Shiden-Kai boasted armour protection, and US pilots noted in their mission reports that it was very difficult to set one on fire, unlike the Zero.

40
N1K2-J Shiden-Kai 21 of the 343rd AG, 301st Squadron flown by squadron leader Lt Naoshi Kanno, Matsuyama airfield, Japan, April 1945
The letter 'A' denotes the 301st Squadron, whilst the number'15', painted inside the red 'meatball', was temporary for training and maintenance purposes – it was never used during combat missions. Lt Kanno flew 'AI5' during the No 3 Kikusui Operation to Okinawa on 16 April 1945.

41
J1N1-S Gekko Model 23 of the Yokosuka AG, 7th Squadron, flown by CPO Juzo Kuromoto (pilot) and Ens Shiro Kurotori (observer), Yokosuka airfield, May 1945
Adorned on the rear fuselage are eight victory markings (six probables and two destroyed), Kuromoto and his observer claiming five B-29s destroyed and one damaged in this aircraft on the night of 25 May 1945.

42
A6M5 Model 52 of the 203rd AG, 303rd Squadron, flown by CPO Takeo Tanimizu, Kagoshima Prefecture, Japan, June 1945
The unusual kill markings on this aircraft made it the most cel-ebrated Zero ever depicted in postwar publications. The two head-on silhouettes of B-29s represent one probable and another jointly shot down with CPO Tetsuzo Iwamoto. The five stars with arrows indicate kills, whilst the single unpierced star denotes a probable or damaged aircraft. Tanimizu had these markings painted on to inspire his inexperienced men. The broken up hulk of this aircraft was photographed in a Nagasaki hangar in November 1945.

43
A6M7 Model 63 of the 302nd AG, flown by

squadron leader lt Yutaka Morioka, Atsugi airfield, Japan, 3/8/45

Lt Morioka flew No 106 (accompanied by three wingmen) in a desperate attempt to thwart the rescue of P-51 pilot Capt Ed Mikes Jr of the 458th FS, who had parachuted into Tokyo Bay. Morioka downed 2Lt John J Coneff of the 457th FS, who had been covering Mikes, and before returning to base from their unsuccessful sortie, he and his men strafed the American pilot in his life-boat, although Mikes escaped with minor splinter wounds.

FIGURE PLATES

1

This is what the completely outfitted carrier pilot looked like in 1941-42. P03/c Sadamu Komachi is seen ready for action whilst serving aboard Shokaku at the time of the Pearl Harbor raid, wearing his one-piece winter flightsuit, which was waterproofed, but not fireproof, and trimmed with a white rabbit fur collar. His headgear comprised a woolen toque and winter helmet, whilst over his kapok life jacket (which offered its wearer some protection from flying shrapnel) he wears a Type 97 parachute harness with a white cloth name tag on the right vertical strap. Komachi's gauntlets, which are stuffed into his right leg pocket, are made from deerskin.

2

After having had his hand amputated by the tail gunner of a B-29 in January 1945, Lt Yutaka Morioka of the 302nd AG returned to duty sporting an iron claw! He is seen wearing an early style (button sleeve) brown gabardine summer flightsuit and a winter (rabbit fur-lined) helmet. A small green cloth name patch is sewn onto his left breast, but it has been left unmarked (as was usually the case), for the suits were often reissued to other pilots. Home defence pilots like Morioka did not carry pistols unless their mission took them away from the Japanese mainland - to Iwo Jima or Okinawa, for example. A headphone cord dangles around his neck. JNAF aviators often wore silk scarves (often white, as they were usually made from salvaged parachutes, although other colours were occasionally seen) as part of their attire.

3

P01/c Takeo Tanimizu wears typical JNAF flying gear whilst aboard the carrier Junyo in May 1942. He is attired in a one-piece brown gabardine summer flying suit, which is quilted inside (lined) for additional warmth while at sea. Tanimizu's kapok-filled life jacket is of an early style, boasting a small utility pocket which contains his watch. Many pilots carried a pis-tol, although this was not for personal protection, but instead to be used as an instrument with which to commit suicide in order to prevent capture – Tanimizu's is an 8 mm Nambu (Nagoya 1st series, produced in November 1941 and serialled 2147),

which belonged to the carrier's arsenal. It had an eight-shot capacity, but only five rounds were loaded to prevent magazine spring weakness. Holsters were too bulky, so the usual method of securement was with a rope lanyard. In his hand is a summer issue gauntlet. Unusually for the 1942 period, Tanimizu is wearing a hachimaki (headband) – these were used both to keep the sweat from the pilot's eyes and to symbolise his manly spirit.

4

Winter and high altitude flying over Atsugi made heavy flying gear a must for flight instructor Lt(jg) Sadaaki Akamatsu of the 302nd AG in early 1945. The late style winter flightsuit (zippered sleeve as opposed to the early button sleeve) has a rabbit fur collar and is quilted inside. Of interest is the custom-made winter flying helmet worn by the pilot – some officer pilots, for whatever reason, had custom helmets specially made for them. The standard issue item was made from sheepskin. Akamatsu wears typical short black flying boots with leather soles and rubber heels.

5

Just back from the China War, newly-promoted P01/c Kaneyoshi Muto of the 12th AG gives off the impression of being a seasoned veteran in his petty officer's blues. On his left breast are three medals – the Golden Kite, Rising Sun 1st Class and the China Incident medal. On the lower right-hand side of Muto's tunic is an air medal, whilst his right sleeve carries two Zenkosho (good conduct stripes) and a sleeve rating depicting a naval aviator, Petty Officer 1st Class.

6

P02/c Saburo Sakai of the 12th AG is depicted at Nanchang air base, in southern China in 1939. He is wearing typical two-piece tropical work fatigues and a floppy (but quite functional) 'Daisy Mae' hat. In the heat of the tropics pilots would wear these work clothes beneath their unlined summer flightsuits.

HOME DEFENCE

The loss of both the Philippines and Iwo Jima now positioned Allied forces at Japan's 'front door', and it came as no surprise when Saipan-based B-29s raided the Imperial capital for the first time on 24 November 1944.

It was the turn of US carrier aircraft to strike at Tokyo for the first time since Lt Col 'Jimmy' Doolittle surprise raid of 1942 on 16/17 February 1945, TF58 aircraft attacking airfields across the region. In response, the JNAF and JAAF sortied practically anything that could fly – including fixed-landing gear 'relics' from the China War. Both sides once again distorted their results, with combined claims by the JNAF/JAAF amounting to 275 kills against the loss of 78 fighters in the air, whilst the US Navy claimed 330+ victories for 52 F6Fs and 16 F4Us lost to all causes.

Adm Marc Mitscher swung his task force towards southern Japan after 'slapping' Tokyo, his priority now being to destroy airfields in the Kyushu area in order to prevent *kamikaze*s from taking off.

During these 'dark days' when the JNAF suffered defeat after defeat, one unit would shine. Capt Minoru Genda – who masterminded the Pearl Harbor raid – formed an elite unit composed of veterans armed with the latest naval fighter, the Shiden-Kai ('George'). Officially titled the 343rd AG, the group was dubbed the 'Squadron of Experts' because it had the highest concentration of aces of any unit then in the JNAF.

On 19 March 1945 TF58 aircraft took off for an early morning raid against the great naval bastion of Kure, the pilots involved confident in the knowledge that no serious fighter opposition would oppose them. However, Capt Genda scrambled three squadrons of 'Georges', with first contact being made between VBF-17 F6Fs and elements of the 407th and 701st Sqns. A vicious dogfight erupted and six pilots from both sides went down, this action setting the tempo for the morning battles which ranged far and wide. Few fighters from other JNAF/JAAF units joined in due to a lack of fuel – the day belonged to Genda's 343rd.

According to the group's records, they claimed 53 Hellcats and Corsairs and four SB2C Helldivers against a loss of 13 pilots on this day. CPO Katsue Kato alone was credited with nine victories in the morning combat, and these tremendous claims made headlines throughout Japan, temporarily raising morale.

B-29s continued to raid the industrial centres of Japan, however, although the inaccuracy of high altitude bombing forced USAAF commanders to initiate low altitude bombing at night. Devastating fire raids commenced on the night of

Zero pilots of the 203rd AG study their day's assignment at Kagoshima Naval Air Station in May 1945. On the left is CPO Takeo Tanimizu (32 victories), whilst the he pilot on the right has an 8 mm Nambu pistol in his hand (*T Tanimizu*)

Members of the 303rd Squadron, 203rd AG, in July 1945. This unit was reorganised numerous times, and suffered heavy losses over the Philippines, Okinawa and during home defence missions. CPO Takeo Tanimizu (second row, fifth from left) was the most experienced veteran in the group, the majority of his squadronmates having only just graduated from flying school (*T Tanimizu*)

9/10 March, which resulted in nearly 16 square miles of Tokyo being gutted. In response the JNAF sent up teams of 'Gekko' nightfighters, but they achieved marginal results. The most famous B-29 'killer' of them all was Lt Yukio Endo, who had earlier pioneered the art of nightfighting in the Solomons. He and his observer downed at least eight Boeing 'heavies' before they were killed.

Starting in April, P-51s and P-47s began escorting the B-29s over Japan from their bases on Iwo Jima, and Japanese pilots were hard pressed to compete against these menaces. The navy's most famous Mustang 'tamer' was Lt(jg) Sadaaki Akamatsu of the 302nd AG at Atsugi, who proved to the doubters that the Raiden ('Jack') could 'whip' a Mustang by downing at least two in wild dogfight on 19 April. But it was never easy, as Akamatsu observed in a postwar interview;

'I have witnessed so many splendid enemy pilots. It was towards the end of the war when I had one particular encounter with a P-51. We spotted the enemy planes over the southern end of Tokyo Bay. Five Raidens raced in to fight. The enemy always kept their tail covered with the P-51. I hid behind a P-51 – there was a blind spot. After following a while I had the advantage to attack. I fired my guns from very close range and hit its fuel tank. Suddenly it fell on fire. His comrades saw this and spiralled down to attack me. I couldn't escape so I tried a head-on attack. I could see tracers coming toward me, but I was accustomed to this. The enemy never separated me and finally gave up to save fuel. Maybe because it was a hard fight, I respected the enemy's abilities.'

As the war drew to a close, very few JNAF fighters were seen, orders having been given to conserve fuel and fighters for the one big *kamikaze* attack that would greet the anticipated Allied landings.

Aside from lacking fuel, JNAF pilots also felt that their aircraft were by poor. Lt Cdr Iyozoh Fujita was one such individual who had many complaints about the equipment and armament his pilots had to work with;

169

These A6M5c Zero Model 52s belong to the 252nd AG, and are seen undergoing engine runs prior to their pilots strapping in anticipation of the next home defence sortie. The A6M5c had an additional 13.2 mm machine-gun in each wing, armour plate behind the pilot's seat and a self-sealing fuel tank behind the cockpit. Despite these improvements, the aircraft was still no match for its American fighter opponents (*via Aerospace Publishing*)

'During the early part of the war we felt that the weapons in our Zeroes (two 7.7 mm and 20 mm guns) were adequate, but later on this was not enough. Our pilots wanted 13 and 15 mm guns like the Grummans, but we were unable to have them and I don't know why. Our gunsights were adequate for the veterans, but I requested better ones like those used by the Americans. Again we never received them. I knew about the German Me 262 jet and their rocket fighters. We wanted them too, but couldn't get them.'

The last major dogfight of World War 2 occurred on 15 August 1945 when VF-88 Hellcats encountered a mixed formation of Zeroes and 'Jacks' of the 302nd AG near Atsugi. In a running gunfight, four Hellcats were lost. Two hours later the Emperor broadcast his surrender announcement, but the guns of the JNAF did not remain silent.

On 17 August unescorted B-32 Dominators flew over Tokyo on a photo-reconnaissance mission and were duly intercepted by fighters from the Yokosuka AG. Ens Saburo Sakai and WO Sadamu Komachi chased one bomber to Oshima Island, where it ditched – the loss was recorded as operational. This incident was repeated the following day when the bombers again returned without escorts – this time one B-32 crewman was killed in the attacks, Sgt Anthony J Marchione dying aboard the 312th BG's *Hobo Queen*.

Saburo Sakai explained the rationale for their actions in the following quote;

'It may appear that we committed an illegal act. I investigated this matter after the war. What we did was perfectly legal and acceptable under international law and the rules of engagement. While Japan did agree to the surrender, we were still a sovereign nation, and every nation has the right to protect itself. When the Americans sent over their B-32s, we did not know of their intentions . . . By invading our airspace they were committing a provocative and aggressive act . . . It was most unwise for the Americans to send over their bombers only a few days after the surrender announcement! They should have waited and let things cool down.'

Many Japanese pilots, believing a rumour that the US occupation forces had plans to execute them in reprisal, burned their logbooks, while executive officers destroyed mission reports and other data. In this fashion, much detailed information on units and pilots was lost to history.

Warrant Officer Takeo Tanimizu

'I believe in fate. God determines at the time of birth just when and where a person shall die', recalled Takeo Tanimizu, a truly remarkable fighter ace whose specially-marked Zero is the most easily recognisable of its type due to its unique kill markings.

Tanimizu was born in Mie Prefecture in April 1919, his mother being a pearl diver. He too followed aquatic pursuits by joining the navy – against the wishes of his mother – when the Pacific War started, entering flight training and duly graduating in March 1942. After various assignments (none involving combat), Tanimizu transferred to the *Shokaku* in February 1943. However, it wasn't until 2 November 1943 at Rabaul that he finally engaged the enemy, claiming two P-38s in his first combat.

The daily battles over Rabaul took a tremendous toll of Zero pilots, with Tanimizu considering the Hellcat to be his greatest foe;

'I think the F6F was the toughest opponent we had. They could manoeuvre and roll, whereas planes such as the P-38 and F4U made hit and run passes – they were not very manoeuvrable. It was difficult to make the American planes burn in the air. If you hit them, they may puff some smoke. You could always tell by the way they smoked if it was a Zero or an enemy plane.'

The gull-winged F4U had a ferocious reputation amongst the Americans, who nicknamed it 'Whistling Death'. However, although most

CPO Takeo Tanimizu painted elaborate kill markings on his Zero 03-09 in an effort to bolster the morale of his men. The stars with arrows through them indicate a sure victory, while the single marking below is a probable. His scoreboard also boasted two head-on silhouettes of B-29s, although these are obscured in this photograph by the sun's reflection. This shot was taken in June 1945 in Kyushu (*T Tanimizu*)

In 1945 the 352nd AG flew Raiden ('Jack') fighters against B-29s over western Kyushu from their base at Kanoya. Although the unit trained to use deadly aerial burst bombs, no victories were achieved with the weapon. JNAF ace Lt Yoshihiro Aoki (second from left) is seen briefing his men before a mission in front of his distinctively marked 'Jack' (*K Osuo*)

Zero pilots respected the Corsair, they did not fear it. Tanimizu recalled;

'The only time you could really shoot it down was when it was fleeing. You had to shoot at it from a certain angle, otherwise, the bullets would bounce off. A few times, I would see F4U making low level diving attacks and dive into a coconut grove or the water because it couldn't pull out – the plane was too heavy. We would sometimes chase them into the sea. We didn't have this problem because our planes were so light.'

Despite the 'kill or be killed' philosophy, Tanimizu also showed compassion for the enemy. On 4 January 1944, while returning from combat, he saw a lone Corsair pilot parachute from his damaged aircraft into the waters off Capt St George. Concerned for his opponent, Tanimizu flew down and threw Capt Harvey F Carter of VMF-321 his life ring. Carter retrieved the ring and waved thanks to his foe, but was never recovered.

In March 1944 Tanimizu became an instructor with the Tainan AG in

A Kawanishi N1K Kyofu ('Rex') floatplane of the Sasebo AG flies over Kyushu in September 1944. The Shiden and Shiden-Kai fighters were developed from this advanced, yet temperamental float-plane, of which only 97 were built (*via Aerospace Publishing*)

The pilot of an unidentified N1K1-J runs the aircraft's unreliable Nakajima Homare 21 powerplant up on the ramp whilst his mechanics examine the fighter's undercarriage legs – another of the fighter's problem areas (*via Robert C Mikesh*)

The 'George' was a direct descendant of the 'Rex' floatplane, the 201st AG taking it to the Philippines, where it held its own against the F6F Hellcat (*via Phil Jarrett*)

Japan, although shortly afterwards he was sent to Formosa to perform bomber intercepts and general patrol duties. He also very occasionally flew nocturnal sorties, and on the night of 31 August 1944, he engaged 11 B-24s attacking Takao (now Kaohsiung) Harbour by himself. Tanimizu made frontal passes on a B-24 piloted by Lt Norman B Clendenen of the 425th BS, causing the Liberator crash in flames – there was only one survivor, who was duly captured. He may also have damaged the bomber flown by Lt George Pierpont, the B-24 crashing into a mountain peak on mainland China. The remains of the crew were only discovered in October 1996, being handed over to the US Ambassador in January 1997.

On 3 November 1944, over Amoy Harbour (China), Tanimizu and his

wingman, Manabu Ito, had commenced their landing approach after providing air cover for a convoy of ships entering the harbour when they were bounced by two P-51s of the 74th FS flown by Capt Paul J Reis and 1Lt John W Bolyard. Firing from extreme distance, Reis hit Tanimizu's wing tip, but the ace failed to see the closing Mustangs, assuming instead that his inexperienced wingman trailing behind him had accidentally fired a burst. Bolyard quickly downed Ito and flamed Tanimizu's A6M (these were the Mustang pilot's first in an eventual tally of five kills).

'My Zero was out of control, on fire, and going straight up', he later recalled, 'and then I thought, "so this is where I am going to die!"'

Tanimizu managed to extricate himself from the burning aircraft and parachuted at just 250 ft, his 'chute opening just before he hit the water. He was eventually rescued by two Chinese from a nearby beach nearly two hours later.

The later N1K2-J Shiden-Kai (with its repositioned wing and length-ened fuselage) was a vast improve-ment on the original Shiden (*via Phil Jarrett*)

Raiden fighters of the 1st Squadron, 302nd AG, are seen at Atsugi in 1945 – note that the three fighters in the second row all sport kill markings on their tails. Designed to attack B-29s, the 'Jack' and was not a par-ticularly manoeuvrable aircraft, and most pilots disliked it due to its heavy handling and excessive land-ing speed. However, Ens Sadaaki Akamatsu – and a few others – was able to outfight P-51s in the aircraft

A 302nd AG Raiden scrambles to intercept an incoming raid. Operating a mixed force of both Zeroes and 'Jacks' from Atsugi airfield, the unit was the guardian of the Imperial Capital. However, by May 1945, the 302nd was down to just ten operational aircraft, and it flew its last combat mission on 15 August 1945 – two hours before the surrender announcement – when Hellcats from VF-88 were engaged (*via Aerospace Publishing*)

The 'Jack' was a pugnacious looking design when viewed from almost any angle (*via Aerospace Publishing*)

After spending a month in a hospital in Formosa, Tanimizu was ordered back to Japan, where his request for a *kamikaze* assignment was rejected by an admiral – he was sent instead to the 203rd AG in Kyushu.

On 18 March 1945 Tanimizu fought Corsairs which were strafing his airfield at Kasanbara, shooting one off the tail of a comrade and inflicting serious damage on another, flown by Lt James J Stevens of VBF-83. Stevens fled at low altitude over the sea, trailing a plume of black smoke, and although Tanimizu tried to chase him down, he failed to catch him. The F4U had been fatally wounded, however, Stevens subsequently drowning after ditching his aircraft.

To give the inexperienced pilots in his unit confidence, Tanimizu began applying victory markings to his aircraft. One was for the F4U downed over Kasanbara, whilst others denoted a B-29 shared with Ens Tetsuzo Iwamoto (the top JNAF ace) and a second as a probable.

This candid shot shows a wrestling match underway in a corner of Atsugi airfield in early 1945. Ens Sadaaki Akamatsu (second from left, without a flying helmet) was a champion wrestler, in addition to being a renowned ace (*Sakaida*)

Ens Sadaaki Akamatsu, the JNAF's top Raiden master, demonstrates how to attack an American fighter. He never lost a dogfight in more than eight years of combat, and ended the war without having suffered as much as a scratch (*Sakaida*)

On 10 June 1945 Tanimizu fought against P-47s in a savage battle over Kyushu, and although he seriously damaged a Thunderbolt, his Zero was hit in the oil pipe and he was forced to make an emergency landing.

When the surrender was announced on 15 August 1945 Tanimizu could not accept defeat. For five days, he searched for enemy aircraft and dropped leaflets urging the public to fight on.

By the end of the war Takeo Tanimizu had recorded 1425 flight hours and claimed 32 victories. He is now retired and resides in Osaka.

Lieutenant(jg) Sadaaki Akamatsu

'Outrageously temperamental, eccentric and quite violent!' were the words used by ace Saburo Sakai to describe this fighter pilot. Temei (he preferred this nickname to the formal Sadaaki) Akamatsu was the JNAF's most infamous fighter ace, whose antics became legendary.

Born in Kochi Prefecture in July 1910, the son of a weatherman, Akamatsu entered the navy in June 1928, commenced flight training two years later and graduated in March 1932. The high quality of the prewar training instilled in each pilot an extreme sense of self-confidence, and honed the killer instinct – traits which helped Akamatsu survive the war.

Following the completion of his training, Akamatsu (his name means red pine) served with various air groups, including those on the carriers *Akagi*, *Ryujo* and *Kaga*. When the China War commenced in 1937, he was transferred to the 13th AG and went into combat.

The rogue fighter pilot known as 'Matsu-chan' (little pine) was good from the very start, for on 25 February 1938, during his first action over Nanchang, he claimed four enemy aircraft shot down. In September he transferred to *Soryu* Fighter Squadron. The vicious engagements of the China War helped hone Akamatsu's fighting style to the point where he would take the offensive even when facing a numerically superior enemy.

At the end of his combat tour in China, Akamatsu returned to Japan as a war hero. 'I destroyed over 200 enemy aircraft including confirmed, probables and burned on the ground', he recalled in his postwar years. 'The time before World War 2, the fighter plane didn't have the great speeds; it was the pilot's ability that counted. It was the "one-to-one dog-fight era". The fight was slower and determined; we didn't fight in massed formations.'

The self-proclaimed 'King of Aces' earned a notorious reputation as an undisciplined rebel and womaniser, and it was no secret that he was also an alcoholic. His heavy drinking and violent temper often resulted in fights, landing him in the brig. Despite having his service stripes taken away and being held back in rank, Akamatsu was nevertheless respected by his subordinates for his fighting ability, and tolerated by his superiors.

When Japan went to war on 8 December 1941, WO Akamatsu flew with the 3rd AG on a raid against Iba and Clark Fields, where he fought against 20th PS P-40s and claimed one damaged. Two days later he shared a victory over Manila with two other pilots.

From the Philippines, the 3rd AG fought over the Dutch East Indies, where, according to Akamatsu's recollections, he downed two 'Curtiss Nieuports' over Surabaya, Java, and also shared in the destruction of a fly-ing boat with two other pilots. Over Bali, two more P-40s fell to his guns, and when his unit attacked Darwin (Australia) from their base at Kupang, Akamatsu added a single Spitfire to his tally. It wasn't until May 1942 that the veteran ace returned to Japan.

In July 1943, Ens Akamatsu was posted to the 331st AG, with whom he fought over Calcutta and claimed four enemy aircraft shot down on 5 December 1943. The following month Akamatsu returned to Japan and was assigned to the tough 302nd AG at Atsugi airfield, where he became a division officer within a Raiden ('Jack') unit. His new job brought many responsibilities with it, and he mended his evil ways except for his drink-ing. The old master trained his young subordinates to respect enemy fighters – 'Use hit and run attacks', Akamatsu would advise his men. 'The American pilots have excellent radio communications and group tactics'.

When American carrier fighters raided the Tokyo region on 16 Febru-ary 1945, Ens Akamatsu jumped into a Zero and plunged into the Hell-cat formations. He downed two in the morning sortie and another pair in the afternoon, and by war's end, he had accounted for nine F6Fs (four confirmed and five probables).

Akamatsu's fighting ability reached legendary status with his handling of the J2M Raiden fighter. The aircraft had initially been designed as a bomber interceptor, and was widely despised by navy pilots, who com-plained constantly about its lack of manoeuvrability, high landing speed and oversized cowling. It was often mistaken for the enemy's P-47 Thun-derbolt, and there was a high accident rate amongst trainees. Many vet-eran pilots believed that this aircraft could not survive against Hellcats and Mustangs in a dogfight.

Ens Akamatsu was not intimidated by the American aircraft, however, stating, 'Our dogfighting techniques were superior to any other coun-try's, but the American's shooting average was better than ours.'

In an astonishing display of aerobatics and raw courage, Akamatsu proved that a Raiden could break a Mustang when, on 19 April 1945, the

34-year-old 'Raiden Master' flew his 'Jack' against P-51s of the 45th FS. Fighting on his own terms, he forced his opponents down to low altitude and claimed two or three shot down.

On 29 May, near Yokohama, the 'old man' of the Atsugi Air Corps single-handedly attacked 75 Mustangs in a Zero and shot down 2Lt Rufus Moore, again of the 45th FS. Capt Todd Moore, who witnessed Akamatsu's attack, said later, 'If he had been an American he would have been awarded the Congressional Medal of Honor'.

When the surrender announcement was broadcast by the Emperor on 15 August 1945, Lt(jg) Akamatsu sided with the faction at Atsugi who vowed to continue fighting. However, the air group's fighters were disabled and the rebellion was quashed.

Akamatsu ended his flying career with more than 8000 flight hours, and he often boasted of over 350 victories when he was intoxicated and 260 when he was sober, but almost no one believed him. In addition to the nine F6F Hellcats that he claimed, several Mustangs, one B-24 and seven B-29s (one confirmed and six probables) also appear in his victory list. According to available records, and his peers, he probably scored over 30 victories, and although his fighter was hit many times, Akamatsu was never wounded.

It was only natural that such a 'character' who defied the odds and survived would achieve legendary status within the ranks of the JNAF. Akamatsu was said to have engaged in combat while in a drunken stupor, whilst another story concerning his exploits had the nonconformist bolting from a brothel during an air raid and jumping into his fighter still wearing his kimono and wooden clogs! Saburo Sakai, who knew Akamatsu, replied, 'Don't believe those silly stories – it's all nonsense!'

The postwar years proved difficult for the alcoholic ex-fighter pilot. His old comrades took up a collection and presented him with a small Piper, which he flew as a fish search pilot for the Kochi Fishery Association until he eventually sold it to keep himself in drink. Ruined in health by his alcoholism and ostracised by his friends and former comrades, he ran a small cafe in Kochi City until he died on 22 February 1980 of pneumonia, a broken and dejected man.

Lieutenant Yukio Endo

Yukio Endo was regarded as the navy's top B-29 'killer', his pioneering efforts in nightfighting helping the JNAF to develop tactics that enabled fighters to engage the previously invincible B-29s over Japan.

Born in Yamagata Prefecture in September 1915, the future 'King of B-29 Killers' graduated from flight training in 1933 and went on to become a carrier pilot. Endo flew ground support missions in 1938 during the China War, but failed to score any aerial victories before returning to the homeland and becoming an instructor. This tasking lasted until January 1943, when he was assigned to the 251st AG.

USAAC B-17s from Port Moresby had been pounding Rabaul during their nocturnal sorties with near impunity, the crews considering their missions as mere 'milk runs' due to the inaccuracy of anti-aircraft fire. Cdr Yasuna Kozono, CO of the 251st AG, formulated a plan to counter the Flying Fortresses by arming a twin-engined aircraft with a pair of

Lt Yukio Endo was JNAF's top B-29 'killer' who, having perfected methods of attacking the Superfortress in combat, trained other teams in nightfighting tactics (*K Osuo*)

obliquely-mounted 20 mm cannons, the eccentric, hot-headed, commander forcing his plan into action despite being ridiculed by most of his peers and superiors. Lt(jg) Endo was picked by Kozono to test the first model of the Gekko ('Irving').

When the commander's new weapon made its combat debut, the honour of downing the first B-17 in a night action over Rabaul fell to PO1/c Shigetoshi Kudo on 21 May 1943 – despite repeated sorties, Endo failed to score, while his comrades succeeded in spectacular fashion. He returned to Japan and was assigned to the 302nd AG at Atsugi in March 1944, where his job was to train more Gekko nightfighter crews in anticipation of American bombing raids over the mainland.

When Twentieth Air Force B-29s bombed Japan for the first time on the night of 15/16 June 1944, Lt(jg) Endo transferred to the 352nd AG, based at Omura airfield in Kyushu. With eight fully-trained flight crews, he was anxious to put his men to the test, and on the night of 20 August 88 B-29s raided northern Kyushu and his men sortied in force – in one of the costliest missions of the war, the USAAF lost 14 B-29s to all causes.

Endo succeeded in aligning his aircraft beneath the tail of a B-29 over Sasebo, and with calm precision, proceeded to rake the undersides of the Superfortress, which fell away in flames. He repeated this manoeuvre and heavily damaged another, and by the time Endo had finally finished his mission, his tally stood at two destroyed, one probable and two damaged.

From his first encounter with B-29s until his death, Lt(jg) Endo flew night and day intercept missions, returning to Atsugi in November 1944. On 14 January 1945 Yukio Endo intercepted a daylight raid performed by 73rd BW B-29s on Nagoya. After he had shot down one bomber and damaged another, his aircraft was hit and burst into flames. His observer, WO Osamu Nishio, attempted to parachute to safety but failed to survive, whilst Endo, who had been badly burned trying to control the Gekko, attempted to parachute at low altitude but was killed.

A posthumous citation issued to the team of Endo and Nishio on 11 February 1945 by Adm Funizo Tsukahara, CO of the Yokosuka Naval Station stated;

'You downed eight B-29s and damaged more than eight others with your nightfighter when they came over Nagoya and Tokyo. You intercepted the B-29s over the area piloting a nightfighter of the 302nd AG with high more morale and distinguished skills. You are hereby cited.'

He was promoted two ranks to commander.

Chief Petty Officer Shoichi Sugita

Shoichi Sugita became the top ace of the 204th AG during the Solomons campaign, and was one of the JNAF's five highest scoring pilots. He was born in 1924 in Niigata Prefecture, and at the age of 15, dropped out of agriculture school and joined the Imperial Navy.

In March 1942 Sugita graduated from flight training and arrived at his new base at Buin in October. In his first combat on 1 December 1942, he teamed with up PO2/c Saji Kanda to destroy a B-17 over the airfield, although in the process he struck the bomber with his right wing but nevertheless managed to land safely. On the 28th Sugita shared in the destruction of another B-17 over Buin.

Lt Takashi Oshibuchi was a great fighter-leader who fought with the 201st and 253rd AGs at Rabaul, before being given command of the 701st Squadron of the 343rd AG. Oshibuchi was killed on 24 July 1945 over the Bungo Straits by VF-49 Hellcats, his score at the time standing at six victories (*Sakaida*)

The 301st Squadron of the 343rd AG is seen at Matsuyama Airfield in March 1945, this outfit boasting the highest number of aces of any air group at this time. Sitting in the front row (centre) is Capt Minoru Genda, the mastermind of the Pearl Harbor attack and CO of the unit. Lt Naoshi Kanno (48 victories) is in the front row, second from left, whilst the top ace of the unit, CPO Shoichi Sugita (120+ kills), is third from right in the second row. To Sugita's right is CPO Tomoichi Kasai (10 victories) (*Y Izawa*)

CPO Shoichi Sugita claimed two P-38s on the ill-fated Adm Yamamoto escort mission of April 1943. He was an extremely aggressive pilot to the point of being reckless, and it was this trait that eventually led him to his death on 15 April 1945 over Kanoya airfield (*Maru*)

On 2 January 1943 he fought with Wildcats of VMF-121 over Munda Point and claimed one shot down (two were lost). Before month's end, he had claimed another three F4Fs and shared in the destruction of a B-24.

On 18 April Sugita was one of six Zero pilots selected to fly as escort for two 'Betty' bombers, one carrying Adm Isoroku Yamamoto, Commander in Chief of the Combined Fleet. They were ambushed by P-38s and the two bombers shot down. In the wild dogfight that followed, Sugita hit and damaged a P-38 flown by 1Lt Raymond K Hine and may have shot him down (he was the only American lost on this mission). However, his claim for two P-38s was a hollow victory, for each pilot blamed himself for their collective failure to protect their distinguished leader.

Given every chance to redeem their honour by death in combat, the escort pilots threw all caution to the wind, and within three months four of them were dead, and the fifth, Kenji Yanagiya, had been seriously wounded and sent back to Japan. However, instead of embracing death, sole survivor Sugita relished the increasing levels of combat, honing his already razor sharp fighting skills to the point where he became the deadliest of foes.

Sugita claimed Corsairs for the first time on 12 June when he engaged VMF-112 over Guadalcanal. He downed one and shared another, and four days later claimed another F4U (from VMF-122). Sugita's final F4U kill came on 25 August. Just 24 hours later the Marines got their revenge when Sugita was hit by Corsairs from either VMF-214 or -215 south-east of the Shortlands. Forced to bale out with serious burns, he was sent back to Japan.

In March 1944 Sugita joined the 263rd AG and saw heavy action in the Carolines and Marianas. On 8 July he was in a flight of six Zeroes (led by Lt Yasuhiro Shigematsu – group leader with 10+ victories) on their way to Palau that was overwhelmed by VF-31 Hellcats near Yap. All bar Sugita were shot down, and he barely escaped to Peleliu. Leaderless, and with only a handful of aircraft on Guam, the unit was disbanded ten days later and Sugita and a handful of survivors escaped north to the Philippines.

His next assignment was with the 201st AG in the Philippines. Once again he was in constant combat, claiming victory after victory while his comrades fell all around him, and by the time he returned to Japan in January 1945 he had claimed over 120 kills.

An elite fighter air group was formed by Capt Minoru Genda in December 1944 at Matsuyama, on Shikoku Island, the unit being armed exclusively with the new Shiden-Kai ('George'). Genda personally selected Sugita to be a member, and upon his arrival he was posted to the 301st Squadron. In the unit's first combat on 19 March 1945 over Kure, Sugita and his flight claimed three Hellcats.

CPO Shoichi Sugita finally met death on 15 April 1945. American carrier aircraft raided airfields in Kyushu in an effort to destroy *kamikaze* suicide aircraft which posed a serious threat to American warships in Okinawan waters. VF-46's Lt Cdr Robert 'Doc' Weatherup led his strike group in an attack on Kanoya airfield, and when the Hellcats were seen approaching, Sugita and his wingman, PO2/c Toyomi Miyazawa, ran towards two fighters being prepared for take-off at one end of the flightline. Ens Saburo Sakai yelled at Sugita to take cover, but his warning was ignored, and struggling to build up speed as he climbed through 200 ft, he met his end.

Lt Cdr Weatherup, who had completed his rocket and strafing attack on an aircraft in a revetment, then spotted Sugita taking off. He circled around, pulled a big lead, and waited until the wingspan of the ace's fighter was 35 mils in his sight, then opened fire. Sugita apparently saw the tracers and tried to relax his turn, but it was too late. Weatherup saw flicks where his 'slugs' were hitting armour, then the 'George' nosed over trailing a thin plume of smoke. It crashed in a ball of fire at the end of the airfield, and seconds later Weatherup consigned Miyazawa to a similar fate.

In a personal citation issued to Sugita posthumously on 1 August 1945, he was recognised as having achieved 70 individual and 40 shared victories. Since Capt Genda would not accord Sugita a double rank promotion for distinguished service (he reserved such honours for officers), higher authorities intervened and Shoichi Sugita was duly promoted to ensign.

In May 1982, Saburo Sakai met Robert Weatherup at a reunion in California. 'I was looking up from the air raid shelter when I saw you shoot down my comrade', said Sakai. 'He was a great ace but a little reckless.' The two shook hands in the spirit of friendship, and commented on the loss of a great airman.

An unidentified pilot of the 407th Squadron, 343rd AG, stands by the tail of Shiden-Kai 343-B-03, flown by ace WO Koji Ohara. Of interest is the white '03' just visible in the 'meatball', which was used for training purposes. The small white box on the tail reads '2 Suzuki', which translates to 'Section 2, Suzuki', denoting the aircraft's maintainer. The wooden brace across its tail was used to secure the rudder, thus protecting it from wind damage during violent storms (*Y Shiga*)

CPO Hideo Nakao takes a break on the tail of 343-B-20, a Shiden-Kai of the 407th Squadron of the 343rd AG. The white maintenance assignment box reads 'Section 4 Ochiai' (top), 'Kitagawa' (left), and 'Nakao' (right). Ochiai was the chief mechanic for this aircraft, followed by Kitagawa and Nakao (not related to the pilot). CPO Nakao claimed an F6F on 19 March 1945, followed several months later by a P-51 (*K Osuo*)

WO Katsue Kato was a rare 'double ace-in-a-day', achieving the feat during the 343rd AG's baptism of fire on 19 March 1945. Although he claimed ten kills, his tally was never officially recognised (*K Osuo*)

Lt Naoshi Kanno is seen posing in front of a Zero 21 in 1943 at Oita airfield. Although his 'gung ho' fighting spirit endeared him to his CO, Capt Genda, a number of his men felt that he was reckless (*Y Ikari*)

Warrant Officer Katsue Kato

Katsue Kato became a rare 'ace-in-a-day' while flying the new Shiden-Kai with the 'Squadron of Experts'. Born in March 1924 in Ibaragi Prefecture, young Katsue entered naval flight training in October 1941 at Tsuchiura. Graduating in January 1943, he began specialised training as a seaplane pilot. however, due to the tremendous demand for fighter pilots in the Solomons, Kato switched courses, and after a brief training period, was assigned firstly to the 381st AG, then to the 311th Squadron of the 153rd AG. He advanced with the latter group to western New Guinea, where he participated in combat over Biak. At the end of 1944, Kato returned to Japan and was selected to join the 343rd AG.

When US Navy carrier fighters raided Kure Harbour on 19 March 1945, Kato hurled himself into the massed ranks of F6Fs as the No 3 wingman to Lt Naoshi Kanno, CO of the 301st Squadron. By morning's end, he had claimed a record nine destroyed, but because the dogfights were conducted by formations, Kato's individual score was not announced, nor officially recognised. However, his performance was so outstanding that he was cited in the Naval All Units Proclamation.

On 16 April 1945 CPO Katsue Kato was killed in aerial combat with more F6F Hellcats (from VF-17) over Amami Island. It is uncertain whether his score was in excess of nine kills at the time of his death.

Lieutenant Naoshi Kanno

The Naval Academy's top ace, Naoshi Kanno was born on 13 October 1921 in Miyagi Prefecture. Upon graduation from the Etajima academy in the Class of 70 in December 1941, he entered flight training and became a fighter pilot in September 1943.

Kanno first taste of combat came in April 1944 when he was sent to Micronesia as a division officer for the original 343rd AG, remaining with the unit until it was disbanded on 10 July due to combat losses. He was next transferred to the 306th Squadron of the 201st AG, where he gained considerable fame for his combat prowess.

One of his much-admired tactics saw him fearlessly attacking B-24s, sent to bomb Yap Island, from head-on – while still perfecting his technique, Kanno rammed a Liberator and damaged it, but still managed to survive. His squadron claimed over 60 aircraft destroyed around Yap in July, for which it received a unit citation.

In October 1944 the *kamikaze* corps was formed in the Philippines, and it was widely believed that Lt Kanno would be given the honour of leading it. However, command went to Lt Yukio Seki (another Naval Academy graduate), for Kanno was in Japan procuring aircraft for his unit at the time.

When the 343rd AG was reorganised for the second time, Kanno was given command of the 301st Squadron. The unit was now equipped with the Shiden-Kai ('George') fighters, which were Japan's answer to the Hellcat. In their baptism of fire over Japan, the 343rd intercepted carrier aircraft attacking targets in Kure Harbour on 19 March 1945, the 301st initially engaging F4Us of VMF-123 north of Kure Naval Base, before various divisions became separated as the morning combat raged on.

After a wild dogfight off the eastern coast of Shikoku Island, Lt Kanno reassembled his men to resume the hunt. Within minutes a pair of VBF-10 F4Us, flown by Lt Robert 'Windy' Hill and Ens Roy D Erickson, encountered the 'Georges' from astern, the former pilot squeezing off a burst at the leader who was flying straight and level. Lt Kanno's fighter burst into flames, and the pilot baled out close enough for Erickson to see his astonished face, and his brand new brown flightsuit!

Lt Kanno landed roughly in a farm field not far from Matsuyama Castle, suffering burns to his face and hands. An elderly farmer, mistaking him for an American, advanced on the pilot with a pitchfork, although he soon backed off upon hearing curses aimed at him in Japanese! Quickly appropriating a bicycle, Kanno pedalled furiously back to base.

On 1 August 1945, whilst leading his men against B-24s over Yaku Island, one of his 20 mm cannons blew up due to a mechanical defect, leaving a large hole in his wing. He experienced difficulties in controlling his aircraft and his wingman, WO Mitsuo Hori, offered to stay with him. Kanno kept pointing at the bombers, and when Hori insisted on flying escort, Kanno glared at him and gestured again. The wingman reluctantly left and Kanno was never seen again.

Lt Naoshi Kanno was elevated two ranks to commander and received a posthumous commendation. His bulldog tenacity, while admired by his CO, Capt Genda, worried his subordinates, with some of his men even considering him reckless and overrated. Indeed, of the four squadrons within the 343rd, Kanno's 301st suffered the heaviest casualties.

According to the Naval All Units Proclamation No 214, Kanno had destroyed or damaged 30 enemy aircraft in his combat tour of the Carolines and the Philippines. Additionally, it stated that he achieved another 18 victories while serving with the 343rd, including two B-24s downed on his last mission.

Ensign Kaneyoshi Muto

'Muto was the toughest fighter pilot in the Imperial Navy!' according to comrade Saburo Sakai. That a man so short in height could wield a Zero fighter like a Samurai sword to 'cut down' far bigger opponents with speed and grace is hard to imagine. Yet Muto was likened to Japan's most famous medieval swordsman, Miyamoto Musashi.

Kaneyoshi Muto (his given name could also be pronounced Kinsuke, which he preferred) was born in June 1916 in Aichi Prefecture to a poor farming family. In June 1935 Muto enlisted in the navy at Kure and briefly served aboard the destroyer *Uranami*. Realising that the aviation service offered career advancement, he applied for, and was accepted into, the flight training programme, graduating in July 1936 and being posted to the Omura AG.

With the advent of the China War, Muto found himself in combat with the 12th AG, scoring his first victory – a Soviet I-16 – over Nanking on 4 December 1937. He fought continuously over Hankow and added four more kills before his tour of duty ended. On 30 April 1938 Muto received a rare official commendation for distinguished service.

When the Pacific War broke out, Muto was a member of the 3rd AG. After attacking Iba and Clark Fields with the group in the first days of

Ens Kaneyoshi Muto was considered the 'toughest pilot in the JNAF' by famed ace Saburo Sakai. Although only 5 ft 3 in tall, he was a 'giant' amongst JNAF aces. Muto was also known for his great sense of humour, which made him a favourite with his comrades (*Y Shiga*)

conflict, he ranged over the Dutch East Indies with the unit. However, the end of the Malayan campaign in April 1942 saw him return to Japan.

In November 1942, Muto advanced to Rabaul with the 252nd AG, subsequently participating in the heavy fighting over the Solomons and eastern New Guinea. In April 1943 he received a military decoration for distinguished service.

In November, 'Kin-Chan' (the nickname means 'Little Gold') was transferred back to the mainland to join the Yokosuka AG, with whom he flew as an instructor with old China War comrade, Saburo Sakai. By the summer of 1944 the war situation had deteriorated to the point where the Yokosuka AG – the proud guardian of the Imperial capital – was ordered to Iwo Jima. On 24 June, the island was attacked by Hellcats, and in a staggeringly one-sided combat, the Americans butchered the Zeroes. Muto, however, returned alive with several victories to his credit. In desperation, he and his men were ordered to crash their aircraft in a *kamikaze* style attack on American warships, Muto and two wingman duly launching on their one-way mission on 5 July. Inbound to the target, they were bounced by Hellcats, forcing them to abort their mission and fight their way back to base. The remnants of the unit were evacuated back to Japan shortly afterwards

Upon his return, Muto was assigned air defence duties over Tokyo, and when B-29s started to bomb Japan in November, he tackled the massed formations of four-engined 'heavies' with typical gusto.

On 16 February 1945 the US Navy launched its first carrier raid against the Tokyo area, and Muto, piloting a new Shiden-Kai ('George') from the

Waiting to sortie, WO Yuzaburo Toguchi (left) and Ens Matsuo Hagiri (13 victories, right) relax at Yokosuka airfield's ready area in 1945. Hagiri claimed an F6F Hellcat during the big carrier raid of 16 February 1945 (*M Hagiri*)

evaluation department of his air group, joined his squadronmates in their efforts to thwart the raiders. Muto became embroiled in a fierce dogfight with F6Fs from VF-82 that saw four Hellcats downed.

Desperate to find heroes to help deflect news of the seemingly endless series of military defeats, the Japanese press found WO Kaneyoshi Muto's deeds during this sortie ideal for their propaganda purposes. An exaggerated version of the combat was duly spread that saw Muto single-handedly take on 12 F6Fs, destroying four – this myth survives to this day.

In June Muto was transferred to the 301st Squadron of the 343rd AG as a replacement pilot for the great ace, Shoichi Sugita, who had been killed in April. On 24 July, during his first combat mission with the unit, Muto failed to return from the Bungo Straits. The squadron's mission on this day was to destroy enemy aircraft heading to their carriers after they had attacked warships anchored in Kure Harbour.

Subsequent research in the 1980s revealed that Muto's flight bounced a pair of VBF-1 F4U Corsairs lagging behind a larger group, swiftly shooting down Ens Robert J Speckman and leaving Lt(jg) Robert Applegate to engage the enemy alone. Just as he was on the verge of being overwhelmed, two Hellcats from VF-88 (flown by Lt Malcolm Cagle and his wingman, Lt(jg) Ken Neyer) charged in to help the lone Corsair pilot. Neyer was also shot down, however, leaving the two surviving Americans to fight their way back to their carrier. Applegate was also eventually shot down, parachuting from his damaged Corsair and subsequently being rescued, leaving Cagle as the only pilot to make it back to his ship.

During the action both Applegate and Cagle had downed three 'Georges', one of which was flown by Muto – it is not known which of them shot down the great ace.

Kaneyoshi Muto received a posthumous promotion to ensign. His final tally of kills cannot be ascertained, for some Japanese historians have estimated his score to be around 28, while others have pegged it at 35.

Lieutenant Yutaka Morioka

Slim of build and gentle in character, Yutaka Morioka was a fearless fighter-leader and a late starter in the Zero fighter. He was born on 8 March 1922 to parents whose job was guns and explosives distribution.

Morioka entered the Naval Academy at Etajima and graduated on 11 November 1941 in the 70th Class, after which he trained as a 'Val' dive-bomber pilot, but did not see any combat. He subsequently became a dive-bomber instructor with the Usa AG in northern Kyushu.

When the war situation became critical, Morioka was offered the chance to become a Zero pilot, and in April 1944, as a member of the 302nd AG at Atsugi, he began the conversion with the help of the unit's top fighter ace, Ens Sadaaki Akamatsu. In their first dogfighting session, the master instructor and the eager neophyte engaged in mock dogfights over Atsugi airfield until, after about ten minutes, Akamatsu called over the radio, 'Lt Morioka! I have shot you down four times already!' However, after two months of intensive training Akamatsu presented his pupil with a diploma.

In the wake of his conversion, Lt Morioka became the youngest JNAF squadron leader at age 23 when he was given command of three

Pilots of the 2nd Squadron, 302nd AG, pose for a group shot at Atsugi airfield in late 1944. The squadron CO, Lt Yutaka Morioka, is seated in the front row, centre – his wingmen on the squadron's final wartime combat mission of 15 August 1945, being Ens Mitsuo Tsuruta (second row, third from right), Ens Muneaki Morimoto (first row, second from left) and Ens Tooru Miyaki (first row, third from right) (*Y Morioka*)

squadrons – two equipped with Raidens and one with Zeroes. From November 1944 onwards, they intercepted B-29s over Tokyo and surrounding areas.

On 23 January 1945 Morioka attacked B-29s of the 73rd BW near Nagoya, damaging a Superfortress before its tail gunner shot off his left hand – his comrades later destroyed the crippled bomber. After brief hospitalisation, Lt Morioka was fitted with an iron claw and returned to combat.

Lt Morioka became an ace just two hours before the end of World War 2 when he shot down a Hellcat from VF-88. He is seen here in the cockpit of his Zero 52, his iron claw clutching the throttle (just visible through the windscreen) (*Y Morioka*)

On 3 August 1945 Morioka led four Zeroes in an attempt to thwart the rescue of Capt Edward Mikes Jr of the 458th FS, who had parachuted from his damaged P-51 into Tokyo Bay. A B-17G of the 4th Emergency Rescue Squadron had dropped a wooden life-boat to Mikes, and the submarine *Aspro,* four Mustangs, two Privateers and a B-29 had all been involved in protecting the downed airman.

During the aerial engagement fought above Mikes, Morioka shot down 2Lt John J Coneff in a 457th FS P-51, although the pair of PB4Y-2s (from VPB-121) and the remaining Mustangs forced JNAF pilots to withdraw. However, before leaving the combat area, the four Zeroes twice strafed Capt Mikes in his life-boat, although he survived the harrowing ordeal with only few scratches from wood splinters.

On 13 August Morioka led eight Zeroes in an attack on a PBY which had landed in Tokyo Bay in an attempt to rescue a downed Hellcat pilot. Although the crew of the flying boat succeeded in taking off and racing at wave top height across the bay towards the open sea, they were eventually shot down near Tateyama, at the mouth of Tokyo Bay, following a brief chase.

On 15 August 1945 – just two hours before the surrender announce-

Lt(jg) Shiro Kurotori (right) and Tech/Lt(jg) Minoru Hida of the Yokosuka AG stand beside the impressive scoreboard painted onto the rear fuselage of their Gekko nightfighter – these victory markings were designed by Lt Cdr Yamada of the 7th Squadron. The aircraft's tail number (Yo-101) has been painted over *(via Robert C Mikesh)*

187

The same J1N1-S Gekko (Yo-101) seen in the previous photograph serves as backdrop for this shot of assorted Yokosuka AG air- and groundcrew (*via Robert C Mikesh*)

With its code just visible on the tail, this was the Gekko ('Irving') was flown by Lt(jg) Shiro Kurotori and CPO Juzo Kuramoto on the night of 25 May 1945 when the pair downed five B-29s and damaged a sixth. Note that the elaborate victory marks seen in the previous two photographs have not yet been applied (*K Osuo*)

ment – Lt Morioka achieved his fifth, and final, victory when he and seven comrades fought six F6F Hellcats of VF-88 in what was the last major dogfight between Hellcats and Zeroes in World War 2. He had bounced his victim at the start of the engagement, forcing the Hellcat pilot to take to his parachute. When Morioka and his crew chief went to visit the American three days later, they were turned away, for he had died of his wounds.

Becoming a certified practising accountant after the war, Yutaka Morioka credited his survival to veteran ace Akamatsu. On 4 December 1991, during the 50th Anniversary of the Pearl Harbor attack in Hawaii, he met Edward Mikes, whom he and his men had strafed 46 years earlier. The two old warriors shook hands and became the best of friends. Morioka died in July 1993.

Lt(jg) Shiro Kurotori

Shiro Kurotori (whose surname means 'blackbird'), became an 'ace in-a-night', and an instant hero in Japan, in 1945.

Born in Tokyo in February 1923, young Shiro received his early flight training at Tsuchiura as a reconnaissance pilot, before switching to nightfighters when he was assigned to the Yokosuka AG. Here, he studied the techniques of Shigetoshi Kudo – one of the great nightfighting pioneers – and others who had returned from Rabaul.

Based on the experiences of the same veterans, the group prepared a Gekko with upward firing 20 mm cannon for Ens Kuratori and CPO Juzo Kuramoto. On the night of 15/16 April 1945, the pair sortied from Oppama airfield against B-29s from the 313th and 314th BW sent to attack Kawasaki and downed a Superfortress and damaged another.

The following month Kuratori and Kuramoto scored a spectacular success on the night of 25/26 May, their award citation, dated 1 June 1945, stating;

'Since December 1944, you participated in intercepting enemy planes attacking the mainland, downing six and damaging two others. You did a splendid job. Especially worthy was the results of 25 May 1945. At night, a big formation of B-29s came flying into the Kanto District. You piloted

A 332nd AG J1N1-Sa Type 2 Gekko Model 11 Ko is boarded in mid-March 1945 by its pilot, FPO1/c Nagano, and observer/aircraft commander Lt(jg) Tadashi Maniwa (*via Robert C Mikesh*)

A veritable 'sea' of JNAF single- and twin-engined types ground the Atsugi flightline in this late-1944 view. The five J1N1-Ss seen with their engines idling in the foreground belong to the 302nd AG (*via Robert C Mikesh*)

a Gekko and bravely attacked the waves of bombers, from south-west of Kanto to the north-east. In the fight lasting three hours, you downed five and damaged one. By your distinguished service, you contributed to the defence of the Imperial land. I hereby recognise your military merit and your deeds will be cited in the Naval All Units Proclamation.'

The citation was issued by the Adm Michitaro Tozuka, CO of the Yokosuka Naval Air Station. In addition to the citation, the team of Kuratori and Kuramoto also received ceremonial swords in recognition of their actions, and the former was promoted to lieutenant (junior grade) on 1 June. His CO also forbade him to intentionally ram a B-29.

Lt(jg) Kuratori was still training for the final decisive air battle when the war came to an abrupt end. He had achieved six B-29 victories.

A6M Model 52s of the 653rd AG (a mixed fighter and reconnaissance group) undergo maintenance at an overcrowded Oita airfield in August 1944 (*via Aerospace Publishing*)

Lt Chitoshi Isozaki was a great instructor who produced many aces – one of his most successful students was Ens Saburo Sakai. He is shown here at Meiji Airfield in December 1944 whilst serving with the 302nd AG. He finished the war flying Shiden-Kai fighters with the elite 343rd AG in home defence missions (*Sakaida*)

BIBLIOGRAPHY

Anabuki, S *Soku No Kawa (Pale Blue River)*. Kojinsha Publishers, Tokyo, Japan, 1985

Hinoki, Y *Tsubasa No Kessen (Wings of Bloody Combat)*. Kojinsha Publishers, Tokyo, Japan, 1967

Izawa, Y and Hata, I *Nihon Rikugun Sentoki Tai (Japanese Army Fighter Units)*. Kantosha Publishers, Tokyo, Japan, 1977

Jobo, R *Itsutsu No Sora (Five Stars in the Sky)*. Seiunsha Publishers, Tokyo, Japan, 1985

Kuroe, Y *AA Hayabusa Sento Tai (Alas, Hayabusa Fighter Squadron)*. Kojinsha Publishers, Tokyo, Japan, 1984

Miyabe, H *Kato Hayabusa Sento Tai No Saigo (The Last of the Hayabusa Fighter Squadron Kato)*. Kojinsha Publishers, Tokyo, Japan, 1986

Osuo, K *Rikugun Koku Eiyu Retsuden (Japanese Army Air Force Heroes Biographies, Medaled Pilots of Japanese Army Air Force in World War 2)*. Model Art Co Ltd, Tokyo, Japan, 1993

Sakurai, T *Rikugun Hiko Dai 244 Sentai Shi (History of the Army 244 Air Group)*. Soubunsha Publishers, Tokyo, Japan, 1995

Thorpe, D W *Japanese Army Air Force Camouflage And Markings World War II*. Aero Publishers, 1968

Watanabe, Y *Rikugun Boku Sen (Japan Air Defense, Pictorial History of Air War Over Japan, Japanese Army Air Force)*. Hara Shobo Co Ltd., Tokyo, Japan, 1980

Famous Airplanes of the World, Army Type 97 Fighter, No 29, Bunrindo Publishers, Tokyo, Japan, 1991

Maru Mechanic No 37 Hien and Goshikisen. Maru (Kojinsha), Tokyo, Japan, 1982

Nihon Rikugun Isshiki Sentoki No Toso To 'Markings' (Japanese Army Type 1 Fighter Camouflage and Markings). Model Art Co Ltd, Tokyo, Japan, 1992

APPENDICES

Flying Units of the JAAF

The flying units of the JAAF were organised much like their opposite numbers in Allied air forces. Japan's Army and Navy had their own air service, there being no indepedent air force.

The JAAF was organised into five air armies called Kokugun. Each air army had specific areas of operations. For example, in the spring of 1944 the 2nd Air Army was responsible for all of Manchuria, and had its headquarters in Hsingking, whilst the 4th Air Army administered the area of the Philippines, Celebes and western New Guinea from Manila. Their task was to co-operate with the local area army headquarters and to ensure the flow of equipment, supplies and personnel to wherever they were needed.

The Hikoshidan (air division) was the largest tactical organisation under Air Army control. It exercised operational and administrative control over lower air units in its command.

The Hikodan (air brigade) was the next organisation down from the air division, and there were usually two or more air brigades attached to a single Hikoshiden. This was a highly-mobile, operational, organisation, with a small headquarters staff. It was mostly concerned with tactical matters. The usual strength of each air brigade was three or four Hikosentais (fighter regiment or air group).

The Hikosentai, or simply sentai, was the basic operational unit of the JAAF. It was composed of three or more Chutais (companies or squadrons). Sentais had between 27 and 49 aircraft, with each squadron comprising roughly 16 aircraft and a similar number of pilots, plus a maintenence and repair unit. A fighter regiment would have roughly 400 officers and men.

The Shotai (flight or section) usually had three aircraft. This was the smallest flying unit, and later on in the war, it was sometimes composed of four aircraft – through hard experience, it had been found that the odd man out in a three-fighter flight usually became separated in an engagement and would fail to survive.

JAAF Sentais of World War 2

1st Sentai
Established 5/7/38 at Kagamigahara, Saitama Prefecture, Japan
Aircraft: Ki-27, Ki-43 and Ki-84
Area of operations: Manchuria (Nomonhan), China, Burma, East Indies, Indochina, Rabaul, Solomons, New Guinea, Philippines, Formosa and Japan
Unit disbanded at Takahagi, Saitama Prefecture, at the end of the war
Remarks: First flying unit of the JAAF, it claimed 245 Soviet aircraft shot down and 95 probables at Nomonhan for the loss of 16 aeroplanes

4th Sentai
Established 7/38 in Fukuoka Prefecture, Japan
Aircraft: Ki-10, Ki-27 and Ki-45
Area of operations: Formosa and Japan
Unit disbanded at the end of the war at Ozuki Air Base, Yamaguchi Prefecture, Japan
Remarks: Distinguished itself in home defence of Kyushu. Leading B-29 killers were Capt Isamu Kashiide and 1Lt Sadamitsu Kimura (recipients of the Bukosho)

5th Sentai
Established 31/8/38 at Tachikawa (Tokyo)
Aircraft: Ki-10, Ki-27, Ki-45 and Ki-100
Area of operations: East Indies, western New Guinea and Japan
Unit disbanded at the end of the war at Kiyosu, south-east of Nagoya, Japan

Remarks: Home defence unit. Bukosho recipients were WO Isamu Hotani, WO Yoshio Sakaguchi and Capt Fujitaro Ito

9th Sentai
Established 1/7/38 in China
Aircraft: Ki-10, Ki-27, Ki-44 and Ki-84
Area of operations: Manchuria (Nomonhan) and China
Unit was disbanded at the end of the war at Nanjing
(Nanking), China
Remarks: Flew against B-29s

11th Sentai
Established 31/8/38 at Harbin, Manchuria
Aircraft: Ki-27, Ki-43 and Ki-84
Area of operations: Manchuria (Nomonhan), China, Indochina, East Indies, Burma, Rabaul, Solomons, eastern New Guinea, Formosa, Philippines and Japan
Unit disbanded at the end of the war at Takahagi, Saitama
Prefecture, Japan
Remarks: Lost 19 aircraft at Nomonhan, but claimed over 530 Soviet machines destroyed. Top JAAF ace was WO Hiromichi Shinohara

13th Sentai
Established 7/38 at Kakogawa, Hyogo Prefecture, Japan
Aircraft: Ki-10, Ki-27, Ki-43, Ki-45 and Ki-84
Area of operations: Korea, Rabaul, New Guinea, East Indies, Indochina and Formosa
Unit disbanded at the end of the war in Formosa

17th Sentai
Established 10/2/44 at Kagamigahara, Japan
Aircraft: Ki-61 and Ki-100
Area of operations: Philippines, Formosa and Japan
Disbanded at the end of the war in Formosa

18th Sentai
Established 10/2/44 at Choufu, near Tokyo, from the 244th Sentai
Aircraft: Ki-61 and Ki-100
Area of operations: Philippines and Japan
Unit disbanded at the end of the war at Matsudo, near Tokyo
Remarks: Lt Mitsuo Oyake won the Bukosho for

shooting down four B-29s (one by ramming) on 7/4/45 and damaging three others

19th Sentai
Established 10/2/44 at the Akeno Fighter School in Japan
Aircraft: Ki-61
Area of operations: Indonesia, Philippines, Formosa and Okinawa
Unit disbanded in Formosa at the end of the war

20th Sentai
Established 1/12/43 at Itami, Hyogo Prefecture, Japan
Aircraft: Ki-43 and Ki-45
Area of operations: Okinawa, Formosa and the Philippines
Unit lost nearly all of its pilots by 6/45 in suicide attacks at Okinawa

21st Sentai
Established 15/10/42 at Hanoi, Indochina, comprising the 84th Independent Fighter Squadron
Aircraft: Ki-27 and Ki-45
Area of operations: Philippines, Burma, Indochina and East Indies
Unit disbanded in Formosa at the end of the war

22nd Sentai
Established 5/3/44 at Fussa, near Tokyo
Aircraft: Ki-84
Area of operations: China, Philippines, Korea and Japan
Unit disbanded at the end of the war at Kimpo (Seoul), Korea
Remarks: First sentai to receive the Ki-84

23rd Sentai
Established 11/10/44 at Inba, Chiba Prefecture, Japan
Aircraft: Ki-43, Ki-44 and Ki-61
Area of operations: Iwo Jima and Japan
Unit disbanded at Inba at the end of the war

24th Sentai
Established 1/9/38 at Harbin, Manchuria, from the 11th Sentai
Aircraft: Ki-27, Ki-43 and Ki-84
Area of operations: Manchuria (Nomonhan), China, Formosa, Philippines, New Guinea, East Indies and Okinawa

Unit disbanded at the end of the war in Formosa
Remarks: During Nomonhan Incident claimed 214 Soviet aircraft shot down and 56 probables for the loss of 12 pilots

25th Sentai
Established 11/42 at Hankow, China
Aircraft: Ki-43 and Ki-84
Area of operations: China and Korea
Unit disbanded in Korea at the end of the war

26th Sentai
Established 2/10/42 in Manchuria
Aircraft: Ki-27, Ki-30, Ki-51, Ki-43 and Ki-44
Area of operations: Manchuria, China, Philippines, New Guinea, East Indies, Indochina, Formosa and Okinawa
Disbanded in Formosa at the end of the war

28th Sentai
Established 6/39 in Manchuria
Aircraft: Ki-46, Ki-61 and Ki-102
Area of operations: Manchuria and Japan
Disbanded 7/45

29th Sentai
Established 1/7/39 at Kagamigahara, Gifu Prefecture, Japan
Aircraft: Ki-27, Ki-44 and Ki-84
Area of operations: Manchuria, China, Philippines, Formosa and Okinawa
Disbanded in Formosa at the end of the war

30th Sentai
Established 30/6/43 in Manchuria
Aircraft: Ki-27 and Ki-43
Area of operations: Manchuria, Philippines and Burma
Disbanded 30/5/45 in Thailand

31st Sentai
Established 7/38 in China
Aircraft: Ki-10, Ki-61 and Ki-43
Area of operations: Manchuria and Philippines
Unit disbanded 30/5/45 in Singapore

33rd Sentai
Established 1/8/38 in China
Aircraft: Ki-10, Ki-27, Ki-43 and Ki-44
Area of operations: Manchuria (Nomonhan), China, Burma, India, New Guinea, East Indies and Philippines
Disbanded at the end of the war at Medan, Sumatra

47th Sentai
Established 10/43 at Choufu, near Tokyo
Aircraft: Ki-44 and Ki-84
Area of operations: Japan and Okinawa
Unit disbanded at the end of the war at Ozuki, Yamaguchi Prefecture, Japan
Remarks: The unit was organised from the 47th Independent Squadron

48th Sentai
Established 5/11/43 in Manchuria
Aircraft: Ki-27 and Ki-43
Area of operations: China
Disbanded at the end of the war in Manchuria

50th Sentai
Established 10/9/40 in Formosa
Aircraft: Ki-27, Ki-43 and Ki-84
Area of operations: Philippines, Burma, western New Guinea, and Indochina
Disbanded in Formosa at the end of the war
Remarks: MSgt Satoshi Anabuki (top JAAF ace in WW 2) served with this unit

51st Sentai
Established 28/4/44 at Ozuki, Yamaguchi Prefecture, Japan
Aircraft: Ki-84
Area of operations: Philippines and Japan
Disbanded at the end of the war at Shimodate, Ibaraki Prefecture, Japan

52nd Sentai
Established 28/4/44 at Osaka, Japan
Aircraft: Ki-84
Area of operations: Philippines and Japan
Disbanded at the end of the war at Choufu (near Tokyo)

53rd Sentai
Established 3/4/44 at Tokorozawa, Saitama Prefecture, Japan
Aircraft: Ki-45
Area of operations: Japan
Disbanded at the end of the war at Fujigaya
Remarks: B-29 interception duties. Sgt Nobuo Negishi received the Bukosho

54th Sentai
Established 21/7/41 at Kashiwa, Gifu Prefecture, Japan
Aircraft: Ki-27, Ki-43, Ki-45 and Ki-84
Area of operations: China, Philippines, East Indies and Okinawa Disbanded at the end of the war in Formosa

55th Sentai
Established 30/5/44 at Taisho (near Osaka), Japan
Aircraft: Ki-61
Area of operations: Philippines and Japan Disbanded at the end of the war at Sano, Nara Prefecture

56th Sentai
Established 8/44 at Taisho (near Osaka), Japan
Aircraft: Ki-61
Area of operations: Japan Disbanded at the end of the war at Itami, Osaka Prefecture
Remarks: WO Tadao Sumi was a Bukosho recipient. Unit claimed 11 B-29s destroyed for the loss of 30 pilots

59th Sentai
Established 1/7/38 at Kagamigahara, Gifu Prefecture, Japan
Aircraft: Ki-27, Ki-43, Ki-61 and Ki-100
Area of operations: China, Manchuria (Nomonhan), Indochina, East Indies, New Guinea, Okinawa and Japan Disbanded at the end of the war at Ashiya, Fukuoka Prefecture, Japan
Remarks: 1Lt Naoyuki Ogata was a Bukosho recipient

63rd Sentai
Established 25/2/43 at Hachinohe, Aomori Prefecture, Japan
Aircraft: Ki-27 and Ki-43
Area of operations: New Guinea Disbanded 25/7/44 in New Guinea

64th Sentai
Established 1/8/38 in Manchuria
Aircraft: Ki-10, Ki-27, Ki-43 and Ki-44
Area of operations: Manchuria (Nomonhan), China, Indochina, Burma, Thailand and East Indies Disbanded at the end of the war in Cambodia
Remarks: The 64th was the most famous JAAF unit during WW 2, and had the highest number of aces. They fought against the AVG. Unit claimed 258 victories in WW 2, and received nine unit citations up to 1/45

68th Sentai
Established 3/42 at Harbin, Manchuria
Aircraft: Ki-61.
Area of operations: Rabaul (New Britain), New Guinea, and Halmahera. Unit was destroyed by the USAAF, and disbanded 25/7/44 in New Guinea

70th Sentai
Established 3/41 in Manchuria
Aircraft: Ki-27, Ki-44 and Ki-84
Area of operations: Manchuria and Japan Disbanded at the end of the war at Kashiwa, near Tokyo
Remarks: Capt Yoshio Yoshida and 2Lt Makoto Ogawa both received the Bukosho for their successes against B-29s

71st Sentai
Established 30/6/44 at Kameyama, Shimane Prefecture, Japan
Aircraft: Ki-43 and Ki-84
Area of operations: Philippines and Japan Disbanded at the end of the war at Hofu, Yamaguchi Prefecture
Remarks: Sgt Mizunori Fukuda attacked a flight of P-38s on 7/1/45, which resulted in the death of USAAF's second-ranking ace, Maj Thomas McGuire (38 kills)

72nd Sentai
Established 5/44 at Kita Ise, south-west of Nagoya, Japan
Aircraft: Ki-43 and Ki-84
Area of operations: Japan, Formosa, and Philippines Disbanded in the Philippines 1/45
Remarks: Unit was annihilated. Survivors joined an infantry unit and fought as guerilas until the end of the war

73rd Sentai
Established 5/44 at Kita Ise with the 72nd Sentai
Aircraft: Ki-43 and Ki-84
Area of operations: Japan and Philippines Disbanded (unofficially) 3/45 in the Philippines
Remarks: Unit suffered the same fate as the 72nd

Sentai, fighting on as ground troops

77th Sentai
Established 27/7/38 at Nanjing (Nanking), China
Aircraft: Ki-10, Ki-27 and Ki-43
Area of operations: China, Thailand, Burma, East Indies and New Guinea
Disbanded 25/7/44 in New Guinea
Remarks: Unit was destroyed by the USAAF, not one pilot surviving the war

78th Sentai
Established 31/3/42 in China
Aircraft: Ki-27, Ki-43 and Ki-84
Area of operations: Manchuria, Rabaul and New Guinea. Disbanded 25/7/44 in New Guinea
Remarks: Unit was destroyed by the USAAF

85th Sentai
Established 1/3/41 near Harbin, Manchuria
Aircraft: Ki-27, Ki-44 and Ki-84
Area of operations: Manchuria, China and Korea Disbanded in Kimpo (Seoul), Korea, at the end of the war
Remarks: Claimed over 250 enemy aircraft destroyed/damaged from 7/43 until the end of the war

87th Sentai
Established 1/3/41 at Harbin, Manchuria
Aircraft: Ki-27 and Ki-44
Area of operations: Manchuria, Burma, East Indies and Japan Disbanded in Singapore at the end of the war

101st Sentai
Established 7/44 at Kita Ise, south-west of Nagoya, Japan
Aircraft: Ki-27, Ki-43 and Ki-84
Area of operations: Okinawa and Japan Disbanded at the end of the war at Takamatsu, Kagawa Prefecture, Japan

102nd Sentai
Established 7/44 at Kita Ise, Japan
Aircraft: Ki-43 and Ki-84
Area of operations: Okinawa and Japan Disbanded 30/7/45 at Narimasu, Japan

103rd Sentai
Established 25/8/44 at Kameyama, Shimane Prefecture, Japan
Aircraft: Ki-43 and Ki-84
Area of operations: Japan
Disbanded at the end of the war on Awaji Island (off the coast of Kobe), Japan
Remarks: Capt Tomojiro Ogawa and 1Lt Rintai Miyamoto were both Bukosho recipients

104th Sentai
Established 26/7/44 at Ozuki, Yamaguchi Prefecture, from the 4th Sentai
Aircraft: Ki-43 and Ki-84
Area of operations: Manchuria
Disbanded at the end of the war in Manchuria
Remarks: In 8/44 the unit reorganised as the 25th Independent Squadron

105th Sentai
Established 8/44 at Taichung, Formosa
Aircraft: Ki-61
Area of operations: Okinawa and Formosa
Disbanded at the end of the war in Formosa

111th Sentai
Established 10/7/45 at Akeno in Mie Prefecture, Japan
Aircraft: Ki-84 and Ki-100
Area of operations: Japan
Disbanded at the end of the war at Komaki, near Nagoya, Japan
Remarks: One of the last JAAF units formed

112th Sentai
Established 18/7/45 at Nitta, Japan
Aircraft: Ki-84 and Ki-100
Area of operations: Japan
Disbanded at the end of the war at Nitta
Remarks: The last JAAF unit to form. Their only combat occurred on 10/8/45 when four pilots damaged a B-29 of the 314th Bomb Wing over Tokyo

200th Sentai
Established 12/10/44 at Akeno, Mie Prefecture, Japan
Aircraft: Ki-84
Area of operations: Philippines
Disbanded 30/5/45 in the Philippines
Remarks: Survivors joined an infantry unit and fought as guerillas until the end of the war

204th Sentai

Established 4/42 at Chinsei, Manchuria
Aircraft: Ki-27 and Ki-43
Area of operations: Manchuria, Burma, Thailand, Indochina, Philippines, Okinawa and Formosa
Disbanded at the end of the war in Formosa

244th Sentai

Established 4/42, reorganised from the 144th Sentai
Aircraft: Ki-27, Ki-61 and Ki-100
Area of operations: Japan
Disbanded at the end of the war at Yokaichi, Shiga Prefecture, Japan
Remarks: Unit had nine Bukosho recipients including Maj Teruhiko Kobayashi, the JAAF's youngest sentai commander. It also had an air-to-air B-29 ramming unit. The sentai claimed 73 B-29s shot down and 92 damaged. It was the most famous home defence unit of the war

246th Sentai

Established 8/42 from the 13th Sentai
Aircraft: Ki-27, Ki-44, Ki-84 and Ki-46
Area of operations: Japan and Philippines
Disbanded at the end of the war at Taisho, near Osaka, Japan

248th Sentai

Established 10/8/42 at Ozuki, Yamaguchi Prefecture, Japan, from the 4th Sentai
Aircraft: Ki-27 and Ki-43
Area of operations: Japan and New Guinea
Disbanded 25/7/44 in New Guinea
Remarks: Destroyed by the USAAF

Aerial Victory Claims by JAAF Pilots

In the American and Commonwealth custom, the shooting down of five or more enemy aircraft entitled the pilot to claim the coveted title of 'ace'. He joined an elite fraternity of fighter pilots whose accomplishments were widely publicised in the military and national press. As the victories mounted, his achievements were recognised by medals and promotions.

The Japanese adopted many of the flight concepts from the West (Europe in particular). However, in Japanese culture, the trait of individuality which was so valued by the West, was shunned. Since early school days, Japanese children are taught to work and sacrifice for the benefit of the group. In military training both before and during World War 2, it was common for the drill instructor to line up his trainees and strike them for the shortcomings of a single individual in the group. In war, teamwork was critical, and there could be no prima donnas. When an individual accomplished a distinguished feat, the group received the honours.

As with most fighter pilots, Japanese aviators did keep personal scores, and for morale purposes they would paint victory markings on the aircraft. Since pilots flew aircraft on an availability basis, and most did not have their own personal mount, the number of 'kill' markings on the aircraft could be deceptive. It was the fighter rather than the pilot which recorded the victory.

There was no established rule for determining a victory. Many pilots would claim the destruction of an enemy aircraft which was seen to smoke in the air, believing that it would never reach home. The Japanese did have gun cameras, but they were only used for training purposes. The claim was taken on face value and added to the group's score. Since there were usually no decorations, promotions or publicity based solely upon claims, there was no motive to inflate totals.

The claims by JAAF pilots cannot be taken at face value, however. The inflated totals resulted from both confusion in combat and from a very liberal method of scorekeeping. During the war, some JAAF pilots received official recognition from the government for their victories (taken from individual citations), but this does not imply that these victories were 'confirmed'.

Postwar Japanese historians have recognised the problem of inflated totals, and tried to compensate by systematically reducing the scores by percentages. A case in point would be Maj Yasuhiko Kuroe. He claimed 51 victories in his postwar memoir, but Japanese historians have 'corrected' his claim down to 30. Maj Iwori Sakai has nine recognised victories, although he claimed 15.

WO Hiromichi Shinohara is attributed with 58 victories during the Nomonhan Incident, but the Soviets only admitted losing 207 aircraft during the entire conflict. In analysing Shinohara's score versus the admitted losses, his claim would not seem to be credible.

Since there is no basis for verifying claims, the

postwar reduction of scores seem arbitrary. Likewise, accepting the claims on face value would also be historically inaccurate. The following list of JAAF aces was compiled from numerous sources. These scores are simply unverified claims either made by the pilots, or attributed to them. The numerical scores represent a mixture of confirmed, unconfirmed, probable, damaged and imagined victories

JAAF Aces Listing

Rank	Name	Score	Rank	Name	Score	Rank	Name	Score
WO	Shinohara, Hiromichi	58	WO	Takagaki, Haruo	17	WO	Nomura, Akiyoshi	10
Maj	Kuroe, Yasuhiko	51	Maj	Namai, Kiyoshi	16	WO	Tsubone, Kosuke	10
MSgt	Anabuki, Satoshi	51	Maj	Yonaga, Hyoe	16	MSgt	Asano, Jiro	10
Maj	Sakagawa, Toshio	49+	1Lt	Kuroki, Tameyoshi	16	MSgt	Kobayashi, Taro	10
WO	Nakada, Yoshihiko	45	1Lt	Yajima, Yoshihiko	16	Maj	Hirose, Yoshio	9
Capt	Shimada, Kenji	40	WO	Inouye, Misao	16	Maj	Takiyama, Yamato	9
WO	Kamito, Sumi	40+	WO	Ito, Riichi	16	Capt	Kono, Kensui	9
WO	Sasaki, Isam	38+	WO	Ogura, Mitsuo	16	Capt	Kani, Saiji	9
1Lt	Tarui, Mitsuyoshi	38	MSgt	Motojima, Muneyoshi	16	1Lt	Kawahara, Kosuke	9
Capt	Kashiide, Isamu	33	MSgt	Shimokawa, Yukio	16	1Lt	Nakazaki, Shigeru	9
Capt	Anma, Katsumi	32	Sgt	Igarashi, Tomesaku	16	1Lt	Takiguchi, Hiroshi	9
1Lt	Kanai, Moritsugu	32	Maj	Sakai, Iwori	15	2Lt	Takahashi, Katsutaro	9
1Lt	Koga, Sada	31	Capt	Nakamura, Saburo	15	2Lt	Ogawa, Makoto	9
Capt	Jobo, Ryotaro	30+	Capt	Nango, Shigeo	15	WO	Hayashi, Takeomi	9
Capt	Takeuchi, Shogo	30+	2Lt	Masuzawa, Masatoshi	15	WO	ma, Akira	9
2Lt	Aoyagi, Yutaka	28	WO	Hazawa, Iwataro	15	WO	Kimura, Yutaka	9
Capt	Sumino, Goichi	27	WO	Matsuura, Toshio	15	WO	Shimizu, Takeshi	9
WO	Shibata, Rikio	27	WO	Seino, Eiji	15	Sgt	Kato, Kenji	9
2Lt	Saito, Shogo	26+	MSgt	Ono, Megumu	15	Maj	Kawamoto, Koki	8+
Maj	Kimura, Takaji	26	MSgt	Otake, Kyushiro	15	Capt	Ito, Naoyuki	8
1Lt	Hosono, Isamu	26	Capt	Motomura, Koji	14	Capt	Miyamaru, Masao	8
MSgt	Miyamoto, Goro	26	Capt	Onozaki, Hiroshi	14	Capt	Obara, Tsutae	8
WO	Furugori, Goro	25+	WO	Minami, Takaaki	14	Capt	Tsuchiya, Takashi	8
MSgt	Hanada, Tomio	25	WO	Mune, Noboru	14	2Lt	Kanemaru, Teizo	8
MSgt	Yoshiyama, Bunji	25	WO	Noguchi, Takashi	14	2Lt	Kimura, Sadamitsu	8
2Lt	Saito, Chiyoji	24	MSgt	Hirohata, Tomio	14	2Lt	Terada, Shinobu	8
MSgt	Haraguchi, Kichigoro	24	Sgt	Shono, Tadashi	14	WO	Hida, Hitoshi	8
Sgt	Kajinami, Susumu	24	Corp	Okuda, Jiro	14	WO	Tashiro, Tadao	8
WO	Ishizuka, Tokuyasu	23	Capt	Ito, Fujitaro	13+	MSgt	Okubo, Misao	8
WO	Kato, Shoji	23	Capt	Kurono, Shoji	13	MSgt	Yamato, Mitsuo	8
Maj	Togo, Saburo	22	Capt	Kuwabara, Yoshiro	13	Sgt	Nishioka, Shigetsune	8
Capt	Asano, Hitoshi	22	Capt	Shirai, Nagao	13	1Lt	Fukuyama, Yonesuke	7
Capt	Hasegawa, Tomoari	22	2Lt	Shindo, Norio	13	1 Lt	Gomi, Hiroshi	7
MSgt	Otsuka, Zenzaburo	22	WO	Takahashi, Takeo	13	1 Lt	Sekiguchi, Hiroshi	7
Maj	Iwahashi, Jyozo	21	Maj	Miyabe, Hideo	12+	Capt	Ikuno, Fumisuke	6
WO	Kira, Katsuaki	21	Maj	Eto, Toyoki	12	Capt	Yoshida, Yoshio	6
WO	IShiromoto, Naoharu	21	Maj	Hinoki, Yohei	12	1Lt	Yoshioka, Yoshitaro	6
MSgt	Matsui, Morio	21+	2Lt	Nishihara, Goro	12	WO	Sumi, Tadao	6
MSgt	Sudo, Tokuya	20	WO	Iwase, Koichi	12	Sgt	Negishi, Nobuji	6
Maj	Ishikawa, Kanshi	19	WO	Ishizawa, Koji	11+	Sgt	Noguchi, Yoshinori	6
Capt	Ozaki, Nakakazu	19	Maj	Fukuda, Tokuro	11	Capt	Inayama, Hideaki	5+
WO	Ofusa, Yojiro	19	Maj	Sawada, Mitsugu	11	Maj	Ishikawa, Tadashi	5
WO	Yamaguchi, Bunichi	19	Capt	Shishimoto, Hironojo	11	Capt	Takanashi, Tatsuo	5
MSgt	Kimura, Saburo	19	2Lt	Kanbara, Daisuke	11	Maj	Kobayashi, Teruhiko	5
Capt	Wakamatsu, Yukiyoshi	18+	MSgt	Suzuki, Eisaku	11	1Lt	Ogata, Naoyuki	5
Lt Col	Kato, Tateo	18	Sgt	Kodama, Takayori	11	WO	Kawakita, Akira	5
WO	Ishii, Takeo	18	WO	Tsubone, Kosuke	10+	2Lt	Nishio, Hannoshin	5
WO	Shimizu, Kazuo	18	WO	Yasuda, Yoshito	10+	WO	Sato, Gonnoshin	5
1Lt	Takamiya, Keiji	17	Sgt	Kanazawa, Nobuo	10+	Sgt	Nakano, Matsumi	5
1Lt	Suzuki, Shoichi	17	Capt	Ichikawa, Chuichi	10			
WO	Hanada, Mamoru	17	1Lt	Shimamura, Miyoshi	10			

APPENDICES

Flying Units of the JNAF

The flying units of the JNAF were organised much like their opposite numbers within the Allied air forces. Japan's navy and army had their own air services, there being no independent air force like the German *Luftwaffe* or the British Royal Air Force.

The working component of the JNAF was the Air Group (*Kokutai*). *Kokutai* is used to denote JNAF air groups whereas *Sentai* is used for the JAAF. There were about 90 air groups within the JNAF, and depending on the size of the unit, these controlled between 36-64 (or more) aircraft.

Air Groups were either identified by names or numbers. Named groups are associated with a particular air command or base (Yokosuka Air Group, Sasebo Air Group). With a few exceptions such as the Tainan Air Group, most units that went overseas dropped their names and were given number designations (Kanoya Air Group became the 253rd Air Group for example). Air groups with numbers between 200 and 399 were fighter units, whilst those in the 600 to 699 range controlled a mix of aircraft. Float-plane units were numbered between 400 and 499. Carriers were too small to accommodate entire air groups, so the units on board took their names from the vessel they were embarked on (*Shokaku* Fighter Squadron for example).

The Air Group was divided into three or four squadrons (*hikotai*), with each squadron having between 12 to 16 aircraft. It could be commanded by a lieutenant (junior grade), a warrant officer, or even an experienced chief petty officer.

The majority of the pilots were enlisted men and not officers, unlike many of their Allied counterparts. Contrary to popular belief, while many non-aviation officers did not associate with their enlisted subordinates, officer pilots went to great lengths to form a bond. Said one Zero pilot;:

'These green lieutenants didn't know how to fight and would get shot down right away. So he was assigned a veteran enlisted man to protect him. If he was unpopular, the wingman might become "separated" during combat and the officer would surely die. *Do you understand?*'

The smallest operational unit in the squadron was the flight or section (*shotai*), which consisted of between three and four aircraft – four flights were usually found in the squadron. Initially, the flight consisted of three aircraft.

However, Lt Zenjiro Miyano was the first to effectively copy and refine the four-fighter flight formation from the Americans in 1943. Positions one and three were flown by seasoned veterans, while positions two and four were occupied by neophytes. This combination assured a higher rate of survival for the new pilot, plus allowed him to learn critical combat skills from his mentor. By 1944, the three-fighter flight had been mostly discarded. Through hard experience, it had been found that the 'odd man out' in a three-fighter flight usually became separated in combat and was shot down.

JNAF Air Groups of World War 2

The following list of naval air groups is not presented in numeric order since the establishment of the units was not carried out sequentially. Only fighter air groups of any significance are listed – carrier squadrons are not listed.

Yokosuka
Established 4/30 at Yokosuka. Japan's first naval Air Group fought over Iwo Jima and participated in the home defence. Disbanded at the end of the war

Chitose - 201st
Established 10/39 at Chitose, Japan. Reorganised as the 201st AG 12/42 at Roi, Marshall Islands. Reorganised again 3/44, disbanded at the end of the war

Kanoya - 253rd
Established 4/36 at Kanoya, Japan. The unit helped sink the British battleship HMS *Prince of Wales*. Reorganised 11/42 as 253rd AG. Fought at Rabaul and in the Solomons. Disbanded 7/44

Genzan - 252nd
Established 11/40 at Genzan (Wonsan), Korea. Participated in the Battle of the Coral Sea. Renamed 252nd AG 9/42, disbanded at end of war

1st
Established 4/41 at Kanoya, Japan. Fought briefly in China. Disbanded 9/41

Tainan - 251st

Established 10/41 at Tainan, Formosa. The was the most famous JNAF unit due to its spectacular early successes, it also boasted the most aces, including Saburo Sakai and Hiroyoshi Nishizawa. Reorganised 11/42 as 251st AG. Disbanded 7/44

3rd - 202nd

Established 4/41. First unit to be composed solely of fighter aircraft. It gained a fierce reputation during the early months of the war. Participated in the attacks over the Philippines, Dutch East Indies and Darwin, Australia. Reorganised as 202nd AG 11/42, disbanded 7/44

4th

Established 2/42 on the island of Truk and saw duty over Rabaul and eastern New Guinea. The unit was merged with Tainan Kokutai 4/42

2nd - 582nd

Established 5/42 at Yokosuka Air Base, Japan. Active over eastern New Guinea and Guadalcanal. Reorganised as 582nd AG, it had claimed around 220 victories when the fighter unit was disbanded 7/43

6th - 204th

Established 4/42 at Kisarazu Air Base, Japan. Participated in the attacks at Dutch Harbor (Aleutians), Battle of Midway, eastern New Guinea and Rabaul. Reorganised as 204th AG 11/42. Disbanded 4/44. From inception till the end, the unit claimed over 1000 aerial victories

281st

Established 2/43 at Maizuru Air Base, Japan. Saw limited service in the northern Kurile Islands, then transferred to the Marshall Islands and Rabaul. Unit was totally destroyed by 2/44, their pilots fighting as infantrymen during the invasion of Kwajalein and Roi (Marshall Islands). The top JNAF ace, Tetsuzo Iwamoto, saw much action with this unit

261st

Established 6/43 at Kagoshima Air Base, Japan. Fought over Peleliu Island, Saipan and Yap. Disbanded 7/44

331st

Established 7/43 at Saeki Air Base in Japan. Limited actions in Burma and Calcutta, and also fought over Borneo and the Philippines. Disbanded 5/44

254th

Established 10/43, provided air defence for Hainan Island and Hong Kong. Later fought over Formosa and in the Philippines, where it was destroyed in heavy fighting. Disbanded 1/45

263rd

Established 10/43 at Genzan, Korea. Fought over Tinian, Peleliu and Guam. Disbanded 7/44

321st

Established 10/43 at Mobara Air Base, Japan. First JNAF nightfighter unit. Fought over Tinian and Guam. Disbanded 7/44

381st

Established 10/43. Fought over Biak, Borneo, Celebes and French Indochina. Disbanded at the end of the war

265th

Established 11/43 at Kagoshima Air Base, Japan. Fought at Saipan and the Marianas. Disbanded 7/44

301st

Established 11/43 at Yokosuka Naval Base, Japan. Fought at Tinian and Iwo Jima. Destroyed at Iwo Jima and disbanded 7/44

341st

Established 11/43 at Matsuyama Air Base, Japan. Fought over Iwo Jima, Formosa and the Philippines using the new Shiden ('George') fighter. Some pilots flew *kamikaze* suicide attacks. The unit had been destroyed in the Philippines by 1/45

153rd

Established 1/44, fought over western New Guinea. Reorganised as a reconnaissance and nightfighter unit 7/44. Disbanded at the end of the war

343rd

Established 1/44 at Matsuyama Air Base, Japan. Fought at Guam, disbanded 7/44. Second formation established 12/44 at Matsuyama as an elite unit of hand-picked veterans flying the Shiden-Kai. Disbanded at the end of the war

221st

Established 1/44 at Kasanbara Air Base, Japan. Fought over Formosa and the Philippines. By 1/45 unit was virtually annihilated

256th

Established 2/44 at Lunghwa airfield, Shanghai (China). Fought over Shanghai, Philippines and Formosa. Disbanded 12/44

203rd

Established 2/44 at Atsugi Air Base, Japan. Fought over the northern Kurile Islands of Japan, Okinawa, Philippines, Formosa and home defence. Disbanded at the end of the war

302nd

Established 3/44 at Kisarazu Air Base, Japan. Guarded the Imperial Capital against B-29 attacks and also fought over Okinawa. Disbanded at the end of the war

131st

Established 7/44 at Yokosuka Air Base, Japan. Fought over Okinawa and home defence. Disbanded at the end of the war

332nd

Established 8/44 at Iwakuni Air Base, Japan. Fought over the Philippines and home defence. Disbanded at the end of the war

352nd

Established 8/44 in Japan. Fought in the home defence, disbanded at the end of the war

210th

Established 9/44 at Meiji Air Base, Japan. Fought at Okinawa and the home defence, disbanded at the end of the war

721st

Established 10/44 as a *kamikaze* suicide unit at Konoike Air Base, Japan. Flew suicide attack missions at Okinawa using Zeroes and piloted rocket bombs (Ohka). Disbanded at the end of the war

205th

Established 2/45 at Taichung Air Base, Formosa. Participated in *kamikaze* attacks at Okinawa. Disbanded at the end of the war

Aerial Victory Claims by JNAF Pilots

in the American and Commonwealth custom, the shooting down of five or more enemy aircraft entitled the pilot to call himself (herself in the USSR) an 'ace'. He joined an elite fraternity of fighter pilots whose accomplishments were widely publicised in the military and national press. As the victories mounted, his achievements were recognised with the awarding of medals and promotion through the ranks.

Although the Japanese adopted many of the concepts of flight from the West (Europe in particular), in its culture, the trait of individuality, which was so valued in the West, was shunned. Since early school days, Japanese children are taught to work and sacrifice for the benefit of the group. In a military context, this often manifested itself in basic training – both before and during World War 2 – when drill instructor lined up their trainees and struck them

for the shortcomings of a single individual in the group. In war, teamwork was critical, and there could be no prima donnas. When an individual accomplished a distinguished feat, the group received the honours.

During the China War, and in the early part of the Pacific campaign when Japan was on the offensive, various units did record individual credits in their mission reports. However, in June 1943 navy GHQ issued a directive prohibiting the continuation of this practice, this measure being taken in an effort to promote greater teamwork – most units adhered to the new policy.

As with fighter pilots the world over, Japanese aviators *did* keep personal scores, and for morale purposes they would paint victory markings on the aircraft. Since pilots flew aircraft on an availability basis, the number of 'kill' markings on the aircraft could be deceptive, for it was the fighter, rather than the pilot, who scored the victory.

There was no established rule for determining a victory. Many pilots would claim the destruction of an enemy aircraft which was seen to smoke in the air, believing that it would never reach home. The Japanese did have gun cameras, but they were only used for training purposes. The claim was usually taken on face value and added to the group's score.

As the war turned against the Japanese, and surviving pilots fought with tenacity, trying to hit as many enemy aircraft as possible before their end, many simply stopped counting. Although a few leading aces received rare personal citations and ceremonial swords for outstanding service, in general pilots had no incentive to inflate their claims in the hop of winning such honours because they were literally fighting for their lives.

Despite this, claims by JNAF pilots cannot be taken at face value. The inflated totals resulted from both confusion in combat and from a very liberal method of scorekeeping. During the early part of the war, many pilots received official recognition from the government for their victories (taken from individual citations and unit reports), but this does not imply that these victories were 'confirmed'.

Postwar, Japanese historians have recognised the problem of inflated totals, and tried to compensate by systematically reducing the scores by percentages. WO Takeo Tanimizu claimed 32 victories during the war, but historians have reduced his score to 18. Likewise, the top JNAF ace, Lt(jg) Tetsuzo Iwamoto, claimed 202 victories, although his tally has now been reduced to 'about 80' – It is a fact that no Japanese pilot ever reached 100 victories.

Since there is no basis for verifying claims, the postwar reduction of scores seem arbitrary. Likewise, accepting the claims on face value would also be grossly inaccurate.

The following list of JNAF aces was compiled from numerous sources. These scores are simply unverified claims either made by the pilots or attributed to them. The numerical scores represent a mixture of confirmed, unconfirmed, probable, damaged and imagined victories.

JNAF Aces Listings

Rank	Name	Score
Lt(jg)	Iwamoto, Tetsuzo	202
CPO	Sugita, Shoichi	120+
WO	Nishizawa, Hiroyoshi	86
WO	Fukumoto, Shigeo	72
Ens	Sakai, Saburo	60+
CPO	Okumura, Takeo	54
Lt(jg)	Sasai, Junichi	54
WO	Okabe, Kenji	50
Lt	Kanno, Naoshi	48
WO	Ohara, Ryoji	48
Lt Cdr	Fujita, Iyozoh	42
WO	Komachi, Sadamu	40
Ens	Muto, Kaneyoshi	35
PO1/c	Ota, Toshio	34
WO	Sugino, Kazuo	32
WO	Tanimizu, Takeo	32
Ens	Ishihara, Susumu	30+
CPO	Ishii, Shizuo	28
Lt(jg)	Akamatsu, Sadaaki	27
WO	Ogiya, Nobuo	24
CPO	Hidaka, Yoshimi	20
Lt(jg)	Sugio, Shigeo	20
PO3/c	Uto, Kazushi	19
CPO	Nagano, Kiichi	19
WO	Okano, Hiroshi	19
PO1/c	Nakase, Masayuki	18
Lt(jg)	Matsuba, Akio	18
Ens	Saito, Saburo	18+
CPO	Oki, Yoshio	18
Ens	Honda, Minoru	17+
Ens	Tanaka, Kuniyoshi	17
CPO	Masuyama, Masao	17
Lt(jg)	Kamihara, Keishu	17
WO	Ito, Kiyoshi	17
WO	Katsuki, Kiyomi	16+
CPO	Matsunaga, Eitoku	16
CPO	Matsunaga, Hidenori	16
WO	Takesuka, Toraichi	16
Lt	Miyano, Zenjiro	16
CPO	Nakajima, Bunkichi	16
WO	Nakaya, Yoshiichi	16
CPO	Kato, Kunimichi	16
Ens	Shiga, Masami	16
WO	Watanabe, Hideo	16
Ens	Nakakariya, Kunimori	16
Ens	Minami, Yoshimi	15
WO	Yoshino, Satoshi	15
WO	Nakamichi, Wataru	15
WO	Shibukawa, Shigeru	15
Lt Cdr	Suho, Motonari	15
WO	Tanaka, Minpo	15
CPO	Koyae, Kotaro	15
PO1/c	Endo, Masuaki	14
PO1/c	Yamazaki, Ichirobei	14
PO2/c	Yoshida, Mototsuna	14
Ens	Taniguchi, Masao	14
WO	Ozeki, Yukiharu	14
WO	Takahashi, Kenichi	14
WO	Koga, Kiyoto	13
Lt(jg)	Handa, Watari	13
Ens	Yamamoto, Akira	13
WO	Yamashita, Sahei	13
WO	Matsumura, Momoto	13
WO	Kuroiwa, Toshio	13
WO	Maeda, Hideo	13
CPO	Uehara, Sadao	13
WO	Miyazaki, Gitaro	13
Sup Sea	Shibagaki, Hiroshi	13
Ens	Kondo, Masaichi	13
PO1/c	Omori, Shigetaka	13
Lt(jg)	Hagiri, Matsuo	13
Ens	Miyazaki, Isamu	13
Lt(jg)	Koizumi, Fujikazu	13
WO	Shibayama, Sekizen	13
WO	Kashimura, Kanichi	12
PO1/c	Yoshimura, Keisaku	12
WO	Kanamaru, Takeo	12
CPO	Kikuchi, Tetsuo	12
PO1/c	Shimizu, Kiyoshi	12
Lt	Isozaki, Chitoshi	12
Lt	Yamaguchi, Sadao	12
Ens	Sasakibara, Masao	12
PO1/c	Odaka, Noritsura	12
Ens	Yamashita, Koshiro	11
CPO	Sekiya, Kiyoshi	11
WO	Yasui, Kozaburo	11
CPO	Yamamoto, Tomezo	11
Lt(jg)	Wajima, Yoshio	11
PO2/c	Ichioka, Matao	11
PO3/c	Kokubun, Takeichi	11
Lt(jg)	Hidaka, Hatsuo	11
WO	Oishi, Yoshio	11
Lt(jg)	Iwai, Tsutomu	11
CPO	Shirahama, Yoshijiro	11
WO	Hori, Mitsuo	11
Lt	Fukuda, Sumio	11
Ens	Kodaira, Yoshinao	11
WO	Yamamoto, Ichiro	11
WO	Kitahata, Saburo	10+

WO	Sugiyama, Teruo	10
CPO	Tanaka, Jiro	10
CPO	Tanaka, Shinsaku	10
PO2/c	Banno, Takao	10
CPO	Ishii, Isamu	10
Ldg Sea	Hattori, Kazuo	10+
CPO	Nagahama, Yoshikazu	10+
PO2/c	Kurosawa, Seiichi	10
CPO	Hashiguchi, Yoshiro	10+
Lt	Shigematsu, Yasuhiro	10+
Lt	Kobayashi, Hohei	10+
Ens	Kagemitsu, Matsuo	10+
Ens	Takahashi, Shigeru	10
CPO	Sasai, Tomokazu	10
WO	Atake, Tomita	10
WO	Yoshida, Katsuyoshi	10
Cdr	Aioi, Takahide	10
CPO	Abe, Kenichi	10
PO1/c	Sakano, Takao	10
Lt(jg)	Mochizuki, Isamu	9
LCdr	Shirane, Ayao	9
WO	Sueda, Toshiyuki	9
PO1/c	Suzuki, Kiyonobu	9
PO1/c	Okamoto, Juzo	9
WO	Oda, Kiichi	9
Lt(jg)	Mori, Mitsugu	9
Lt(jg)	Tsunoda, Kazuo	9
Lt(jg)	Morinio, Hideo	9
Lt(jg)	Matsuda, Jiro	9
Lt(jg)	Harada, Kaname	9
PO2/c	Izumi, Hideo	9
PO3/c	Matsuki, Susumu	9
WO	Nakamura, Yoshio	9
PO2/c	Kanda, Saji	9
Ens	Yamanaka, Tadao	9
PO1/c	Shirakawa, Toshihisa	9
CPO	Yoshizawa, Tokushige	9
CPO	Ishida, Teigo	9
Lt(jg)	Higashiyama, Ichiro	9
Lt	Fukui, Yoshio	9
WO	Kato, Katsue	9
Ens	Kudo, Shigetoshi	9
Lt Cdr	Kaneko, Tadashi	8
Lt	Iizuka, Masao	8
Lt(jg)	Ono, Takeyoshi	8
Lt	Nakagawa, Kenji	8
Lt	Endo, Yukio	8+
PO3/c	Moriura, Toyoo	8
CPO	Suzuki, Hiroshi	8
PO1/c	Takaiwa, Kaoru	8
PO1/c	Iwaki, Yoshio	8

WO	Ema, Yuichi	8
PO1/c	Magara, Koichi	8
WO	Shigemi, Katsuma	8
PO1/c	Goto, Kurakazu	8
PO1/c	Yano, Shigeru	8
WO	Tokuji, Yoshihisa	8
Lt(jg)	Ono, Satoru	8
Ens	Muranaka, Kazuo	8
Lt	Nango, Mochifumi	8
CPO	Yoshihara, Hiroji	8
WO	Yanagiya, Kenji	8
Ens	Nakano, Katsujiro	7
Lt Cdr	Shiga, Yoshio	6
A1/c	Yonekawa, Tadayoshi	6
Lt(jg)	Kuratori, Shiro	6
WO	Hayashi, Sakuji	6
Lt	Oshibuchi, Takashi	6
CPO	Sasaki, Yoshiichi	6
Lt	Nishiwaki, Masaharu	5+
Lt	Hayashi, Yoshishige	5
PO	Mitsuda, Masahiro	5
Lt	Yokoyama, Tamotsu	5
CPO	Naka, Yoshimitsu	5
Lt	Morioka, Yutaka	5
PO1/c	Tsujinoue, Toyomitsu	5
PO1/c	Arita, Yoshisuke	5
WO	Takenaka, Yoshihiko	5
CPO	Ishikawa, Seiji	5
PO2/c	Kakimoto, Enji	5

INDEX

References to illustrations are shown in **bold**. Colour Plates are prefixed 'pl1.' or 'pl2.' and Figure Plates 'fig.pl1.' or 'fig.pl2.', with page numbers and caption locators in brackets.